SOVEREIGN WEALTH FUNDS
Threat or Salvation?

Edwin M. Truman

Peterson Institute for International Economics
Washington, DC
September 2010

Mixed Sources
Product group from well-managed
forests and other controlled sources
www.fsc.org Cert no. BV-COC-070702
© 1996 Forest Stewardship Council

FSC

Edwin M. Truman, senior fellow since 2001, was assistant secretary of the Treasury for international affairs (1998–2000). He directed the Division of International Finance of the Board of Governors of the Federal Reserve System (1977–98). He also served as one of three economists on the staff of the Federal Open Market Committee (1983–98) and as a member of numerous international working groups on international economic and financial issues. He is author, coauthor, or editor of *International Economic Policy Coordination Revisited* (forthcoming), *A Strategy for IMF Reform* (2006), *Reforming the IMF for the 21st Century* (2006), *Chasing Dirty Money: The Fight Against Money Laundering* (2004), and *Inflation Targeting in the World Economy* (2003).

PETER G. PETERSON INSTITUTE FOR INTERNATIONAL ECONOMICS
1750 Massachusetts Avenue, NW
Washington, DC 20036-1903
(202) 328-9000   FAX: (202) 659-3225
www.piie.com

C. Fred Bergsten, *Director*
Edward A. Tureen, *Director of Publications, Marketing, and Web Development*

Typesetting by BMWW
Printing by United Book Press, Inc.
Cover photo: © khz—Fotolia

Printed in the United States of America
12 11 10   5 4 3 2 1

Library of Congress Cataloging-in-Publication Data
Truman, Edwin M.
Sovereign wealth funds : threat or salvation? / Edwin M. Truman.
    p. cm.
Includes bibliographical references and index.
    ISBN 978-0-88132-498-3
    1. Sovereign wealth funds.   2. Investment of public funds.   3. Investments, Foreign.   4. International finance.   I. Title.

HJ3801.T78 2010
332.67'252—dc22

2010031393

4957855415

To the memory of
Edward M. ("Monty") Graham
1944–2007
Friend, colleague, and mentor

Contents

Figures

Boxes

Preface

Sovereign wealth funds (SWFs), large pools of government-owned funds that are invested in whole or in part outside their home country, burst upon the policy consciousness only three years ago. Their explosive growth up until 2007 fanned widespread anxieties about shifts of global economic wealth and the roles of governments in managing that wealth. On the other hand, SWF investments helped some major Western financial institutions weather the recent global financial crisis.

Edwin M. Truman is one of the pioneers of independent, policy-oriented research on SWFs. In 2007, he advocated a voluntary set of international best practices in accountability and transparency for the SWFs and developed a prototype in the form of an SWF "scoreboard." His SWF scoreboard helped to inspire the Santiago Principles for SWFs that were agreed by the International Working Group on SWFs and released in October 2008, setting out the first international agreement on these institutions and their practices.

Sovereign Wealth Funds: Threat or Salvation? is the culmination of a three-year research program at the Peterson Institute for International Economics on this topic. The study reviews the origins of SWFs, the potential for their future growth, the policy issues that they raise, and various proposals for the regulation of SWFs. Truman concludes that the best approach is a robust set of best practices for SWFs and increased compliance with that standard. To this end, he updates the SWF scoreboard and extends it to 53 pension and nonpension funds in 37 countries. He reviews the considerable progress since 2007 in SWF compliance with the 33 elements in the scoreboard.

The study provides a positive assessment of the Santiago Principles as a first step toward high quality best practices for SWFs. It also reviews the less-than-satisfactory response of members of the Organization for Economic Cooperation and Development in recent years with respect to their openness to foreign direct investment, including by governmental entities such as SWFs. Many countries have raised the bar on incoming foreign investments over the past several years in response, at least in part, to the rise of SWFs. The United States, in its Foreign Investment and National Security Act passed in 2007, updated the legislation governing the Committee on Foreign Investment in the United States (CFIUS),

Against the background of his analysis, Truman makes four broad recommendations: (1) countries with SWFs should promote adherence to and implementation of the Santiago Principles and progressive improvement of their content; (2) countries receiving SWF investments should monitor and endeavor to roll back their increased financial protectionism; (3) to prevent regulatory and institutional arbitrage, countries should increase their collaborative efforts to improve other related standards of accountability and transparency such as those governing the management of international reserves; and (4) the long-term objective should be a comprehensive international agreement governing all types of cross-border investments by governments.

This study draws upon two strands of previous work at the Institute. The first strand is pioneering work on foreign direct investment in the United States by Edward M. Graham and Paul Krugman dating back to 1988, Monty Graham's subsequent work with David Marchick on US national security and foreign direct investment published in 2006, and Theodore Moran's more recent work on the CFIUS and China's foreign investment strategy. The second strand is the Institute's work on international standards best exemplified by Morris Goldstein's successful advocacy in 1997 of an international banking standard. Truman's pioneering work on SWFs has brought these two strands together and established a new area of Institute intellectual and policy leadership.

The Peter G. Peterson Institute for International Economics is a private, nonprofit institution for the study and discussion of international economic policy. Its purpose is to analyze important issues in that area and to develop and communicate practical new approaches for dealing with them. The Institute is completely nonpartisan.

The Institute is funded by a highly diversified group of philanthropic foundations, private corporations, and interested individuals. About 35 percent of the Institute's resources in our latest fiscal year was provided by contributors outside the United States. Support for this study was provided by the Revenue Watch Institute.

The Institute's Board of Directors bears overall responsibilities for the Institute and gives general guidance and approval to its research program, including the identification of topics that are likely to become important over the medium run (one to three years) and that should be addressed by the Institute. The director, working closely with the staff and outside Advisory Committee, is responsible for the development of particular projects and makes the final decision to publish an individual study.

The Institute hopes that its studies and other activities will contribute to building a stronger foundation for international economic policy around the world. We invite readers of these publications to let us know how they think we can best accomplish this objective.

C. Fred Bergsten
Director
August 2010

Acknowledgments

This study is the product of more than three years of research on sovereign wealth funds. I have learned a great deal while studying this multifaceted topic. In the process I incurred too many obligations to people and institutions to catalogue each of them. However, several deserve special mention.

First, I thank C. Fred Bergsten for his ongoing support for this project including permitting me to bring it to a conclusion with this volume. I am also greatly in debt to Madona Devasahayam for her excellence in shepherding the production once I had finally finished.

Second, without the assistance of Doug Dowson and Daniel Xie, in particular with the three editions of the SWF scoreboard, this project would never have been completed. It is indicative that I have burned through two, dedicated research analysts.

Third, the comments I received at a study group meeting at the Peterson Institute for International Economics in March 2010 were invaluable in shaping the final result. I want to thank William Cline, Anna Gelpern, Jennifer Harris, Mohsin Khan, Nicholas Lardy, Russell Munk, Larry Promisel, Steven Weisman, and John Williamson.

Fourth, in the course of my work on this topic, I have benefited from interactions with many people around the world. I have had the opportunity to present my thinking on more than two dozen occasions. In particular, I would like to mention generically my friends and former colleagues at the US Treasury and the encouragement I received from many at the International Monetary Fund. Finally, Moreno Bertoldi of the European Commission has been a constant source of advice and insight.

I started this project in early 2007 and frequently consulted my colleague Edward "Monty" Graham for advice. On September 18, 2007, as we celebrated Monty's contributions at the Peterson Institute for International Economics, I expressed my regret that his struggle with cancer did not permit him to see my finished product. In his broad interests, he is the closest to a renaissance economist that I have known. He was also the author of an excellent piece of advice, "Take the time to do it right." I am sorry that this project took so long. I hope it comes close to the Graham standard. I am honored to dedicate this study to his memory.

1

Sovereign Wealth Funds and the Global Economy

Five years ago, sovereign wealth funds (SWFs) were so unknown that there was no common term to describe government-owned funds that invested in whole or in part outside their home country. Andrew Rozanov (2005) of State Street Corporation coined the term "sovereign wealth fund" in May 2005. At that time, assets under management of SWFs were about $1.5 trillion. By 2007, they had doubled to $3 trillion and were projected to reach $12 trillion by 2015.[1]

Although SWF assets represented only a tiny fraction of total reported international financial assets of $92 trillion as of 2007, their rapid growth and government control became a source of substantial economic and political anxiety in many countries that were actual or potential recipients of their investments. The SWFs were also a source of considerable controversy in their home countries. The SWFs came to be viewed as "big money," and big money is distrusted, whether in the hands of banks, other private investors, or governments. In the case of SWFs, policymakers and observers in countries receiving their investments raised understandable concerns about the motivations of the governments making the investments. Policymakers in the countries with the SWFs, not inappropriately, focused on the policy responses of countries receiving the actual or potential SWF investments. Concerns were also expressed about the

---

1. This figure for assets under management by SWFs includes only nonpension SWFs as classified by the definition adopted by the International Working Group on SWFs. Chapter 2 elaborates on the distinction between conventional pension funds and nonpension SWFs and argues that many of the public policy issues that pension funds raise are essentially the same as those raised by pure SWFs.

possible impact of SWF investments on markets and the integrity of the processes governing investment decisions. In this context, conflicts of interest between countries with the SWFs and those receiving their investments are a real possibility.

Anxieties about the threats posed by SWFs were fed by the attempted purchase in 2006 by Dubai Ports World of US ports operated by the Peninsular and Steam Navigation Company and by the prospect of aggressive expansion in Europe by Russia's Gazprom—despite the fact that these are government-owned companies, not SWFs. In some countries, critics also questioned the rationale behind transferring government ownership of a business or activity to the private sector by sales in whole or in part to foreign government-controlled firms or investment funds.

Sovereign wealth funds are symbolic of two major, recent trends in the global political economy: (1) a redistribution of wealth and economic and financial power from the United States, Europe, and other mature industrial economies to countries perceived to be less firmly grounded in similar economic, financial, and political mores; and (2) an increasing role of governments in managing wealth and economic power.

The rapid expansion of SWFs was fueled before 2008 by high and rising prices of natural resources and other commodities and by policies that led to massive accumulations of foreign exchange and financial resources in government coffers. Accelerated transfers from foreign exchange reserves to SWFs, with their more aggressive investment strategies and higher expected returns, were projected to continue to boost the size of SWFs. To a significant degree, this wealth was accumulating under the control of governments that were unfamiliar to citizens of the United States and Western Europe and that, perhaps, were hostile to the interests of those countries. Excluding pension funds, six countries have SWFs with assets of more than $100 billion.[2] Only one country, Norway, is currently a member of the Organization for Economic Cooperation and Development (OECD), the traditional grouping of wealthy nations. Thus, the rise of SWFs is symbolic of the growing disenchantment in the United States and many other mature industrial countries with globalization, which no longer is seen as delivering the dividends that it once did. Globalization is increasingly seen as a lopsided process, and China with its SWF of $300 billion on top of $2.5 trillion in foreign exchange reserves is exhibit A.

The associated fear was that governments would use their SWFs to buy control of large "national champion" firms in key sectors. This dynamic would contribute to the creation of "sharecropper societies" in the West as foreign government investment would pour into industrial countries

---

2. In order of the estimated size of their SWF assets, the economies are the United Arab Emirates, Norway, Singapore, China, Hong Kong, and Kuwait. Saudi Arabia's international investment holdings often are placed in the same category.

that had lost control over their own affairs.[3] In the United States, if somewhat less so in Europe, there was at best ambivalence and at worst deep suspicion and mistrust of many forms of government investments and economic interventions. These perceptions were illustrated by the delayed, negative reaction to the Troubled Asset Relief Program even after it succeeded in stabilizing the US financial system. In addition, the SWFs were viewed by many as vehicles with which other countries could appropriate sensitive proprietary commercial and technical information and threaten the economic and national security of countries in which they were investing.

Symptomatic of interpretations of a rapidly changing world, Gerard Lyons (2007) of Standard and Chartered wrote about the rise of state capitalism in which SWFs would play an active role and Diana Farrell and colleagues (2007) from the McKinsey Global Institute wrote about a broader set of new global financial power brokers, including SWFs. According to these disquieting reports, economic and financial power would no longer rest with the traditional actors in the private sector or their governments that had dominated international finance during the post–World War II era. At the extreme, the perceived threats from SWFs were exaggerated, but those perceptions were illustrative of a distrust of change, particularly when that change is associated with unfamiliar and opaque foreign governments.

Sovereign Wealth Funds and the Global Financial Crisis

In the fall of 2007, as the global financial crisis gained momentum, views about SWFs moderated somewhat. In the fourth quarter of that year and the first quarter of 2008, several SWFs invested substantial amounts in Western financial institutions that were under financial stress. Their actions were motivated by the potential for financial rewards, but they also generated political side benefits: sovereign wealth funds to the rescue! For example, on August 21, 2007, during the month that the financial crisis broke, Steven R. Weisman in the *New York Times* quoted US Treasury Secretary Henry M. Paulson, Jr. as saying: "I'd like nothing more than to get more of that money." Weisman also reported my view that in a future global crisis, and perhaps even during the crisis unfolding at the time, the US Treasury secretary might be wise to place calls to SWF managers as

---

3. Warren Buffett raised this concern in his letter to his Berkshire Hathaway Company shareholders in 2005, directing it toward the large US fiscal and external deficits at that time (see letter at www.berkshirehathaway.com/letters/2005.html). As described in chapter 3, observers were quick to make the link to a threat from foreign investment and to ignore Buffett's policy prescriptions to reduce fiscal deficits and reign in overspending by the country as a whole.

well as to central bankers and finance ministers around the world in an effort to manage the financial crisis.[4]

The perception of SWFs as saviors of the Western financial system was as exaggerated as that of the SWF as threats that preceded the financial crisis. The new perception was based upon a flawed, partial-equilibrium understanding of SWF investment practices and balance sheets. In managing their portfolios, SWFs may buy government or corporate securities, invest in hedge funds, buy real estate, buy stocks of commodities, or purchase stakes in financial institutions. SWFs have to invest in some asset and generally do not hold substantial proportions of their portfolios in low-yielding cash investments. The particular governments, corporations, hedge funds, real estate developers, commodity producers, or financial institutions benefit financially from the SWFs' investments via access to funds in large volume often for a price. However, other governments and potential recipients of SWF investments, at most, benefit indirectly.[5] To the extent that the SWF disinvests from some assets to make new investments, the issuers of the assets from which the SWF disinvests are net losers. SWFs were not positioned in 2007 to save everyone.

SWF investments in Western financial institutions soured as the financial crisis deepened in the fall of 2008 and winter of 2009. Along with other global investors, SWFs saw reductions in the mark-to-market value of their portfolios on the order of 20 to 30 percent. Their managers were heavily criticized for investment decisions that, with the benefit of hindsight, were seen as unwise. SWFs in 2007 and 2008 proved to be neither an unqualified threat nor an unqualified salvation for anyone involved.

Meanwhile, the SWFs' continued and still-rapid growth raised issues that were not going away. They remained controversial and contentious in North America and Europe, and numerous suggestions were made to regulate SWF investments or refine existing regulations as they applied to such investments by foreign governments.

As researchers and analysts explored the SWF phenomenon, policymakers in North America and Europe discovered that their own countries had SWFs too, often operating at the subnational level, such as Alaska's Permanent Fund, as well as the functional equivalent of SWFs in the form of government pension funds.[6] Both types of governmental investment vehicles diversify their investments globally. Moreover, in the United States, observers are familiar with large government pension funds that use their

---

4. Steven R. Weisman, "A Fear of Foreign Investments," *New York Times*, August 21, 2007. Weisman became editorial director and public policy fellow at the Peterson Institute for International Economics in July 2008.

5. For example, they may benefit from the stability that a specific SWF investment in one financial institution brings to the financial system as a whole.

6. Policymakers in countries with large foreign exchange reserves, such as Japan, India, and Brazil, also began to think about setting up SWFs. Brazil subsequently has done so.

financial muscle to achieve political objectives, often under the guise of ethical investment policies. Meanwhile, policymakers in non-Western countries with SWFs became concerned that jurisdictions would erect barriers to SWF investments. The associated tensions led to more finger pointing.

Response to Sovereign Wealth Funds

As is appropriate and desirable when international controversies emerge, responsible policymakers sought multilateral solutions and, to that end, the involvement of multilateral institutions—the International Monetary Fund (IMF), World Bank, and OECD. Outside observers, including myself, suggested the development of a voluntary code of conduct or set of standards or best practices for SWFs.[7]

This suggestion was initially resisted by officials of some of the countries that would be affected. They argued that hedge funds, private equity firms, and other large pools of capital were not subject to international standards. The arguments from the countries with SWFs were somewhat undercut by the fact that authorities in the United States, United Kingdom, and other jurisdictions were moving at the same time to promote the establishment of standards or codes of conduct for such private investment vehicles. Standards were emerging for all the big money players.

Some also argued that the public sector should set a strong example for the private sector in demonstrating accountability and transparency. The fact that this argument took time to catch on reflected the reality that the many countries that are home to SWFs have diverse and differing political and cultural histories. Their funds were established to serve a wide range of economic and financial policy objectives derived from their own unique circumstances. They did not from the start perceive themselves as part of a coherent group, let alone one that could benefit from self-regulation. Moreover, the countries that were home to SWFs were legitimately seeking a quid pro quo in the form of a commitment from countries receiving their investments not to subject SWF investments to special restrictions or higher standards.

In October 2007, the Peterson Institute for International Economics released my prototype of an international standard for SWF accountability and transparency in the form of an SWF scoreboard.[8] In April 2008, my refined and updated SWF scoreboard was released in the form of a

---

7. Edwin M. Truman, "What Should the Fund's Role Be Now?" Remarks at the Bretton Woods Committee 2007 Annual Meeting, June 12, 2007, available at www.piie.com (accessed on July 12, 2010).

8. See Edwin M. Truman, "Sovereign Wealth Fund Acquisitions and Other Foreign Government Investments in the United States," testimony before the US Senate Committee on Banking, Housing, and Urban Affairs, November 14, 2007.

blueprint for SWF best practices (Truman 2008a). The blueprint was designed to prod and inform the multilateral, collaborative project that became the International Working Group of Sovereign Wealth Funds (known as the IWG), which was about to be established under the aegis of the IMF. The first meeting of the IWG was on May 1, 2008.

The IWG completed its work in September 2008 and the result of its effort was a set of Generally Accepted Principles and Practices of SWFs (known as the Santiago Principles or the GAPP). The release of the Santiago Principles in October 2008 was drowned out by the cascading crescendos of the global economic and financial crisis.

In parallel with the IMF-facilitated process, during 2007–08 many of the countries that are recipients of SWF investments, as well as those that are home to SWFs, met under the aegis of the OECD to reexamine the issues raised by international investments by governments or government-controlled entities. This examination concluded that there was no case for establishing a new, separate regulatory framework for SWF investments. Members of the OECD in effect recommitted themselves to the existing framework of OECD codes and declarations governing foreign government investments. Nevertheless, over the past several years the authorities in a number of OECD countries, including the United States, have implemented, and in a few cases established for the first time, regimes governing foreign investments in their countries that, in their practical application, raise the potential bar for such investments. Countries with SWFs are justified in their concern that the quid pro quo for greater accountability and transparency by SWFs has not been delivered.

All the multilateral activity addressed, but hardly dispensed with, the SWF challenge. The funds continue to raise a host of economic, financial, and political issues, which is why they are both fascinating and contentious, attracting observers and scholars in many disciplines and with many different perspectives. Everyone has an opinion and gets into the act.

Structure of the Book

This volume is designed to describe the state of play for SWFs as of mid-2010. It pulls together the insights and information I have gathered since late 2006, when I expanded my research interests from patterns of reserve diversification to other closely related forms of international financial investment by governments.

Chapter 2 provides background information on SWFs and their many different origins, objectives, and investment strategies. I examine prospects for the continued expansion of SWFs and conclude that these funds will continue to expand, although probably not at the pace of the 2002–07 period, which was more than 30 percent per year. SWFs are part of the international financial system and are here to stay.

Chapter 3 examines five broad areas of principal concern about SWFs: (1) mismanagement of investments by SWFs to the economic and financial detriment of the country with the fund; (2) pursuit of political objectives, economic power objectives, or both together, via SWFs; (3) exacerbation of financial protectionism inspired by SWFs; (4) the potential for financial market turmoil and uncertainty associated with SWF activities; and (5) conflicts of interest between countries with SWFs and countries in which they invest. Some argue that these are largely hypothetical concerns and unsubstantiated. However, fear of the unknown is still fear.

Chapter 4 reviews a range of possible policy responses to SWF investments by the authorities of the countries receiving their investments. These responses include (1) a comprehensive regulatory regime covering all aspects of SWF activities; (2) prohibitions on specific SWF investments, as, for example, in certain industries or sectors; (3) limitations on SWF investment activities such as voting their shares; and (4) reciprocal arrangements with the country of origin of an SWF investment. I conclude that none of these approaches is likely to be effective in dealing with the issues described in chapter 3, and each would be economically costly to implement. Thus, I argue that an approach to increase the accountability and transparency of SWFs and their government owners is preferable in the absence of strong evidence that tighter measures are required.

Against this backdrop, chapter 5 provides an updated and slightly revised SWF scoreboard with coverage expanded to 53 nonpension and pension SWFs. The objective is not only to describe the rationale behind the elements of the scoreboard as it has evolved, but also to demonstrate two key points. First, not all SWFs are alike in their accountability and transparency or in their lack thereof. Second, since I first presented the scoreboard in 2007, the scores of the SWFs have increased, in some cases substantially. To some extent (I have been assured) the attention given to the SWF scoreboard has enhanced incentives to improve the accountability and transparency of individual SWFs. This recorded progress is a strong argument in favor of the scoreboard approach to promoting SWF best practices. The scoreboard approach also helps to address each of the five broad concerns outlined in chapter 3 and summarized above.

The Santiago Principles are an agreed-upon and voluntary international application of the SWF scoreboard approach. They are a significant first step toward establishing and implementing a responsible response to concerns raised by SWFs via increasing their accountability and transparency. The specific application of the SWF scoreboard approach was the result of a negotiation that necessarily involved compromises. Chapter 6 examines the Santiago Principles using the SWF scoreboard as a yardstick. Three tests are applied. First, was there broad participation by the countries with large SWFs? The answer is yes, with a few prominent exceptions. Second, do the Santiago Principles cover most of the elements in the scoreboard? The answer is a qualified yes. In particular, the Santiago Principles fall short in not systematically recommending public disclosure to demonstrate implementation by each fund. Third, are the SWFs already implementing the Santiago Principles? The answer is that to date the record of implementation of the principles as a scaled-down mechanism for accountability and transparency is as diverse as that recorded on the full SWF scoreboard. The Santiago Principles are the start, not the end, of enhanced SWF accountability and transparency.

Chapter 7 looks at the investment policies, procedures, and practices of countries that receive SWF investments and the review of those policies conducted in 2007–08 under the aegis of the OECD. The good news is that the OECD exercise did not result in a formal tightening of the existing framework applied by OECD members to SWF investments. The OECD members agreed that no special regime for SWF investments is required because those investments are (rightly) seen as not inherently different from other government-owned or controlled investment vehicles. The bad news is that the OECD countries did not address how to strengthen their current codes, procedures, and practices to reinforce their openness to foreign investments, including by governments and their SWFs. Instead, and partly as a consequence of the rise of SWFs, we have seen a tangible increase in financial protectionism in OECD countries in recent years via a tightening of laws, standards, and procedures.

Chapter 8 concludes and looks to the future. SWFs are here to stay. As a result of the Santiago Principles and other parallel efforts at education such as the SWF scoreboard that I have featured in my research, a substantial amount of distrust surrounding SWFs has been defused. Unfortunately, reciprocal actions by host countries to SWF investments have been less than impressive.

On the basis of my analysis, I make four broad recommendations. First, countries with SWFs should promote adherence to and implementation of the Santiago Principles and the progressive improvement of the quality and content of those principles. Second, recipient countries should take reciprocal steps to monitor more closely incipient financial protectionism put in place in recent years with a view to rolling it back. Third, to prevent regulatory and institutional arbitrage, governments should step up their collaborative efforts in order to improve other accountability and transparency standards, such as those on the management of foreign exchange reserves, and to collect more comprehensive data on all cross-border government investments. Fourth, the long-term goal should be a comprehensive, internationally agreed-upon framework governing all types of cross-border investments by governments.

2

What Are Sovereign Wealth Funds?

There is no single, accepted, fully operational definition of sovereign wealth funds. How long have they existed? For more than five decades. What is the source of their financing? Predominantly, but not exclusively, they are funded from excess accumulations of foreign exchange, often but not in all cases derived directly or indirectly from revenues from the export of natural resources. What issues are raised by SWFs? They raise many issues about globalization and the role of governments in today's world. How do they fit into the international financial system of the 21st century? Awkwardly, potentially contentiously, in ways on which there is less than total agreement. This chapter expands upon these brief answers.

What, When, and How?

Governments are involved in a wide range of economic and financial activities. Some of those activities involve the accumulation of financial assets in various structures in anticipation of the use of those assets, or some or all of the earnings on them, to finance and otherwise support various governmental activities in the near or distant future. In some cases, governments invest abroad. In 2005, governments discovered that their pools of such financial assets were what had come to be called "sovereign wealth funds." They had become members of a club to which they had not applied. Nor was it clear what defined their membership qualifications, because there was and still is no single, accepted definition of an SWF. Anna Gelpern (forthcoming) argues that they are an artificial category and a jumble of contradictions, but I would not go quite that far.

I use "sovereign wealth fund" as a descriptive term to identify separate pools of government-owned or controlled assets that include some international assets.[1] I treat government pension funds as SWFs to the extent that they manage marketable assets.[2] Government pension funds raise many of the same issues for public policy in the home and host countries.[3] For the same reason, I do not distinguish between SWFs that exist at the national level and those at a subnational level, such as those of states or provinces.

Sovereign wealth funds may have a number of different objectives. One classification (IMF 2008b) lists five: (1) stabilization funds designed to insulate the budget or the economy against price swings; (2) savings funds for future generations often transferring wealth that is underground into financial wealth aboveground; (3) reserve investment funds that are an adjunct to other arrangements for managing foreign exchange reserves and sometimes include a portion of the country's foreign exchange reserves; (4) development funds that are organized to achieve various socioeconomic objectives at home or abroad and may resemble financial hold-

---

1. In some contexts, "sovereign wealth fund" necessarily is more than a descriptive term. For example, in drawing up a set of recommended principles to apply to SWFs, the IWG (2008b, 3) adopted a precise definition: "SWFs are special purpose investment funds or arrangements that are owned by the general government. Created by the general government for macroeconomic purposes, SWFs hold, manage, or administer assets to achieve financial objectives, and employ a set of investment strategies that include investing in foreign financial assets." The IWG noted that "general government includes both central government and subnational government." It added, "SWFs are commonly established out of balance of payments surpluses, official foreign currency operations, the proceeds of privatizations, fiscal surpluses, and/or receipts resulting from commodity exports." This language on the funds used to establish and expand SWFs is also found in the IMF's *Sixth Balance of Payments and International Investment Position Manual* (IMF 2009a).

2. Some make a distinction between pension funds that mainly invest the surpluses of employee and/or employer contributions over current payouts (social security reserve funds or pension reserve funds) and those that are financed mainly from fiscal transfers from the government (sovereign pension reserve funds); see Blundell-Wignall, Hu, and Yermo (2008). These authors classify Norway's Government Pension Fund-Global as a sovereign pension reserve fund, which is difficult to justify given that the fund's current payments to the government are unrelated to pension obligations. The IWG included sovereign pension reserve funds in its definition.

3. It is difficult to see why any distinctions should be made among government-owned or -controlled investment vehicles as long as the government has some role, for example, in appointing board members. Such distinctions may have some merit for certain legal or analytical purposes, but even in the latter case pension SWFs in their structure, governance, accountability and transparency, and behavior are useful analytically for reference purposes. (A distinction can be made between funds that operate at the national level and those that operate at the subnational level in that the former may more easily be positioned to pursue national strategic objectives. However, this is only one of several policy concerns about SWFs; see chapter 3.) The only distinction I make in this study is to exclude pension structures where the individual account holder chooses investments in particular subfunds and the role of the government is limited to assembling choices among such funds and to executing the decisions of the individual.

ing companies; and (5) contingent pension reserve funds that are intended to backstop government pension funds. In practice, most funds have a mixture of objectives that often change over time with economic and financial circumstances. For example, a stabilization fund may grow sufficiently in size that it becomes more like a savings fund.[4]

Table 2.1 provides a list of 83 generic SWFs of 54 countries; the date when each fund was first established; the principal sources of its financial resources; its size, or an estimate of its size, in late 2009 or the most recent prior or subsequent date for which information is available; and the amount of its foreign assets or an estimate thereof. The table includes 70 nonpension SWFs, the universe that we or others have identified, and 13 pension and pension-reserve SWFs (each separately identified).[5] The total size of these entities is $5.9 trillion.[6] Of the entities listed in table 2.1, 23 have estimated assets of more than $50 billion, and they account for 91 percent of the total assets. The 10 largest entities account for 70 percent of the total.

A reasonable estimate of total assets of pension SWFs is $5.7 trillion, including the $2.4 trillion reported in table 2.1.[7] Adding this figure to the total assets of nonpension SWFs in table 2.1 produces a grand total of $9.2 trillion in SWF assets.

As a group, the pension SWFs listed in table 2.1 hold 28 percent of their portfolios in foreign assets, ranging from 5 percent for China's National Social Security Fund and 14 percent for Thailand's Government Pension Fund to 100 percent for Chile's Pension Reserve Fund and 75 percent for New Zealand's Superannuation Fund. Non-US pension funds hold about

---

4. Bortolotti et al. (2009) argue that many SWFs started out with a stabilization purpose and evolved into something else, which is a plausible scenario. The appendix to their paper presents a valuable timeline for SWFs. Hammer, Kunzel, and Petrova (2008) summarize a survey of the SWFs participating in the IWG, which published an almost complete version of the survey of 20 of the funds (IWG 2008a). The results of the survey illustrate the diversity of SWFs in their legal frameworks and objectives, institutional and governance structures, and investment policies and risk frameworks. The results rely in part on confidential information, but are broadly consistent with the patterns that emerge from the scoreboard presented in chapter 5.

5. The memorandum items list four other entities that I use later in this study for comparison with SWFs: the Teachers Insurance and Annuity Association–College Retirement Equities Fund (TIAA-CREF), a US private-sector pension organization; Blackstone, a publicly traded US private equity firm; the Harvard University endowment; and Terra Firma, a UK private equity fund that is not publicly traded.

6. Excluding the pension SWFs of both types reduces this figure to $3.5 trillion. Table 2.1 uses the midpoint where only a range of estimates of the size of these entities is available.

7. This estimate is based on national sources, the OECD's pension indicators database that covers pension reserve funds, and the US flow of funds accounts. Assets in US state and local government pension funds were estimated at $2.8 trillion at the end of 2009 (Board of Governors of the Federal Reserve System 2010, table L.119).

Table 2.1 Sovereign wealth funds (billions of dollars)

Country	Current name	Date established	Source of funds	Total assets[a]	Foreign assets[b]
Japan	*Government Pension Investment Fund (P)*	1961	Employee contributions	1,264	260
UAE (Abu Dhabi)	Abu Dhabi Investment Authority	1976	Natural resources	620[c]	620
Norway	Government Pension Fund-Global	1990	Natural resources	432	432
Saudi Arabia	Saudi Arabian Monetary Agency[d]	1952	Foreign exchange reserves	414	414
China	China Investment Corporation	2007	Foreign exchange reserves	298	98
Netherlands	*Stichting Pensioenfonds ABP (P)*	1922	Employee contributions	254	125
Singapore	Government of Singapore Investment Corporation[e]	1981	Foreign exchange reserves, fiscal surpluses, employee contributions	248[c]	248
Canada	*Caisse de dépôt et placement du Québec (P)*	1965	Employee contributions	220	84
Hong Kong	Exchange Fund[e]	1993	Foreign exchange reserves, fiscal surpluses	205	174
Kuwait	Kuwait Investment Authority	1953	Natural resources	203	203
United States	*California Public Employees' Retirement System (P)*	1932	Employee contributions	199	48
Canada	*Ontario Teachers' Pension Plan (P)*	1917	Employee contributions	135	29
Singapore	Temasek Holdings	1974	Government enterprises	120	74
Canada	*Canada Pension Plan (P)*	1966	Employee contributions	106	57
Russia	Reserve Fund[e]	2004	Natural resources	95	95
China	National Welfare Fund[e]	2004	Natural resources	90	90
China	*National Social Security Fund (P)*	2000	Fiscal surpluses	83	4
UAE (Dubai)	Investment Corporation of Dubai	2006	Natural resources	82	82
Libya	Libyan Investment Authority[d]	1981	Natural resources	70[c]	70
Qatar	Qatar Investment Authority	2005	Natural resources	70	70
Australia	*Future Fund (PR)*	2006	Fiscal surpluses	66	19
	Queensland Investment Corporation[d]	1991	Fiscal surpluses	65	34
Algeria	Revenue Regulation Fund	2000	Natural resources	55[c]	55
France	*Fonds de réserve pour les retraites (P)*	2001	Fiscal surpluses	38	13
Brunei	Brunei Investment Agency	1983	Natural resources	35	35

Country	Fund	Year	Source		
United States	Alaska Permanent Fund	1976	Natural resources	34	7
Kazakhstan	National Fund	2000	Natural resources	33	33
Australia	Victorian Funds Management Corporation[d]	1994	Fiscal surpluses	30	8
France	Strategic Investment Fund[d,f]	2008	Fiscal surpluses	28	0
Ireland	National Pensions Reserve Fund (PR)	2001	Fiscal surpluses	27	10
Malaysia	Khazanah Nasional	1993	Fiscal surpluses	27	2
UAE (Abu Dhabi)	Mubadala Development Company	2002	Natural resources	21	8
Chile	Economic and Social Stabilization Fund	1985	Natural resources	18	18
Korea	Korea Investment Corporation[e]	2005	Natural resources	18	18
Venezuela	National Development Fund	2005	Natural resources	16[c]	16
Taiwan	National Stabilization Fund[d,f]	2000	Pension funds and government-run funds	15	0
Bahrain	Mumtalakat Holding Company	2006	Natural resources	14	11
Canada	Alberta Heritage Savings Trust Fund	1976	Natural resources	14	5
UAE (Abu Dhabi)	International Petroleum Investment Company	1984	Natural resources	14	14
New Zealand	Superannuation Fund (PR)	2001	Fiscal surpluses	13	10
Azerbaijan	State Oil Fund	1999	Natural resources	13	13
Iran	Oil Stabilization Fund	2000	Natural resources	13	13
UAE (Dubai)	Dubai International Capital	2004	Natural resources	13	12
	Istithmar	2003	Natural resources	12	12
Nigeria	Excess Crude Account[e]	2004	Natural resources	11	11
Thailand	Government Pension Fund (P)	1996	Employee contributions and fiscal surpluses	11	2
Brazil	Sovereign Wealth Fund of Brazil[d,f]	2009	Fiscal surpluses	8	0
Oman	State General Reserve Fund	1980	Natural resources	8	8
Botswana	Pula Fund[e]	1993	Natural resources	6	6
Mexico	Oil Income Stabilization Fund	2000	Natural resources	6	6
Saudi Arabia	Public Investment Fund[d,f]	1971	Natural resources	5	0
Timor-Leste	Petroleum Fund	2005	Natural resources	4.8	4.8
Taiwan	Executive Yuan, Development Fund[d,f]	1973	Fiscal surpluses	4.5	0

(continued on next page)

Table 2.1 Sovereign wealth funds (billions of dollars) *(continued)*

Country	Current name	Date established	Source of funds	Total assets[a]	Foreign assets[b]
United States	Permanent Mineral Trust Fund (Wyoming)	1974	Natural resources	4.0	0.8
Chile	*Pension Reserve Fund (PR)*	1985	Fiscal surpluses	3.5	3.5
United States	Severance Tax Permanent Fund (New Mexico)	1973	Natural resources	3.2	0.5
Malaysia	Terengganu Investment Authority[d]	2008	Natural resources	3.0[c]	3.0
Norway	Government Petroleum Insurance Fund[d]	1986	Natural resources	3.0	1.5
Trinidad and Tobago	Heritage and Stabilization Fund	2007	Natural resources	2.9	2.9
UAE (RAK)	RAK Investment Authority[d]	2004	Natural resources	2.5[c]	2.5
United States	Alabama Trust Fund	2000	Natural resources	2.5	1.8
Colombia	Oil Stabilization Fund[d]	1995	Natural resources	2.1	2.1
China	Shanghai Financial Holdings[d]	2007	Fiscal surpluses	1.0	1.0
Venezuela	Macroeconomic Stabilization Fund	2003	Natural resources	0.8	0.8
Canada	Fonds des générations[d]	2006	Renewable resources (water)	0.6	0.2
Turkmenistan	Stabilization Fund[d]	2008	Fiscal surpluses	0.5	0.5
UAE	Emirates Investment Authority[d]	2007	Natural resources	0.5[c]	0.5
UAE (Dubai)	DIFC Investments[d]	2006	Natural resources	0.5	0.5
Vietnam	State Capital Investment Corporation	2005	Fiscal surpluses	0.5	0.5
Gabon	Fund for Future Generations[d]	1998	Natural resources	0.4	0.4
Kiribati	Revenue Equalization Reserve Fund	1956	Natural resources	0.4	0.4
Uganda	Poverty Action Fund[d]	1998	Savings from the Heavily Indebted Poor Countries (HIPC) debt relief initiative, donor contributions, and fiscal surpluses	0.4	0.4
Mauritania	National Fund for Hydrocarbon Reserves[d]	2006	Natural resources	0.3[c]	0.3
Angola	Reserve Fund for Oil[d]	2007	Natural resources	0.2	0.2
Micronesia	Compact Trust Fund of Micronesia[d]	2004	Foreign aid	0.2[c]	0.2
Papua New Guinea	Mineral Resources Stabilization Fund[d]	1974	Natural resources	0.2	0.2

Marshall Islands	RMI Trust Fund[d]	2004	Foreign aid	0.2[c]	0.2
Sudan	Oil Revenue Stabilization Account	2002	Natural resources	0.1	0.1
Tuvalu	Tuvalu Trust Fund[d]	1987	International donors	0.1	0.1
Nauru	Phosphate Royalties Stabilization Fund[d]	1968	Natural resources	0.06	0.06
Equatorial Guinea	Fund for Future[d]	2006	Natural resources	0.03	0.03
Tonga	Tonga Trust Fund[d]	1988	Receipts from issue of passports, foreign aid	0.03[c]	0.03
São Tomé and Príncipe	National Oil Account	2004	Natural resources	0.02	0.02
Nonpension total[c]				3,524	3,037
Pension total[c]				2,414	666
SWFs total[c]				5,938	3,703
Memorandum					
United States	TIAA-CREF	1918	Plan contributions	363	38
	Blackstone	1985	Equity and other investors	96	10
	Harvard University Endowment	1974	University's endowment	26	7
United Kingdom	Terra Firma	1994	Pension fund, insurance companies, SWFs, and endowments	6	5
Total				492	59

a. As of mid-2009 or the most recent date before or after.
b. Foreign assets are estimated for some funds.
c. Total uses the midpoint of a range of estimates.
d. Excluded from the SWF scoreboard presented in chapter 5.
e. Some or all assets are included in reserves.
f. Currently invests exclusively in domestic assets.

Note: Pension funds (P) and reserve pension funds (PR) are shown in italics.

Sources: National authorities; International Monetary Fund; other public sources.

25 percent of their portfolios in foreign assets, and US state and local pension funds hold about 15 percent.[8] Thus, the total foreign assets of pension and nonpension SWFs can be estimated at $4.2 trillion, compared with the $3.7 trillion listed in table 2.1.

The 54 countries with the 83 SWFs listed in table 2.1 differ substantially in many dimensions, as do their funds. In the United States, four subnational, nonpension SWFs hold $44 billion in assets, of which 23 percent is invested abroad. Including US state and local government employee pension funds and my estimate of their foreign holdings would raise US total SWF assets to $3.2 trillion, with about $425 billion invested abroad. These are larger totals than for any other country with the probable exceptions of SWFs in the United Arab Emirates and Norway. It follows that the United States has an interest in SWFs not only as the recipient of SWF investments but also as a home country to such funds.

The United Arab Emirates, including subnational governmental units, has nine SWFs identified in table 2.1 with an estimated $766 billion in assets, assuming that the listed figure of $620 billion in assets of the Abu Dhabi Investment Authority (ADIA) is approximately correct.[9] The China Investment Corporation (CIC) had almost $300 billion in assets as of the end of 2009, but less than a third of its assets were invested abroad. In contrast, almost two-thirds of the assets of Singapore's Temasek, said to be a model for the CIC, are invested abroad. Singapore has two SWFs: Temasek, which was founded in 1974 and is a holding company for equity-type investments, and the Government of Singapore Investment Corporation (GIC), which was founded in 1981 and whose portfolio more closely resembles that of a university endowment and is entirely invested outside the country.

Some of the 70 nonpension SWFs listed in table 2.1 do not have an identifiable, independent structure. For example, the Saudi Arabian Monetary Agency is that country's central bank and the assets often listed as its SWF portfolio are the longer-term investment component of its foreign exchange holdings. Similarly, the Queensland Investment Corporation and Victorian Funds Management Corporation in Australia, which do invest abroad, manage a range of governmental funds for a variety of purposes. Some of the smaller funds listed in the table, such as those of Uganda, Micronesia, the Marshall Islands, and Tuvalu, manage funds that are largely derived from donors and intended ultimately for domestic investment. On the other hand, several of the funds listed in table 2.1 invest exclusively domestically, as indicated by the footnote to the table. Excluding these types

---

8. The source for this estimate is the US Census Bureau's summaries of state and local public employee retirement system finances.

9. Setser and Ziemba (2009) estimate that the ADIA's assets were only $328 billion as of the end of 2008. The Institute of International Finance (2009a) uses a figure of $395 billion for 2009.

of funds and funds with a lack of information from an analysis, as I do in chapter 5, reduces the number of nonpension SWFs from 70 to 41.

The combined size of SWFs sextupled over the five years ending in 2007. An imprecise proxy for investments in the United States by SWFs from other countries suggests that such investment also quadrupled over the five-year period.[10] In 2007, estimates by various investment banks projected growth of SWF assets to as much as $7.9 trillion by 2011, $12 trillion by 2015, and $17.5 trillion by 2017.[11]

Market estimates of the potential growth of SWFs were subsequently scaled back. Steffen Kern (2010) of Deutsche Bank in mid-2010 estimated that SWF assets under management would be in a range of $7.1 trillion to $8.3 trillion by 2017.[12] SWFs along with other investors suffered losses, generally unrealized and not always reported, as a consequence of the global financial crisis that began to affect financial markets in August 2007 and continued into 2009. Meanwhile, although inflows continued to many funds, the scale of those inflows was reduced compared with 2006 and 2007. Moreover, outflows from some funds accelerated as governments drew on them to finance fiscal deficits, support domestic financial institutions, or stimulate domestic consumption or investment. It is difficult to parse each of these influences on the growth of SWFs, but it is clear that the growth of SWFs has slowed. In Truman (2008a) I estimated that 34 nonpension SWFs held $3 trillion in total assets and $2.7 trillion in foreign assets as of the end of 2007. The estimates in table 2.1 suggest increases of 18 and 14 percent, respectively, over the subsequent two years, including new funds, substantially slower than average annual increases of more than 30 percent over the previous five years.

Because of the range of different origins and objectives of SWFs, it is challenging to generalize about the nature of their investment activities. Most generalizations are either empty or off the mark. As described by Das et al. (2009) in a prescriptive paper, an SWF's investment strategy and

---

10. The United States records most, but not all, SWF investments in its published data on US international transactions and on the US international investment position in the line "other foreign official assets." Although that line includes some other investors, the amount was only $82 billion in 1997, grew to $107 billion in 2002, and exploded to $433 billion by the end of 2007. The amount declined by the end of 2008 to $383 billion, reflecting reduced inflows of $88 billion and valuation losses of $161 billion, accounting for 37 percent of the total stock as of the end of 2007. In 2009, the recorded net inflow was only $22 billion, but valuation effects pushed the value of the total stock back to $495 billion.

11. These high-end estimates are from Merrill Lynch (2007) and Morgan Stanley (2007b, 2007c), respectively. Citi Global Banking (2007) estimated only a modestly lower amount of $7.5 trillion in SWF assets as of 2012.

12. These estimates are based on annual growth rates of foreign exchange reserves over the past 5 to 30 years of 9.7 to 12.3 percent from a base of $3.7 trillion in SWF assets under management at the end of 2009. In late 2008, Steffen Kern's (2008) estimate was that SWF assets under management would reach $10 billion by 2015.

strategic asset allocation depend on its organizational objectives in determining its investment horizon, risk tolerance, risk management strategy, and preference for liquidity. Individual SWFs will differ in each of these elements. The result can be a near-infinite number of possible portfolio allocations for a particular fund or across funds.

One frequent generalization is that SWFs prefer equities in their asset allocations, but how dominant that preference is depends on the fund. Mansoor Mohi-uddin (2010) of UBS reports that the equity share in major SWFs ranges from 100 percent for Singapore's Temasek to only slightly more than 40 percent for Australia's Future Fund, which at the time he was reporting had almost 40 percent of its assets in cash, while Singapore's GIC had more than 30 percent of its assets in cash.

In general, as with US university and college endowments, SWFs may invest in a wide range of assets, including equities, bonds, hedge funds, private equity firms, and infrastructure projects. In its first-ever annual report, for 2009, the ADIA reported that its benchmark for equities ranged from 40 to 70 percent of its portfolio (35 to 45 percent in equities of developed economies, 10 to 20 percent in equities of emerging markets, and 1 to 5 percent in small cap equities) (ADIA 2010). At the same time, government bonds may attract 10 to 20 percent of the ADIA's portfolio, credit extensions 5 to 10 percent, hedge funds and other managed funds 5 to 10 percent, real estate 5 to 10 percent, private equity 2 to 8 percent, infrastructure 1 to 5 percent, and cash 0 to 10 percent. Preqin Equity (2010) reported that 79 percent of SWFs invest in public equities, and a similar percentage of SWFs invest in fixed-income securities. It reports lower percentages for other asset classes: private equity (55 percent), real estate (51 percent), infrastructure (47 percent), and hedge funds (37 percent).

In contrast, until 2007, Norway's Government Pension Fund-Global aimed to hold only 40 percent of its portfolio in equities and 60 percent in bonds (NBIM 2010). In a masterstroke of timing, the Norwegian fund then reversed its target proportions of equities and bonds, and began to invest up to 5 percent of its nonequity portfolio in real estate. As is well known, Norway diversifies its investments widely within each asset class, with its average equity holdings at about 1 percent of the world's listed companies as of the end of March 2010, when its total portfolio reached $465 billion. However, the Norges Bank Investment Management (NBIM) does not follow a passive buy-and-hold strategy in managing its portfolio, but rather uses a sophisticated active management strategy, though this approach has been questioned in Norway (NBIM 2009).

A few SWFs take controlling stakes in firms, though most often only in their domestic investments. Where they take significant equity stakes, the purchases show up in various databases, and researchers can exploit those databases to derive inferences about the SWFs' changing investment strategies. One example is the report of the Monitor Group by Miracky and Bortolotti (2010). Another is Bernstein, Lerner, and Schoar

(2009), who assembled a database of 2,662 transactions of 29 SWFs between 1984 and 2007, although the total value of those investments in 2008 was $298 billion, less than 10 percent of the international assets of all SWFs. We can learn something from these reports and related research, but they do not provide an overall picture of the nature of SWF activities.

In bad periods like 2008 and early 2009, SWF portfolios perform in general like other large, diversified investment portfolios. For example, Norway's Government Pension Fund-Global reported a negative return of 23 percent in 2008.[13] Singapore's GIC, which does not report the size of its portfolio, reported a loss of more than 20 percent in Singapore dollar terms for the year ending March 2009. Setser and Ziemba (2009) estimate the capital losses of Persian Gulf country SWFs, including the Saudi Arabian Monetary Agency, at $350 billion in 2008 or 30 percent of the value of the assets at the end of 2007, larger than the inflows in 2008 and comparable to the losses at the Norwegian SWF. They estimate that the ADIA shrunk by about a quarter in 2008. Bortolotti et al. (2009) report that the $122.7 billion in listed-firm SWF investments in their database suffered $57.3 billion in losses through March 27, 2009—near the bottom of the market—mostly due to investments in Western financial institutions. For comparison, the National Association of College and University Business Officers (NACUBO) and Commonfund reported that in the fiscal year ending June 30, 2009, US colleges and universities had a negative return on their endowments of 18.7 percent (NACUBO and Commonfund 2010). Assets of US state and local government employee pension funds are estimated to have shrunk by 27 percent in 2008 before increasing 14 percent in 2009 (Board of Governors of the Federal Reserve System 2010). It is reasonable to presume that SWFs on average performed similarly. An exception to this pattern is China's CIC, which recorded a substantial gain in 2008 on its investments in domestic banks.

The earliest government investment pool that today is described as an SWF was founded in 1953 and is now the Kuwait Investment Corporation, which was established before Kuwait regained its full independence from the United Kingdom in 1961.[14] Of the 70 nonpension SWFs listed in table 2.1, four were established before 1970. A larger number (nine) were established in the 1970s, mostly in the context of the rise in oil prices during that period, and include three of the four SWFs of US states as well as the SWF of the Canadian province of Alberta. A few more (15) were established between 1980 and the mid-1990s, but the bulk (60 percent) were

---

13. Norway's Government Pension Fund-Global subsequently reported a record return in 2009 of 25.6 percent.

14. The Saudi Arabian Monetary Agency was established in 1952, but for my purposes it is not considered an SWF. Hildebrand (2007) notes that the French Caisse des Dépôts et Consignations set up in 1816 could be regarded as an SWF, but that institution generally does not invest abroad (Demarolle 2008).

established since that time as oil and other commodity prices rose and countries built up large balances of foreign exchange reserves. About half of these SWFs were established in 2004 or later. In this respect, SWFs are a new phenomenon.

Although the vast majority (about 70 percent) of nonpension SWFs listed in table 2.1 receive their financing from earnings on the sale of natural resources, primarily oil or natural gas, such earnings are not the only source of SWF financing. A small number of countries have diverted, or otherwise deployed, their foreign exchange reserves to fund their SWFs, including some of the largest funds.[15] Sometimes the foreign exchange reserves used to fund an SWF are counted as part of the country's international reserves. However, in a number of countries (about 20 percent of the total), the nonpension SWFs are funded from sources other than earnings from natural resources or foreign exchange reserves. In the particular case of pension SWFs, they are funded from fiscal revenues or the contributions of employers and employees.

The variety of sources of funding for SWFs points to several important features of such entities.

First, even when some of their investments are outside the home country, SWFs need not be funded in the first instance with foreign exchange. The governmental investment entity may receive its funding in domestic currency and use that currency to buy foreign currency to invest abroad.

Second, a country investing abroad via its government-owned SWF need not even have a current account surplus to have an SWF. Several of the countries with SWFs that invest abroad that are listed in table 2.1 have current account deficits, starting with the United States. Six other countries with SWFs listed in table 2.1 also had current account deficits on average over the 2004–08 period: Australia, Azerbaijan, France, Kazakhstan, Mexico, and Sudan. When Singapore established Temasek Holdings and the GIC in 1974 and 1981, respectively, the country had a current account deficit and was operating with a more flexible exchange rate regime than it does today. Thus, in their foreign investments, SWFs are just like other governmental and nongovernmental investment entities.

Third, even in the case of SWFs that are nominally funded from earnings from natural resources, those earnings may be either channeled through the domestic economy or diverted from the domestic economy. Four cases are presented in box 2.1.

Many observers also distinguish among SWFs on the basis of their liability structures (IMF 2007d): for example, an SWF that is tied to a pension system and its disbursements, an SWF that is used primarily to stabilize fiscal and/or foreign exchange revenues, or an SWF that has issued liabilities to its government. The liability structure of SWFs is relevant to

---

15. As discussed below, funding an SWF out of reserves versus funding one from the proceeds of exports of natural resources is a distinction without a clear economic difference.

Box 2.1 Funding a sovereign wealth fund

Case A

The country taxes a domestic natural resource producer (in the public or private sector) in domestic currency because it has decided that this type of tax is appropriate or, in the case of a nonrenewable resource (petroleum, gas, diamonds, or copper), it wants to retain the right to transform a part of the country's wealth that was underground into financial wealth aboveground and not immediately spend the financial resources on goods and services. In this first stage, all the transactions would be in domestic currency. If the country wants its SWF to invest abroad, the SWF would use its tax revenues in domestic currency to buy foreign currency to make the investment. The country might have a number of reasons for investing abroad. One is to diversify its investment portfolio. A second is to recycle some of the country's foreign exchange earnings abroad in order to reduce upward pressure on the exchange rate, which would disadvantage the nonresource sectors of the economy or otherwise distort the economy's development via monetary, fiscal, or financial overheating.[1] In other words, the country is trying to avoid the "Dutch disease" associated with an excessive appreciation of the real exchange rate in response to the discovery and exploitation of a natural resource or a sustained rise in the price of an exported commodity. The real appreciation in turn has detrimental effects on the performance and development of the economy by inducing increased spending and/or distorting the allocation of resources away from nontradables and other tradables.[2] Recycling the export earnings is one means of addressing this problem, but it is not the only instrument. Moreover, the effectiveness of this strategy requires supporting macroeconomic and financial policies and institutions. Even if they are present, the country, in effect, is engaging in sterilized foreign exchange market intervention. The sustained effectiveness of such intervention in influencing exchange rates for advanced countries such as Norway, Canada, and the United States is far from agreed upon within the economics profession.

Case B

The country taxes the domestic natural resource producer, but the tax is denominated in foreign currency. In this case, the producer either pays the tax to the government and its SWF in foreign currency, which is most likely, or conducts the foreign exchange market transaction itself to the extent that its revenues are in domestic currency. This may avoid some of the policy risks identified in case A. The net result could be the same, but the mechanism in case B runs through the fiscal authorities. If the SWF invests domestically, the foreign exchange has to be converted into domestic currency.

(box continued on next page)

Box 2.1   Funding a sovereign wealth fund *(continued)*

Case C

The country directs an entity, perhaps because it owns the natural resource producer, to deposit all or a percentage of its gross revenues in the SWF. This mechanism does not run through the fiscal authorities, although, as in Norway, for example, those authorities may be entitled to a fixed or variable annual withdrawal from the SWF that is used to finance the government's nonoil budget.

Case D

The natural resource producer may be government owned or privately owned, but it is not taxed directly on its net earnings or revenues, a large portion of which may come from sales abroad. However, the country's exchange rate policy, executed by the central bank, involves heavy foreign currency purchases that are added to the country's foreign exchange reserves and may be used, in turn, to provide financing to one or more of the country's SWFs.

   In each of these four cases—and a number of additional cases could be imagined—the net result is that the SWF receives funding. How that funding is channeled into domestic and foreign investments depends on the country and how its SWF is organized. There may be more and less preferred ways of institutionalizing the funding of an SWF, but each country makes its own choices based on its own history, institutions, and circumstances. For purposes of this study, these distinctions are not material.

---

1. Although this case assumes that the government would save the tax revenues, if they were spent on either real or financial investments in the country this could distort the macroeconomic development of the economy. This is one reason why it is important that the SWF's investment strategy be appropriately integrated into the country's overall fiscal and financial strategy. Alternatively, the government, in effect, is running a second budget.

2. The literature on Dutch disease is vast and somewhat controversial, as it overlaps with the issue of the existence of the resource curse. For primers on Dutch disease, see Ebrahim-zadeh (2003) and Brahmbhatt, Canuto, and Vostroknutova (2010). Two classic works are Corden and Neary (1982) and Gelb and Associates (1988). For an extensive, collected set of papers on the associated issue of the resource curse, see Humphreys, Sachs, and Stiglitz (2007).

some aspects of the investment policies of the fund (e.g., the date at which it might be expected to make scheduled or unscheduled disbursements), to specific governance aspects of the fund, and to public perceptions of its activities. However, the liability structure is of little relevance in thinking about a government's balance sheet as a whole. For example, an SWF may have issued liabilities to its central bank in exchange for foreign exchange inflows that were mopped up by the central bank and end up in the fund.

As an accounting matter, the fund is required to service those liabilities, but aside from accounting niceties, it is not appropriate to evaluate the fund's return net of servicing those liabilities, nor to condition its investments on achieving such a return. Contrary to the advice in IMF (2007d), the SWF's return is its return, and everything else is a matter of internal government bookkeeping, including the coverage of any potential currency mismatches. There are reasons why an SWF's return on equity or return on assets is relevant, but they are not linked to its particular liability structure. Moreover, the liability structure of an SWF has only marginal or indirect relevance to its role in the global economy, the principal focus of this study. The view here is that too many observers make too much of this aspect of SWFs.

Potential for Growth

Notwithstanding the fact that SWFs may receive financing from their governments from many sources, and regardless of whether or not the country in question is in current account surplus or deficit, the fact is that SWFs are disproportionately associated with countries that either have large sustained current account surpluses generally (but not exclusively) from exports of natural resources, have built up large foreign exchange reserves, or both. Aizenman and Glick (2008) look at this relationship statistically, focusing on 29 countries with SWFs using probit regressions for the probability that a country will have had a fund in 2006 or 2007. They find the ratios of foreign reserves to GDP and fuel exports to total exports have very strong explanatory power at the 1 percent level of significance, and the country's current account surplus as a percent of GDP in 2002–06 is almost as significant (5 percent). Ore and metal export ratios do not show up as significant, nor does GDP per capita. However, GDP per capita is significant for developing countries alone. It is reasonable to surmise that this pattern will continue in the future, but of course history is not always the best guide.

Table 2.2 provides some background information to help evaluate this potential. The 26 countries with the largest SWFs from table 2.1 on the basis of at least $35 billion in combined foreign exchange reserves and SWF international assets are listed in the first column along with 15 other countries with holdings of foreign exchange reserves of more than $35 billion at the end of 2008.[16] The table also lists those reserves as a percent of GDP and each country's average 2004–08 current account balance as a share of GDP. Both large stocks of reserves and continuing current

---

16. The 41 countries account for 98 percent of all SWF international assets from table 2.1 and 85 percent of total foreign exchange reserves as of the end of 2008.

Table 2.2 Potential for expansion of sovereign wealth funds (billions of dollars)

Country	SWF international assets[a] (1)	Foreign exchange reserves, 2008 (2)	SWF international assets + foreign exchange reserves (3)	Foreign exchange reserves as a percent of GDP, 2008 (4)	Current account as a percent of GDP, 2004–08 average (5)
China	103	1,946	2,049	45	8.2
Japan	260	1,004	1,264	20	3.9
United Arab Emirates	751	32	783	12	16.3
Russia[b]	184	411	596	25	8.5
Singapore[b]	322	174	496	95	20.9
Norway	433	50	484	11	16.3
Saudi Arabia	419	28	447	6	26.0
Hong Kong[b]	174	182	357	85	11.9
India	—	247	247	20	−1.1
Kuwait	203	17	219	11	42.4
Canada	175	42	217	3	1.4
Korea[c]	18	200	218	22	1.2
Algeria	55	143	198	90	20.9
Brazil	0	193	193	12	0.6
Libya	70	91	161	101	37.2
Netherlands	125	9	134	1	7.8
Thailand	2	108	110	40	0.8
United States	58	50	107	0	−5.5
Mexico	6	94	100	9	−0.8
Malaysia	5	91	96	41	15.3
Australia	61	30	90	3	−5.6
Qatar	70	10	80	9	28.5
Turkey	—	70	70	10	−5.2
France	34	30	65	1	−0.7
Nigeria[b]	11	53	64	26	15.6
Poland	—	59	59	11	−3.6
Kazakhstan	33	18	51	13	−1.2
Iraq	—	50	50	54	n.a.
Venezuela	17	33	49	10	13.5
Indonesia	—	49	49	10	1.2
Chile	22	23	44	13	2.1
Argentina	—	44	44	14	1.8
Switzerland	—	44	44	9	10.6
Israel	—	42	42	21	2.7
United Kingdom	—	42	42	2	−2.5
Denmark	—	40	40	12	2.4
Germany	—	39	39	1	6.0
Romania	—	37	37	18	−10.7
Czech Republic	—	36	36	17	−3.1
Brunei	35	1	36	5	51.8
Italy	—	35	35	2	−2.2
Total	3,646[d]	5,895[d]	9,541[d]	22[e]	8.3[e]
Memorandum	3,703[a]	6,908[f]	10,611		

n.a. = not available.

a. From table 2.1. Dashes indicate no SWFs.
b. SWF international assets include an unknown amount of foreign exchange reserves producing some double counting.
c. SWF holds international reserves that are netted out from the total in column (3).
d. Total.
e. Average.
f. Global foreign exchange reserves as of December 2008.

account surpluses are potential sources of funding, or additional funding, for SWFs.

The data in the table present a mixed picture. The countries with large combined holdings of foreign assets in their portfolios do not each have large current account surpluses in recent years; the United States, with the 18th largest holdings, had huge deficits. Countries with large SWF holdings of foreign assets do not necessarily have large reported reserves, in particular many of the countries in the Persian Gulf, such as the United Arab Emirates, Saudi Arabia, Kuwait, and Qatar.[17] These countries apparently channel their foreign exchange earnings directly into their SWFs, leaving relatively small amounts in their reported foreign exchange reserves. However, a number of other countries have more international assets in their SWFs than they have foreign exchange reserves, including Canada, the Netherlands, the United States, Australia, and France. Countries with large cumulative current account surpluses, such as Germany and Switzerland, have substantial reserves, but do not have SWFs. Moreover, a country (e.g., India) can have large reserves without a current account surplus or an SWF.

Nevertheless, countries with excess foreign exchange holdings are likely candidates to establish or augment their SWFs using those holdings.[18] At the political level, the size and currency composition of a country's foreign exchange reserves is a topic that interacts with and helps to fuel the SWF debates. At the analytical level, the challenge is the lack of consensus about the point at which reserve holdings become excess.

The literature on the demand for and appropriate level of international reserves dates to the 1960s (Frenkel and Jovanovic 1981, Hamada and Ueda 1977, Heller 1966, Heller and Knight 1978). In the wake of the more than 200 percent increase in the foreign exchange reserve holdings from 2001 through the end of 2008 of all countries, and the almost 450 percent increase over that period in holdings excluding those of the so-called mature industrial countries, this literature has experienced a resurgence (Aizenman 2007, Flood and Marion 2002, García and Soto 2006, Genberg et al. 2005, IMF 2003, Jeanne 2007, Jeanne and Rancière 2006, Mohanty and Turner 2006, and Rodrik 2006). Rules of thumb have been developed for determining the adequacy of reserves. They are expressed in terms of (1) months of imports of goods and services; (2) a ratio to short-term debt

---

17. Of course, for some countries, all or part of the SWF may still be included in reserves, so there is some double counting in the table as indicated by the footnote.

18. Aizenman and Glick (2008) find that, in a regression explaining the ratio of foreign exchange reserves to GDP in 1985–2006, a dummy variable for oil-exporting countries with older SWFs shows up as negatively significant, though for countries with newer SWFs the relationship is positive. At the same time, they find significant positive relationships with the ratio of imports to GDP, M2 to GDP, and the incidence of currency crises, but no significant influence from the variability of reserves.

immediately coming due, or in total, to total external debt of the government or country, or to external obligations; (3) a ratio to GDP or to some measure of the money supply; or (4) combinations of the above. Theoretical and empirical analyses also have sought to explain the behavior of countries in building up their reserves and to determine the appropriate cutoff for "excess" reserves (Aizenman 2007; Aizenman and Lee 2005; Aizenman, Lee, and Rhee 2004; Aizenman and Marion 2003; Garcia and Soto 2006; IMF 2003; and Jeanne 2007).

My reading of this literature is that, first, there is no consensus about the optimal level of foreign exchange reserves and, second, it follows that there is no consensus about the level at which foreign exchange reserves become excessive. One simple explanation for this negative interpretation is that because countries have continued to add to their international reserves, and it is assumed that these decisions are rational within the context of the models employed, more reserves are found to be better. As in flipping coins, there is always a small probability that the bank will be broken, or that "more than adequate reserves" may be insufficient.

A more straightforward explanation for large reserve holdings is that for most countries the level of reserves is a byproduct of other economic and financial policies, in effect the residual. Countries' exchange rate policies are the most likely suspects, driven by a desire to maintain an undervalued currency and support the tradable goods sector of the economy. In the wake of the global economic and financial crisis of 2007–09 and the associated dislocations of exchange rate relationships, this motive is likely to be strengthened, along with the motive of building up an even larger war chest of foreign exchange reserves. Morgan Stanley (2007a) published an analysis in July 2007 estimating that major emerging-market countries held $1.5 trillion in excess foreign exchange reserves. Korea accounted for more that $100 billion of that estimate. In light of the events of 2008, the Korean authorities reportedly now think that their reserves were inadequate. These facts drive concerns about the new mercantilism.

Some authors, such as Caballero, Farhi, and Gourinchas (2007) and Mendoza, Quadrini, and Ríos-Rull (2007), attempt to explain the accumulation of foreign exchange reserves by certain countries in terms of the weaknesses of the countries' domestic financial systems and the strength of financial systems and the rule of law in other countries through which savings in the first group of countries is intermediated. This analysis is built on a flimsy empirical base and fails to distinguish between actions by the private and public sectors.

In their writings on Bretton Woods II, Dooley, Folkerts-Landau, and Garber (2003, 2007) are more imaginative. They implicitly assume that governments know better than their citizens how to manage international financial investments. For them, the government is the only relevant actor, and its aim is to provide collateral in the form of foreign exchange reserves, for example for foreign direct investment in China. These are rationalizations, not explanations, and they fail to pass the test of common sense.[19]

Nevertheless, a few countries such as Chile and Mexico (Jadresic 2007, Ortiz 2007) have undertaken efforts to examine the optimal level of their foreign exchange reserves and as a result have implemented policies to limit their accumulation. However, those strategic decisions are now being reconsidered. As described in Bakker (2007) and Bakker and van Herpt (2007), a number of European countries have taken steps to reduce their foreign exchange reserve holdings or to hedge them into local currency. This is a response to the exchange risk associated with those holdings as well as to pressures by their fiscal authorities to increase the return on foreign exchange holdings and pressures on central banks managing those holdings to limit the asymmetric risks involved. In many cases, the central bank absorbs capital losses at the same time that it is mandated to pass on positive returns to the fiscal authorities.

A slightly more pragmatic view of international reserves distinguishes between reserves held for liquidity purposes and reserves held as longer-term investments. Often the reserves continue to be managed by one institution as two accounts either formally or de facto. Sometimes the tranche of longer-term investments is split formally between the reserve holdings of the monetary authorities—the central bank and/or the finance ministry—and reserves held in an SWF or the equivalent. This strand of the literature recognizes, at the level of the government of a country, that the continuum of purposes in holding international assets ranges from managing exchange rates and meeting short-term external financial obligations to investing for the long term. Working out the associated arrangements in practice is more difficult because the foreign exchange reserves are normally held on the books of the central bank, at least in developing countries, while it is more rational that policies gov-

---

19. The fact base on which the Bretton Woods II authors ground their analysis was always weak. Four examples can be cited. First, in recent years, external financing has accounted for less than 5 percent of fixed investment in China and for similar percentages in other Asian countries. Second, all the US government asset seizures they cite were motivated by political, not private financial, considerations (the use of Iranian assets to pay off non-American commercial or personal noncommercial claims are exceptions that prove the rule, as they were driven by US domestic politics). Third, countries are slowly diversifying away from the dollar (based on IMF COFER data, IMF 2009b; Truman and Wong 2006; and Wong 2007). The dollar's value share in the reserves of developing countries declined by 13.3 percentage points from the end of 2001 to the third quarter of 2009; more than two-thirds of the decline had occurred by the end of 2005, and the quantity share declined by only 7.5 percentage points. Fourth, the events of 2007–09 have finally put an end to the myth of consistency in the foreign exchange policies of Asian countries. Bretton Woods II, if it ever existed, lasted less than half the decade predicted for it at the outset.

erning longer-term investments should be set by the government with associated returns and losses accruing to the fiscal authorities.[20]

The basic question facing countries with huge hoards of foreign exchange reserves is: Once the reserves are there, what does a country's government do with them? One approach is to limit their further accumulation, net of earnings on the existing stock, by adopting a currency policy directed at exchange rate appreciation and flexibility supported by macroeconomic and microeconomic policies directed toward maintaining sustainable domestic growth and price stability.[21]

A second approach is to try to use the foreign exchange reserves for domestic "development" purposes. This approach may be attractive for a developing country, in particular one where the accumulation of foreign exchange reserves does not reflect the conversion of wealth in the form of nonrenewable resources underground into wealth in the form of financial assets aboveground. The motivation for this approach is understandable, but its execution is problematic. If a country is to use its foreign exchange reserves to finance domestic investment or government expenditures, not only does it have to halt or modify the course of its accumulation of reserves, but it also has to reverse, or significantly modify, the course of that accumulation in order to repatriate the principal into domestic financial resources. The former requires economic and financial policies to be recalibrated at the margin; the latter requires a comprehensive reorientation of economic and financial policies.

China has implemented and India has considered implementing the indirect use of foreign exchange reserves to support domestic policies.[22] In

---

20. In Canada, Japan, and the United Kingdom the great bulk of foreign exchange reserve holdings are on the books of the finance ministry rather than the central bank. In the United States, they are split essentially evenly between the Federal Reserve and the exchange stabilization fund of the US Treasury.

21. This is the approach implicitly favored by Rodrik (2006) when he questioned the social return to a developing country of excess foreign exchange reserves. His answer to the Summers (2006) problem of low returns on reserves is not to accumulate them.

22. Montek Ahluwalia, deputy chairman of India's Planning Commission, several years ago raised the issue of how India's growing foreign exchange reserves could be used in a non-inflationary way to finance domestic expenditure. Press reports suggested that the idea would be to borrow abroad against India's foreign exchange reserves as collateral in order to finance investment in domestic infrastructure. However, to do so without recalibrating the country's macroeconomic policies in the direction of current account deficits, India would have to convert the foreign exchange into domestic currency, which either expands the money supply and lowers interest rates or requires the central bank to purchase the foreign exchange with domestic currency and sterilize the monetary effects via sales of government debt. In effect, the infrastructure investment has been financed by an increase in government debt in the hands of the public. Nevertheless, the government of India has continued to consider some variant of the idea (Committee on Infrastructure Financing 2007). Palaniappan Chidambaram, at the time the Indian finance minister, explained at the Peter-

China, an amount of foreign exchange reserves was used initially to fund the Central Huijin Investment Company, which in turn funded the recapitalization of major government-owned banks and financial institutions. In 2007, the Central Huijin Investment Company became part of the CIC. As a result, about half of the initial $200 billion in CIC investments nominally were domestic and that share subsequently rose.[23]

This approach to the use of foreign exchange reserves is problematic. First, it is unclear where the exchange risk lies. Second, except in the limiting cases where the banks involved have foreign-currency-denominated liabilities that they were otherwise unable to hedge or have asset holdings that they are otherwise unable to fund, for the capital injections to be useful to the banks they have to be converted into domestic currency. To the extent that the banks convert the foreign currency in the market into domestic currency supplied by the central bank, the foreign exchange is returned to the books of the People's Bank of China (PBoC), the country's central bank, and there has been an increase in the combined domestic and foreign assets of the CIC and PBoC. To the extent that the PBoC supplies cover to the banks, it absorbs the exchange risk.

A third approach is to use a country's accumulated foreign exchange holdings to meet its international objectives. For example, a country may make loans to or invest in countries through government-owned or -controlled financial or nonfinancial institutions.[24] The investments may be for economic or political purposes, illustrating an additional ambiguity vis-à-vis the country's own citizens as well as the international community.

---

son Institute for International Economics on September 25, 2007 that foreign exchange reserves would be used to finance the import content of infrastructure investments in India. However, there is little difference between the government buying foreign exchange from the central bank to finance imports and buying it in the private market, as long as the central bank pegs the exchange rate. Even well-placed and highly qualified economists gloss over some of the subtleties involved in using foreign exchange reserves to finance domestic investment. In March 2009, Justin Lin, chief economist of the World Bank, was reported by the press to have advocated in a speech in Mumbai that India should use its foreign exchange reserves to fund domestic infrastructure projects.

23. See Truman (2008c, 2008d) for a more extensive discussion of the CIC during its first year. As of early 2010, the press reported that the CIC may be augmented further by additional financing from China's foreign exchange reserves, which had reached $2.4 trillion by the end of 2009. A more recent press report (Henny Sender, "Beijing in Wrangle over Key State Fund," *Financial Times*, July 6, 2010) suggests that the CIC may be stripped of its stakes in domestic banks as part of a turf battle between China's finance ministry and central bank and to lift the Federal Reserve's possible actions limiting CIC investments because the CIC is a bank holding company.

24. Such an operation could take the form of recycling: the government or a government-owned entity makes a loan to a foreign borrower denominated in foreign currency and it purchases the foreign currency from the central bank (directly or indirectly via the market) to fund the loan.

Fundamentally, the preferable approach to the management of "excess" foreign exchange reserves is to apply strict economic and financial criteria, and to maximize their return over a relevant horizon subject to whatever constraints may be imposed for risk management purposes, or as close to such an approach as is possible.[25] As Lawrence Summers (2006, 2007a, 2007b) has argued with his characteristic force and eloquence, to do anything else amounts to financial malpractice. More concretely, Summers has pointed out that for a country like China, a difference of 100 basis points on average over time on its holdings of cross-border financial assets, with foreign exchange reserves at 45 percent of GDP as of the end of 2008, amounts to about half a percentage point of GDP per year. Such calculations apply regardless of whether the cross-border assets are held in the central bank as foreign exchange reserves, in an SWF (or the equivalent), or in some looser structure on the books of some government entity. In all cases the authorities face political or policy incentives to increase the rates of return on their foreign assets.

Going forward, it is an open question whether SWFs are likely to receive large increases in their funding out of accumulations of foreign exchange reserves or out of current account surpluses associated with rising prices of commodities. Much depends on the evolution of the global economy and financial system and cooperative mechanisms designed to maintain a reasonable balance in that evolution, factors that are beyond the scope of this study.

Sovereign Wealth Funds and the International Financial System

The increased international investment activities of governments in managing their foreign exchange reserves and other international assets reflect trends in economic and financial globalization and diversification. Over the past two decades at least, total global cross-border investments have expanded at a more rapid rate than international trade in goods and services, which has expanded at almost twice the rate of global GDP.[26] During 2002–07, global GDP at current prices and exchange rates increased

---

25. Formally, the return that is maximized may be net of the cost of any liabilities associated with the external assets, though, as argued earlier, this is largely an accounting distinction as far as the government as a whole is concerned.

26. I use 2007 as the end point in these comparisons to avoid the distortions introduced into 2008 and 2009 data by the international financial crisis, but recognizing that the 2007 data themselves are distorted by influences that may have contributed to or reflected the crisis once it was fully blown.

63 percent and global trade in goods and services increased 116 percent.[27] Over the same period, reported international financial assets (excluding foreign direct investment) of countries increased 188 percent to $92 trillion.[28]

These broad trends reflect the increased integration of the global economy as well as a process of portfolio diversification that, at least through 2007, had the effect of loosening the "home bias" in individual, institutional, and governmental investment portfolios. The reduction of home bias has facilitated the financing of global imbalances at the same time that it has contributed to more balanced global asset portfolios.

At least until recently, emerging-market and other developing countries have not shared in these trends. Over two decades ending in the early part of this century, the expansion of cross-border investment (assets plus liabilities) of nonindustrial countries had only slightly exceeded their combined GDP growth rate. It was at about the same rate as their (rapid) growth in trade in goods and services (Lane and Milesi-Ferretti 2006). This pattern has changed recently. The international investment assets of developing countries that report their international investment positions to the IMF for publication in its *International Financial Statistics* (including the three Asian economies now often classified with advanced countries—Hong Kong, Korea, and Singapore) expanded by 198 percent over 2002–07, while those of the advanced countries increased by 185 percent.

From 2002 to 2007, the estimated size of global capital markets (stock market capitalization, debt securities, and bank assets) increased by 60 percent to $241 trillion.[29] As noted above, the estimated international financial assets of all countries increased by almost 200 percent. Over the same period, total foreign exchange reserves increased by 166 percent to $6.4 trillion, and international assets of nonpension SWFs increased by at least 300 percent to about $3 trillion. Thus, international assets controlled by governments increased at about the same rate as total international assets but substantially faster than capital markets as a whole. Although the total of reserves and SWF assets (despite double counting) understates the total of government-controlled international assets, their share in the total

---

27. IMF, *World Economic Outlook* database, October 2009, available at www.imf.org (accessed on July 12, 2010).

28. IMF, *International Financial Statistics* database, which includes 129 countries but excludes some important countries such as most in the Persian Gulf region, available at www.imf.org (accessed on July 12, 2010).

29. IMF, *Global Financial Stability Report*, various issues, available at www.imf.org (accessed on July 12, 2010).

remains quite small, though growing.[30] Moreover, the countries accumulating these assets in private or official holdings are largely, though not exclusively, not the mature industrial countries.

Consequently, SWFs in 2007 emerged as symbolic of two tensions involved in the globalization of the international financial system.[31]

The first tension reflected the dramatic redistribution of income and wealth (cross-border as well as national) from the mature industrial countries to countries that historically have not been major players in international finance. The newcomers had little or no role in shaping the practices, norms, and conventions governing the system. Consequently, the leaders and citizens of many of those countries felt they had little stake in the health and stability of the international financial system, or so it has been perceived by many of the leaders and citizens in the mature industrial countries.

The second tension reflected the fact that governments own or control a substantial share of this new wealth. This redistribution from the private to the public sector implies a potential decision-making reorientation by the SWF as well as other institutions and actors that are owned or controlled by the relevant government that is at variance with the traditional private-sector, market-oriented framework with which leaders and citizens in the mature industrial countries are most comfortable, even though many of their own systems do not fully conform to that ideal, in particular in the wake of the 2007–09 global financial crisis. Lyons (2007) captured this visceral concern by linking SWFs with state capitalism as practiced by many of the governments that are home to them and the redistribution of income and wealth associated with the first major concern.[32] John Gieve, also speaking relatively early in the SWF debates, noted that "the switch of reserve rich countries from lenders to owners of financial or real assets is likely to lead to tensions and pressures for protectionism."[33] More recently, Bremmer (2010) wrote about the end of free markets in the strug-

---

30. To illustrate from US data, at the end of 2007, US government assets were only 2.4 percent of US-owned assets abroad (excluding financial derivatives) of $15.7 trillion. (Adding the estimate of foreign assets owned or controlled by state and local pension funds, which are reported as private assets, would boost this figure to 5 percent.) At the same time, foreign official assets in the United States were 19 percent of total foreign assets. Again, this is an underestimate; although foreign official assets include in principle assets of SWFs and other similar government financial institutions, they do not include portfolio or other investments by government-controlled nonfinancial institutions.

31. In Truman (2007), written relatively early in this emergence, I went into more detail describing these trends and differences among SWFs, as they came to be known.

32. Setser (2008b) provides a representative articulation of the potential threat to the United States from the concentration of increasing wealth in the hands of sovereigns of other countries.

33. John Gieve, "Uncertainty, Policy and Financial Markets," remarks at the Barbican Centre, July 24, 2007, available at www.bankofengland.co.uk (accessed on July 12, 2010).

gle between states and democratic capitalism dominated by private, not public, corporations. He comes down on the side of markets and private corporations.

SWFs are one manifestation of broader changes in the global economic and financial system of which they are a part. Their activities affect many interests: the citizens and governments of the home countries, the citizens and governments of the countries that are actual and potential hosts to SWF investments, and financial markets more generally. The funds themselves can be viewed as power brokers, as Farrell et al. (2007) use that term. They should not be viewed as existing outside the financial system. They are not net providers of capital to global financial markets. For the most part, they are recyclers of global financial flows. The financial resources that SWFs invest internationally already are or largely would have been invested internationally. Citigroup's gain was General Motors' loss. In proper perspective, SWFs are neither a threat nor a salvation, but they do reflect the changing shape of the international financial landscape.

3

Issues and Concerns

Governments have established sovereign wealth funds in many different forms to achieve a range of objectives with financing derived from a variety of sources. In their international investment activities, SWFs are a manifestation of globalization as well as of shifts in economic and financial power relationships in the world economy. They are not the most important such manifestations, but the issues and concerns that they raise are important in their own right and indicative of more general concerns about the role of governments in international economic and financial matters. A government's decisions about its international investments, including decisions by an SWF under its control, affect the interests of at least four groups: its own narrow governmental interests, those of its citizens, financial market participants at home and abroad, and the interests of governments and citizens in other countries.[1]

This chapter discusses five areas of concern about SWFs: (1) mismanagement of investments by SWFs to the economic and financial detriment of the country with the fund; (2) pursuit of political or economic power objectives via SWFs; (3) exacerbation of financial protectionism inspired by SWFs; (4) the potential for financial market turmoil and uncertainty associated with SWF activities; and (5) conflicts of interest between countries with SWFs and countries in which they invest. The first two concerns primarily involve the policies and behavior of the countries that are home to SWFs. It can be argued that these concerns are shared by all government-sponsored investment institutions, but SWFs tend to be larger and more consequential for many countries. The second two concerns primarily

---

1. See Truman (2007). Gelpern (forthcoming) expands on this matrix by considering four types of accountability of SWFs: public internal (citizens), private internal (beneficiaries), public external (following international norms or standards), and private external (laws and norms).

involve the attitudes, policies, and markets of the host country. The last concern involves relationships between both groups of countries. Some argue that these concerns are largely hypothetical—in particular concerns (2) and (4)—and not broadly supported by what we know about the behavior of SWFs. The second part of this statement may be correct, but the potential concerns are real. In a survey of attitudes of 1,000 representatives of national elites in seven advanced and emerging-market countries, Hill & Knowlton and Penn Schoen Berland (2010) report that 50 percent are either much more (16 percent) or somewhat more (34 percent) concerned about SWFs as a source of finance than other sources of investment such as investment banks, insurance funds, private equity, and family wealth.[2] Only hedge funds generate more concern.

Mismanagement of Investments

The most serious risk associated with SWFs is to the economic and financial stability of the countries accumulating the huge stocks of assets in the funds—that is, the risk that the wealth will be wasted. The accumulation poses enormous political and policy challenges for the authorities. The understandable temptation for the political authorities in many countries, including advanced countries with SWFs, is to try to use the assets to promote domestic economic development or social objectives. In the United States, officials associated with the Alaska Permanent Fund and Wyoming's Mineral Trust Fund have testified to these tensions (Cowper 2007, Lummis 2007).[3] Moreover, the economics literature is replete with findings suggesting that investments by state-owned enterprises lead to relatively inefficient outcomes (Dewenter and Malatesta 2000).

In principle, the economic inefficiencies associated with state management of firms can affect other countries as well. Park (2008, 18) writing from the perspective of someone at the Asian Development Bank, notes "There is no a priori reason why the public sector is better than the private sector at investing a country's current account surplus." He goes on to argue that the aggressive pursuit of higher returns by SWFs without the benefit of a gradual buildup of experience could "not only impose costs on the SWF but the entire financial system" by dissipating assets that, in

---

2. The figure for US elites is 47 percent, while that for Chinese elites is 97 percent. Germany and the United Kingdom are at 26 and 30 percent, respectively.

3. The Alberta Heritage Savings Trust Fund in Canada has gone through a similar process of pushing and hauling on the objectives of that SWF. See Warrack (2007) for some of that history and a commentary on a proposal to adopt the Alaskan model, which involves paying annual dividends to the state's citizens. Since early 2007, the Alberta fund has been part of a portfolio of government investment funds managed by the Alberta Investment Management Corporation.

effect, serve as a backstop to that system. Berrigan, Bertoldi, and Bosma (2008) argue that the acquisition of companies by SWFs is inconsistent with the trend toward reduced state involvement in the production side of economic activity, which underpinned privatization trends in Europe over recent decades. They argue that the risk of management inefficiency increases because of the governance structures of SWFs and the fact that they are not subject to the normal market disciplines. These arguments have some merit, but the inefficiency of state enterprises in the public utility area is generally associated with domestic political pressures to hold down prices and increase employment, pressures to which foreign investors from the private or public sector may be less susceptible. One suspects that the European concern about SWF investments has more to do with antiprivatization forces in general and with controlling investments through government-controlled investments other than SWFs. Few SWFs have substantial amounts of controlling interests outside their own countries.

More generally, as discussed in chapter 2, trying to use international assets to promote domestic development at the macroeconomic level on a significant scale is essentially impossible without significantly modifying or reversing the fiscal, monetary, and exchange rate policies that gave rise to the initial accumulations of the assets. With the possible exception of exchange rate policies, such reversals are likely to boost inflation, create wasteful distortions in domestic economies, and contribute to slower, not faster, growth and development.

The management of domestic assets or international assets via SWFs also creates enhanced potential for corruption. Corruption involves money. Corruption and kleptocracy are major interconnected issues for many countries today as well as for the global financial system (Reuter and Truman 2004, 148–55). Sovereign wealth funds in most countries involve enormous pools of money. Consequently, the possibility that some of this money may be siphoned off into investments that benefit specific individuals, rather than the citizens of the country as a whole, is ever present. The corruption may be small in scale, such as giving an investment mandate to a friend or relative, or large in scale, such as investing in a white elephant project in a developing country, but the risk is there.

US citizens have evidence of the potential problems in the pension funds of state and local governments and associated units. One recent example is the former pension commissioner for Los Angeles, Elliott Broidy, who pleaded guilty in New York to a pay-for-play felony involving his fund.[4]

Allegations of corruption are not uncommon in nonpension SWFs as well. In the early 1990s, the Kuwait Investment Office, part of what is now the Kuwait Investment Authority, had to defend itself against fraud charges in connection with a collapsed Spanish investment company.

---

4. Stephen Grocer, "Former LA Pension Fund Board Member Pleads Guilty to Felony," *Wall Street Journal*, December 3, 2009.

More recently, in 2007, Kuwait Investment Authority Director Bader M. Al-Sa'ad was charged by opposition members of parliament with benefiting financially through a fund held by the authority he headed. In November 2007, Russian Deputy Finance Minister Sergei Storchak was arrested for embezzling from the budget, but he also managed the Russian Oil Stabilization Fund. The vice chairman of Dubai's Istithmar World SWF, Adel Shirawi, was arrested as part of an anticorruption probe in August 2008. Some of these cases involved only allegations, but that in itself illustrates one of the problems: because of the large amounts of money involved, corruption or mismanagement may be alleged even if there is none.

In an international context, the focus of corruption concerns has been on natural resources and funds derived from their export. Arezki and Brückner (2009) establish the empirical link between oil rents, corruption, and state stability. They endorse the Extractive Industry Transparency Initiative (EITI), a global standard promoting transparency in managing revenues from natural resources that represents a promising policy response. Le Borgne and Medas (2007) detail the macroeconomic policy challenges facing Pacific Island countries and the not entirely successful role that SWFs have played in meeting those challenges.

In June 2002, a group of nongovernmental organizations initiated a publish-what-you-pay campaign directed at the foreign companies that exploit natural resources, principally in developing countries. In September of that year at the World Summit on Sustainable Development in Johannesburg, South Africa, former UK Prime Minister Tony Blair put forward a broad set of principles that became the EITI.

The EITI was codified and received broad official endorsement a year later. Organizations such as the Revenue Watch Institute have worked actively to monitor the adoption of and compliance with such standards and to promote better management of public revenues, in particular those derived from natural resources. These initiatives were initially focused on natural resource funds (NRFs) (Humphreys and Sandbu 2007), considered by most people today to be a subcategory of SWFs. All subcategories share the potential for mismanagement and corruption.[5] Humphreys and Sandbu

---

5. Collier (2007) argues forcefully that for the countries about which he is concerned, home to the bottom billion poorest people, it is inappropriate to save the proceeds from the exploitation of natural resources in government-controlled accounts located abroad rather than invest them wisely domestically. However, the emphasis should be placed on the word "wisely" because Collier advocates his own "Charter for Natural Resource Revenues." Whether the revenues from natural resources should be invested at home today in investment and other government expenditures or invested in financial instruments abroad (or at home) for expenditures tomorrow depends on the social return on those expenditures. Similarly, Heuty and Aristi (2009) argue that SWFs focused on saving resource windfalls abroad and drawing upon those funds using a framework narrowly based on the permanent income hypothesis undermine economic diversification and are politically and institutionally unsustainable. However, these same authors praise the orientation of the SWFs of Botswana, Chile, Norway, and

emphasize the importance of unified or integrated budgetary treatment of NRFs and SWFs, as does the IMF in its advice to members (IMF 2007b; Davis et al. 2001, 2003). In developing the SWF scoreboard described and presented in chapter 5, we have found that somewhat more than half (57 percent) of the funds have guidelines integrating the use of their earnings or principal with the country's budget. However, of those that have such guidelines, about a quarter of them do not consistently follow them.

With respect to mismanagement, in general governments do not have strong records as skilled investors. They are not good at picking winners. Government-owned banks tend not to be the most profitable. A number of countries have established SWFs only to squander and liquidate the resources that have been set aside under short-term political pressures. Two examples are Ecuador's Stabilization Fund and Nigeria's Petroleum (Special) Trust Fund. However, in 2004 the Central Bank of Nigeria established the National Investment Fund to manage its new Excess Crude Account. Venezuela is running down financial resources invested in its two SWFs. Two other examples are the SWFs of Chad and Papua New Guinea; both have been wound down. The circumstances in each country differ, but the common thread is that political forces led to the dissolution of the funds. For funds still in full operation, Bernstein, Lerner, and Schoar (2009) statistically identify one reason why some SWFs may obtain lower returns: a higher degree of politicians' involvement with those funds, in particular in their domestic investments.

In light of the losses that many SWFs experienced in 2008 and 2009, domestic concern about their mismanagement has increased in many countries. Unfortunately, that concern is more likely directed at the quality of the returns on the managers' actual investment decisions rather than at issues of efficiency and corruption, though there is probably scope to raise questions in both respects. How these developments will affect the funds and their behavior in the future remains to be seen.

One might think the mismanagement of SWF investments is principally a matter of concern to the citizens of the host country, in particular to the extent that any corruption involved does not spill across national borders. However, that is too narrow a view. A country that squanders its SWF through corruption, unwise investments, or building white elephant edifices is a country that is poorer and less stable economically, financially, and politically, with adverse implications for its global partners.

Trinidad and Tobago for their development orientation, including in handling volatility in prices of natural resources. Other critics argue that governments should not be allowed to manage the proceeds of natural resource wealth because they inevitably will mismanage the wealth. One alternative is to pass the proceeds directly to citizens as advocated by Moss and Young (2009) for Ghana and Birdsall and Subramanian (2004) for Iraq. The problem with this approach is that it does not entirely eliminate the curse of oil overheating the domestic economy and thereby bringing on the real exchange rate appreciation component of Dutch disease. Clearly, the circumstances of countries differ, as should the objectives of their SWFs.

Pursuit of Political or Economic Power Objectives

A country's foreign assets may be employed to achieve its external economic or political objectives, and viewed through some prisms the two categories are the same or indistinguishable. Such investments might be funded indirectly out of foreign exchange reserves or via an SWF or an equivalent to which the foreign exchange effectively has been transferred. It is often protested that SWFs are invested purely for economic motives. However, the fact is that the boards and managers of SWFs are pressed by the general public and their political authorities to increase their financial returns and to favor certain types of investment, including in the domestic economy. By construction, SWFs are political as has been documented by Jürgen Braunstein (2009) from the perspective of an international political economist.

A survey of 113 respondents from SWFs and private equity and other investors conducted by Norton Rose (2008) found that as a whole they viewed SWFs as investing for the highest economic return. However, the non-SWF respondents saw the funds as giving greater weight to strategic benefits, which can have a variety of implications ranging from promoting technical training to something more sinister. The division of views should not be too surprising. SWFs see themselves as motivated by longer-term, nonstrategic, cooperation considerations. Other investors from private equity funds or even managers of university endowments sometimes see them as competitors driving down returns and scooping up the best investments. This is borne out in the survey: a significant number of non-SWF respondents saw SWFs investing increasingly independently rather than via co-investments.

In debates about SWFs in 2007 and 2008, US Treasury officials (Kimmitt 2008, Lowery 2008) insisted that the funds should formally state that their investment decisions are based solely on economic considerations rather than political, commercial, or foreign policy considerations. The emphasis generally is on discouraging investments or the management of investments to achieve foreign government policy objectives. However, some governments, such as the United Kingdom (UK Treasury 2007), have stressed the economic power dimension and possible effects of SWF investments on competition via mergers and acquisitions. In the United States, former Securities and Exchange Commission (SEC) Chairman Christopher Cox (2007b) noted the potential leverage and market distortion that might be associated with an SWF's information advantage and the ability to profit from inside information.

In either dimension—economic or political power—perceptions matter. Hill & Knowlton and Penn Schoen Berland (2010) found that more than 50 percent of survey respondents were concerned that the motives of SWF investments, as opposed to the motives of other sources of investment from 17 of 19 countries with SWFs, might be to try to assert political influence. The only exceptions were Singapore and Norway. Fifty-eight percent of respondents in the United States were concerned about Singapore. Russia and China led the list as sources of SWF investments that might be politically motivated at 87 and 84 percent, respectively. Interestingly, respondents in China were relatively more concerned about Norway and Singapore, at 74 and 72 percent, respectively, than for the average of 18 countries. The least concern was about Abu Dhabi at 53 percent.

The *Washington Post* editorial staff on October 24, 2007 opined, "Sovereign wealth funds . . . offer governments a way to take over businesses for political as well as economic purposes. That's a benign prospect if the buyer is Norway, a member of NATO. It is more troubling if the government behind the money is that of China, Russia, or Venezuela." This view was echoed in US Director of National Intelligence J. Michael McConnell's 2008 annual threat assessment: "[There are] concerns about the financial capabilities of Russia, China, and OPEC countries and the potential use of their market access to exert financial leverage to gain political ends" (McConnell 2008, 5). Unfortunately, the unclassified version of the report did not elaborate on his statement. The Hill & Knowlton and Penn Schoen Berland (2010) survey identified a close connection between perceptions about a country and about SWF investments from that country. The authors conclude that SWFs have an interest in encouraging their home governments to improve their country images with respect to stability, the rule of law, and the adoption of international standards.

The reality is that governments own SWFs, governments are political organizations, and it is naïve to pretend that they are not. Drezner (2008) argues that "Sovereign wealth funds sit at the intersection of high finance and high politics." As detailed by Steil and Litan (2006), financial statecraft, often involving the private sector or governments influenced by the private sector, is a feature of today's world. It all depends on whose government is on the delivery end and on the impulses to which it is responding.

Even if the actions of an SWF are not motivated by noneconomic considerations, noneconomic motives will be read into the SWF's decisions just the same. Consider four examples.

First, it was reported that in early 2006, at the time of Iceland's mini-financial crisis prior to the 2008–09 crisis, Norway's Government Pension Fund-Global sold or hedged its holdings of Icelandic government bonds. It has been widely reported that the government of Iceland protested to the government of Norway that it had participated in an unfriendly act and undermined Nordic solidarity.

Second, in June 2006, Norway's SWF announced it had disinvested from Wal-Mart because of its labor practices in Mexico. US ambassador Benson Whitney issued a strong indictment of the process by which Norway applied its SWF's ethical guidelines to the investments in US companies. Aside from the merits of the criticism of Norway's procedures, which have since been modified somewhat, Ambassador Whitney stressed the political

nature of the SWF's actions: "Through divestment the Norwegian government has accused a number of American companies of failing to meet its
ethical standards. I want to repeat it is the government of Norway, through
the Finance Ministry, making these allegations, and not just a private person, making accusations of bad ethics."[6]

Third, consider the investments by SWFs of tens of billions of dollars in
late 2007 and early 2008 in US and other financial institutions. Is it reasonable to imagine that the managers of those funds did not at least consider the implications of their actions for relations between their own
countries and the countries in which they were investing? Unlikely. No responsible official of a major private-sector or quasi-private-sector institution would be doing his or her job if he or she ignored such realities. We
know in the case of the ADIA's investment in Citigroup, announced on
November 27, 2007, that at a minimum Citigroup informed key members
of the US Congress in advance of the announcement and obtained as a result statements blessing the investment.[7]

Fourth, consider Temasek's controlling-stake purchase of the Shin Corporation in Thailand from the family of then–prime minister Thaksin
Shinawaatra in January 2006. The subsequent political furor in Thailand
surely is something that Temasek and Singapore in retrospect could have
done without.

Most of these examples involve portfolio or noncontrolling investments, although in the case of the SWF investments in financial firms they
were significant stakes. But the more sensitive cases involve controlling
stakes, such as the famous Dubai Ports World acquisition of Peninsular
and Oriental Steam Navigation Company in 2005, which was an acquisition not by an SWF but by a government-owned entity, Dubai World. In
this connection, it is important, but not widely appreciated, that only a
few SWFs currently follow acquisition strategies. We have collected reasonably complete information on the investment strategies of the largest
SWFs. At present, fewer than a dozen of them state that their investment
strategies involve the acquisition of significant or controlling stakes in
companies: Brunei, Canada, China, Kuwait, Malaysia, the Netherlands,
Qatar, Singapore, the United Arab Emirates, and Vietnam.[8] In the cases of

---

6. Benson K. Whitney, "Pension Fund Divestment: Meeting Norwegian Fairness Standards?"
Remarks to the Norwegian Institute of International Relations, September 1, 2006. The ambassador also noted that, as of the time he spoke, a disproportionate number of these divestment decisions involved US companies, suggesting to him an anti-US bias.

7. Pistor (2008) offers a more nuanced view of the motivation of SWFs in investing in Western financial institutions. She argues that it is buying insurance via "institutional hedging,"
exploiting networks of global finance in particular in times of stress.

8. Bortolotti et al. (2009) argue that SWFs invariably take minority stakes or significant noncontrolling stakes, though they site Miracky et al. (2008) as saying that SWFs do take majority stakes in domestic firms. A distinction can be made between controlling and majority

Canada and Malaysia, the companies involved are domestic. A number of SWFs, including more than half of the pension SWFs that we have examined, have announced policies limiting the size of their investment stakes. Four of the eight nonpension SWFs with announced limits on their stakes are US funds.[9] Those who have extensively searched sources to construct databases on acquisitions by SWFs (Bernstein, Lerner, and Schoar 2009; Bortolotti et al. 2009; Miracky et al. 2008) are unable to come up with more than about $350 billion in acquisitions of significant stakes over several decades, but most of their information is for recent years, substantially less than 20 percent of all SWF investments on the definitions of SWFs that these researchers apply.[10]

Nevertheless, regardless of the small number of such cases, individual acquisitions by SWFs may raise national security concerns, which sometimes morph into economic concerns. In the United States, the enactment of the Foreign Investment and National Security Act (FINSA) in 2007 revised the framework and procedures of the Committee on Foreign Investment in the United States (CFIUS). With these changes and the existing powers of the financial and other regulators, the United States is reasonably well positioned to evaluate and, if necessary, block any US acquisitions by an SWF or other foreign government entity that threatens to impair US national security.[11] One countervailing force familiar to all students of foreign direct investment is that there is always a risk that the host country could expropriate an investment. Graham and Krugman (1995) and Graham and Marchick (2006) have extensively examined US history on foreign direct investment. They distinguish between cases in which hostilities break out between the United States and the home country, where expropriation or the

---

stakes in this context, but the relevant concept, including for the Bortolotti study, is control, not majority control. I suspect that the authors were misled by relying on the particular dataset they assembled; see footnote 10. Their statement does not conform to information from the SWFs themselves.

9. This result may tell us more about the US disclosure culture than about SWFs in general.

10. The database assembled by Bortolotti et al. (2009) incorporates the work of William Miracky and his colleagues (2008) at the Monitor Group and covers domestic and international investments made by 35 SWFs between January 1986 and September 2008 from public source announcements and databases on deals and new issues. It should be noted that their $357.1 billion figure for 1,216 investments includes only 379 investments for $141.2 billion in listed equities, of which only 23 for $667 million are investments in the open market. The database excludes, for example, investments by Norway's Government Pension Fund-Global. Bortolotti et al. (2009, 18) hypothesize that this is due to Norway using intermediaries, because it subcontracts out all its investments, which is not true. The Norwegian fund invests continuously over time and as a result its investments do not show up in databases associated with "deals" of one sort or another. The fund also limits the cumulative size of its stakes.

11. One relevant issue is the definition of control, where US procedures do not specify a bright-line test or provide the regulators with scope to probe deeply. As discussed below, an investor can have substantial influence without exercising control.

equivalent is semi-automatic, often providing unintended benefits to the host country; and cases in which the foreign investment is a "fifth column" operating in the United States. They conclude that there are issues in both categories, but none of them reach the level that would justify blanket prohibitions.

Of course, the current pattern could change, as foreign-government-owned or -controlled financial and nonfinancial institutions do acquire some stakes in companies in other countries, including controlling stakes. Where the host country has weak standards of behavior, or is openly corrupt, other risks are involved.

My conclusion is that SWFs are political by virtue of how they are established, and by their nature are influenced to some degree by political considerations. SWFs could be used to achieve economic or commercial power objectives. However, in this context, SWFs have largely attracted concerns displaced from other forms of investment by government-owned or -controlled entities. If a country were to conduct political or economic espionage, it could use more efficient and clandestine means than to set up an SWF. However, once established, the risk is there.

Financial Protectionism

The issue of financial protectionism with respect to SWFs is both real and complex. On the one hand, many observers share a widespread presumption that capital markets generally should be open to foreign direct investment as well as to other forms of capital flows. On the other, many countries maintain barriers to various types of capital flows and there is substantial skepticism about the virtues of open capital markets and the wisdom of the principle of national treatment of foreign direct investment.

Moreover, for countries like the United States, global trends toward breaking down home bias and increasing portfolio diversification interact with concerns over the US current account deficit and perceptions that a flawed global adjustment process is contributing to the impoverishment of the United States, creating a "sharecropper's society," to use the term made famous in this context by Warren Buffett in his 2005 annual letter to shareholders in his Berkshire Hathaway Company.[12] In his 2008 letter, Buffett was dismissive of criticism of SWFs as "some nefarious plot by foreign governments," and he instead again blamed US policies that led

---

12. A representative expression of these grouped considerations is found in testimony by Patrick A. Mulloy, "Sovereign Wealth Fund Acquisitions and Other Foreign Government Investments in the US: Assessing the Economic and National Security Implications," US Senate Committee on Banking, Housing, and Urban Affairs, November 14, 2007.

to large deficits, national debts, and weak currencies.[13] He might have added that countries with current account deficits, including the United States, also are home to SWFs. Steven Schwartzman, writing in the *Financial Times* in 2008, was more apocalyptic, warning that countries, starting with the United States, would reject SWF investments at their peril.[14] Except for the signaling effect of financial protectionism, he was exaggerating, because as we saw in chapter 2, the annual flows (more appropriately reflows) via SWFs on the order of, say, $500 billion a year globally are small relative to gross annual financial flows of more than $50 trillion into and out of the United States.[15]

Protectionism in all forms lies just below the surface in all countries. A Pew Research Center survey released on February 9, 2009 found that two-thirds of respondents said that it is a good idea to require US stimulus funds be spent on US goods in order to keep jobs in the United States; only a quarter of them said it is a bad idea because it risks trade retaliation (Pew Research Center 2009). The questions might have been phrased differently and, as a result, elicited a narrower margin between the two responses. Nevertheless, the interesting point is that there was no significant difference between the views expressed by self-described Republicans, Democrats, or independents. If one puts these reported views alongside those in a poll a year earlier by Public Strategies (2008)—which found that only 6 percent of 1,000 US respondents had seen or heard anything recently about SWFs, but that 49 percent thought that investments in the United States by foreign governments have a negative effect on the US economy and 55 percent thought that they have a negative effect on national security—one can appreciate that financial protectionism is just below the surface in the United States. It is foolish to think that the United States is unique in this regard. The survey by Hill & Knowlton and Penn Schoen Berland (2010) found that only 57 percent of elites on average in seven countries were familiar with SWFs, and that once informed about them, only 19 percent were favorable.

In addition to these macroeconomic issues, there are microeconomic and national security considerations that are often linked to economic security concerns. With respect to economic security, the greatest risk to recipient economies is that they will erect unnecessary barriers to the free flow of capital and, in the process, contribute to the erection of similar barriers in

---

13. Buffett's letters to shareholders are available at www.berkshirehathaway.com/letters/letters.html.

14. Stephen Schwarzman, "Reject Sovereign Wealth Funds at Your Peril," *Financial Times*, June 20, 2008.

15. The source for the US figure is the Treasury Department's report on international capital data for April 2010.

other countries to the detriment of the health of the recipient countries' and to global prosperity. We may not in all cases be comfortable with the consequences of the free flow of finance and investment either internally or across borders, but on balance it promotes competition and efficiency. Moreover, not all potential host countries have as robust or flexible a framework for dealing with foreign direct investment issues as does the United States.

Nevertheless, domestic economic interests may exploit anxieties about foreign investment to erect barriers to capital flows, including portfolio flows as well as foreign direct investment.[16] Domestic economic interests may also highlight both the lack of a level playing field in national investment regimes and the potential economic power disparities when a direct investment by foreign competitors is undertaken or backed by foreign governments. Further complicating these issues for the SWFs is the fact that they apply in greater force to investment activities of other government-owned or -controlled financial or nonfinancial entities. SWFs are tarred with a brush that generally belongs in another pot.

The risk is that the activities of SWFs will contribute to a rise in financial protectionism around the world either in anticipation of a surge of investments by SWFs or in response to them. In the words of Hildebrand (2007, 4), "the most important challenge associated with the rise of SWFs is therefore to ensure that the policy reactions in recipient countries of potential and actual SWF investments do not degenerate into what ultimately amounts to financial protectionism." To date we have seen some evidence of the tightening of investment regimes in response; this evidence is reviewed in chapter 7. We also have heard some calls for the imposition of reciprocity restrictions on SWFs, which are reviewed in chapter 4.

Market Turmoil and Uncertainty

Roeller and Véron (2008) distinguish between microeconomic concerns about SWFs in terms of their potential impact on competition and economic efficiency, and macroeconomic concerns about the potential impact of such funds on the overall economy and financial markets. This section primarily considers the latter dimension.

On the basis of past behavior of the owners and managers of SWFs, many experienced observers do not see the activities of these funds as posing a threat to financial market stability. An example is O'Neill, Nielson, and Bahaj (2008): "Recent attention among Western policy makers has focused largely on the limited disclosure by SWFs with respect to their risk management and investment strategies, including whether investments

---

16. Mezzacapo (2009) makes this point and links it to the need for the SWFs to build trust through transparency to limit the uncertainty and suspicions about their activities.

are always undertaken on a purely economic—as opposed to a politically-motivated—basis. In reality, many SWFs are as sophisticated investors as the most enlightened private investors in the West."[17] Demarolle (2008, 2) in his report to the French government, stated without qualification, "SWFs play a fundamentally stabilizing role in the international financial system, a view clearly in evidence in the course of the current liquidity crisis." He argued that their investments are positive for both home and host countries.

To cite another example, El-Erian (2008, 198) commented on the first release of my scoreboard for SWFs (Truman 2008c):[18]

> If the underlying concern relates to the impact of SWF on global stability, funds such as those mentioned above [Abu Dhabi Investment Authority, Singapore's Government Investment Corporation, and the Kuwait Investment Authority] have simply not behaved in a manner that their low scores [on the Truman scoreboard] might suggest. If anything, the recent deployment of their patient capital has been a highly stabilizing influence on a global economy that has been increasingly sensitive to balance-sheet excesses and extreme financial alchemy in industrial countries. The catalyst to and aftermath of the liquidity dislocations and market turmoil that started this summer [of 2007] are yet another example of this duality.

The fact and problem are that observers such as El-Erian are not the women and men on Main Street. In today's world, in many societies, citizens are reluctant to accept the testimony of experts at face value. They want to have the facts themselves and be in a position to evaluate those facts. As Setser (2008a, 202) commented in response to El-Erian, "growing public attention to SWFs suggests that it is no longer sufficient for their activities to be known and understood by market insiders while remaining indecipherable to the broader public."[19] Discerning the potential impact of SWFs on financial market stability is complicated by their opacity. As many argue, the funds may take longer-term views and have a generally stabilizing influence on markets. Hill & Knowlton and Penn Schoen Berland (2010) found that only 26 percent of respondents felt that SWF investments were more reliable than other sources.

Without clarity about SWF investment strategies and behavior, it is difficult to assess claims about the longer-term views of SWFs and how the funds might react, for example, to losses on their portfolios (IMF 2007d).

---

17. O'Neill and his colleagues were writing in May 2008. By the end of the year the sophistication of enlightened private investors was under considerable question.

18. The referenced scoreboard scores in 2007 are included with the update in chapter 5.

19. In my own response to El-Erian, not included in the conference volume, I used an anecdote about Federal Reserve Chairman Arthur F. Burns. During discussions in the 1970s about whether the Fed should announce its target for the Federal Funds rate, Chairman Burns said his neighbors in Vermont did not need to know about the Federal Open Market Committee's target as long as "market participants" knew from the actions of the open-market desk at the Federal Reserve Bank of New York. Times have changed!

Moreover, SWFs are inherently problematic to the extent that they are financed with the proceeds of global imbalances that are perceived to be a threat to the stability of the global economy and financial system. The Commission of the European Communities (2008, 4) pointed to this concern:

> At the macroeconomic level, the rise of SWFs illustrates the seriousness of current-account imbalances in the global economy that have their origin in the managed exchange rates operated by some of the countries in surplus. The accumulation of reserves for investment by SWFs should not become an end in itself. SWF owners need to show that they are not holding back appreciation of their currencies to accumulate foreign assets for their SWFs.[20]

However, in the same document, the commission noted that "SWF investment could support the international role of the euro over the medium term. For foreign exchange reserves, the goal is liquid and safe assets denominated in a currency with low foreign exchange conversion costs—which tends to favour the US dollar" (p. 3).

With respect to volatility, former SEC Chairman Cox (2007b) noted the potential for increased volatility in markets associated with investors, such as SWFs, whose actions are not transparent and the associated effects on the determination of market prices. The IMF (2008b) notes that large investors can have disproportionate effects in smaller and shallower markets even via rumors of transactions. It is also the case that without strong risk management systems, rogue traders in institutions with the potential for substantial leverage can disproportionately damage small markets. Press reports that Singapore's Temasek was disinvesting in two large Chinese banks (Bank of China and China Construction Bank) in November 2007 described that action as a signal of concern over the health of the institutions or a signal that the Chinese economy was about to experience a substantial slowdown.[21]

Sun and Hesse (2009) find no significant destabilizing effect of SWFs investments on the basis of 166 event studies, but they caution that to reach conclusions about the broader impact of SWF investments would require much more information about their investments, including their timing and amounts. They note that SWF investments in US and European financial institutions did not fully buffer those institutions from losses. Mauck, Knill, and Lee (2009) find that SWF investment causes firm-level risk-return relationships to deteriorate for some firms, and they speculate that media reports may play a role in this process. However, they are unable to establish this relationship empirically.

In recent years, a cottage industry of analysts has sought to anticipate SWF portfolio preferences and how those preferences and changes in them

---

20. This theme is reiterated in Berrigan, Bertoldi, and Bosma (2008).

21. John Burton, "Temasek Sale a Fresh Sign of China Doubts," *Financial Times*, November 30, 2007.

will affect prices and relative returns on assets over time, as when, for example, countries shift their reserves into SWFs with higher expected returns. Morgan Stanley (2007c) posited an expansion in SWF assets from $2.5 trillion to $17.5 trillion by 2017 and foreign exchange reserves from $5.1 trillion to $9.9 trillion over the same period as global financial assets roughly double from $100 trillion to $209 trillion. Using different assumptions about asset preferences and a simple capital asset pricing model, they derive an impact of 30 to 40 basis points on bond yields and a reduction in the equity risk premium of 80 to 110 basis points relative to what otherwise would prevail.

The IMF (2008b) examines a slightly different scenario in which between 25 and 50 percent of available foreign exchange flows to governments are invested via SWFs rather than via normal foreign exchange reserve holdings with a lower dollar share. They estimate an increase in US real interest rates of 10 to 20 basis points, a depreciation of the dollar of 2 to 5 percent, and a narrowing of the US current account deficit of ¼ to ½ percent of GDP.

A subsequent analysis by Kozack, Laxton, and Srinivasan (2009) projects growth of SWF assets from $4 trillion to $6 trillion by 2014, with these assets less heavily invested in dollar or euro-denominated assets than the pattern for foreign exchange reserves. The authors work back from a presumed impact on the net capital inflows to the United States and, they assume, on the US current account balance of ½ to ¾ percent of GDP on average. They use the IMF's Global Integrated Monetary and Fiscal Model (GIMF) to derive a 100 basis point shock to the risk premium on US assets. With the GIMF, they then trace out the short- and long-run effects on the US external position and domestic economy. For example, the dollar initially depreciates by 7 percent in real effective terms, but over the long term the dollar appreciates because of the improvement in the US current account position relative to the initial norm, which is treated as the equilibrium.

This analysis, as applied to the investments by SWFs, suffers from two problems. First, the dollar-for-dollar link between net capital inflows to the United States and the US current account deficit is an extreme assumption; we know there will be substitution effects in investors' portfolios, which the authors ignore in setting up their model simulation. That substitution attenuates the effect on the US current account position. Second, the GIMF simulations assume a shock to the risk premium on dollar assets, but in fact there will be a gradual adjustment over time as SWF portfolios expand, diluting any observed impacts.

Trying to quantify the global macroeconomic effects of SWF portfolio strategies with any precision is essentially a futile exercise, although the signs of the partial equilibrium effects can be indicative. The portfolio reallocations are likely to be spread over time and swamped by other influences. In general, predictions about the prospective performance of the

US Treasury yield curve, the largest and most sophisticated market in the world, are essentially worthless beyond a few quarters, and these results are likely to be swamped by other unidentified or unidentifiable factors.

Late in 2007 and early in 2008, cheerleaders for the substantial investments by SWF in financial institutions around the world frequently made analytical mistakes on the other side. They spoke as if the investments involved fresh inflows of capital. As far as the investing country is concerned, the SWFs' foreign investments are already outside the country.[22] Only the form of those investments is changed when they buy a stake in a financial institution. More likely the currency and location of the investments are not changed. The fund sells one foreign asset, and it buys another asset denominated in the same currency and located in the same country.

Nevertheless, as with any large investor, SWFs, which manage large holdings of financial assets, potentially can affect markets as they redeploy their portfolios. One example is the spate of investments by SWFs in foreign financial institutions in 2007–08. The market reaction to those investments was generally positive, in terms of the stock prices of the institutions.[23] However, consider what would have been the reaction if those announcements had been that the relevant SWF intended to sell 5 to 10 percent of the stock of the relevant financial institutions.[24] Defenders of the stabilizing influence of the activities of SWFs have replied (see El-Erian above) that SWFs typically are long-term investors and it would be foolish, in any case, for an SWF to announce its intentions in this area. That leaves out the case of announcing a sale after the fact, which would likely have similar effects on financial markets while limiting the scope for front running by other investors.[25]

Moreover, defenders of the stabilizing influence of the activities of SWFs have been quoted also to the effect that they are not like hedge funds and private equity firms in their speculative activities and their use of leverage. For example, CIC Chairman Lou Jiwei was quoted in a Reuters report on October 16, 2007, shortly after the CIC opened for business, as saying that SWFs are "a stabilizing force in the international mar-

---

22. It is logically possible, but unlikely on a large scale, that the SWF is moving investments from the domestic market to the foreign market (see chapter 2).

23. As reported in chapter 5, Kotter and Lel (2010) find that markets generally respond positively to any investment by an SWF in a publicly traded financial or nonfinancial investment.

24. Beck and Fidora (2008) examine 28 disinvestments by Norway's Government Pension Fund-Global under the application of the SWF's policy on ethical investment. They find no significant impact on the stock prices of the companies involved during the period of disinvestment or after the announcement that the disinvestment has occurred. However, they note that the fund is careful in executing its investments and disinvestments. Such an announced policy is one of the elements in the SWF scoreboard presented in chapter 5.

25. See the discussion in chapter 5 of the influence of SWF accountability and transparency on returns following public announcements of SWF investments.

ket."[26] He reportedly drew a contrast with hedge funds, which he characterized as being "a source of instability." In a speech on April 9, 2008, Kuwait Investment Authority Managing Director Bader M. Al-Sa'ad said that "There is no evidence over the past many decades of any wrongdoing by any sovereign wealth fund."[27] He added: "There should be a common and level playing field for all," including hedge funds, private equity funds, pension funds, and other nonlisted private pools of capital. This was the continuation of debates held at the World Economic Forum in January 2008 about the merits of developing a code of conduct for SWFs.

The argument that SWFs are different from hedge funds is somewhat tarnished by the facts. SWFs are different in that they generally use less leverage than hedge funds, they may not be as aggressive in pursuing absolute return goals, they face less in the way of pressures for redemptions, and they may be subject to a greater degree of implicit regulation at home. On the other hand, SWFs invest in hedge funds, private equity firms, and regulated financial institutions, whose use of leverage and range of activities in recent years make them indistinguishable from hedge funds and private equity firms.[28] In effect, they are providing the capital that those firms can leverage to make their investments. SWFs are no different from other investors in hedge funds except that their stakes may be measured in the billions rather than the hundreds of millions of dollars. Once SWFs invest in hedge funds, they become part of the problems, if any, associated with those investment vehicles.

Moreover, some researchers who have looked at SWF structures and portfolio practices argue that they share many characteristics with hedge funds in that they are stand-alone, unregulated pools of capital managed by investment professionals who are known to take large stakes in publicly traded corporations (Bortolotti et al. 2009).[29] Then-governor of the Reserve Bank of India Yaga Reddy agreed that foreign asset funds, including SWFs, are similar to hedge funds and invest in hedge funds. He

---

26. Zhou Xin, "China wealth fund aims for stability, openness," Reuters, October 16, 2007.

27. Bader al-Sa'ad, Overview on the Kuwait Investment Authority and Issues Related to Sovereign Wealth Funds, keynote speech at the First Luxembourg Foreign Trade Conference, April 9, 2008.

28. Investment in financial institutions in the form of deals that involve taking discrete stakes, which shows up in the databases assembled by Bortolotti et al. (2009) and Miracky et al. (2008), is predominantly a phenomenon of 2007 and 2008. That type of investment can be explained by several factors. First, the SWFs were accumulating large amounts of funds during this period that were more difficult to manage internally, or using outside managers. Second, by investing in financial institutions, the SWFs were effectively outsourcing some of the management of their investments. Third, they may gain some indirect management experience as a result, in particular via investments in hedge funds and private equity firms.

29. The irony, as documented by Bortolotti et al., is that SWFs appear not to do as well as hedge funds in their investment returns.

said the major issue is whether there should be a presumption for or against such funds based on whether they were managed by the public or private sector. His answer was that the degree of comfort depends on the standards of governance and transparency that they adopt.[30]

About 40 percent of the SWFs we reviewed in constructing the scoreboard presented in chapter 5 have policies on derivatives. About half of those funds report that they use derivatives only for hedging purposes, despite the moderate involvement of most SWFs in high-profile finance. The situation could change in the future. The Abu Dhabi Investment Company (also known as Invest AD) is owned by the Abu Dhabi Investment Council, which is an investment arm of Abu Dhabi that is separate from the ADIA. Invest AD was founded in 1997 but in 2007 was given a mandate to attract and manage funds received or invested from sources outside of the council's normal governmental source of funds, in effect acting as an investment manager.

On July 29, 2009, Bloomberg News reported that Singapore's Temasak was considering going into the business of managing money for outside investors, though this development may take up to eight years with respect to funds from sophisticated investors seeking to co-invest with Temasek and up to 10 years for funds from retail investors.[31] The Bloomberg report linked this decision to a desire to help overcome foreign governments' concerns about SWF investments by commingling public and private funds. On the other hand, the active involvement of SWFs in financial markets is likely to raise concerns among some authorities and observers about the overall contribution of SWFs to market stability and increase uncertainty about the activities of SWFs in financial markets.

Thus, the potential for SWFs to contribute to market turmoil and uncertainty is there, as is the case with any class of financial entities in which a few people manage large amounts of money. It is in the interests of those investors to behave responsibly, but that need not always be the case, and accidents do happen. For the general public, it is not sufficient for the owners and managers of the funds to say "trust us."

Conflicts of Interest

Investments by SWFs and similar government-owned or -controlled entities raise a number of possibilities of conflicts of interest between public

---

30. Yaga V. Reddy, "Forex Reserves, Stabilization Funds and Sovereign Wealth Funds: Indian Perspective," remarks at the Golden Jubilee Celebrations of the Foreign Exchange Dealers' Association of India, Mumbai, October 8, 2007.

31. Shamim Adam, "Temasek's Public Co-Investors Plan May Ease Suspicion," Bloomberg News, July 29, 2009.

and private sectors and between governments. Such conflicts may be economic, financial, political, or all of the above.[32] Former SEC Chairman Cox (2007a, 2007b) traced these conflicts to the fact that government ownership of SWFs makes them both a market referee and a market player, and as a referee they are likely to side with the home-country player on enforcement issues without the countervailing influence of public opinion in the host country.[33]

With respect to relations between governments, the growth of SWFs and the associated reallocation of wealth among countries and from the private sector to the public sector can indirectly affect international relations. The United States, for example, not only will find it more challenging to promote its vision of the operation of the global economic and financial system based on a reliance on market mechanisms, accountability, and transparency, but also may find it more difficult to advance its model of government of the people, for the people, and by the people. The United States and other countries with similar philosophical orientations also may be challenged by the influence of SWF investments in countries without those philosophical orientations, in particular where the countries or what they produce is of strategic importance. This is one of the themes of Lyons' (2007) emphasis on SWFs as manifestations of state capitalism. Cohen (2008) writes about these issues in terms of the organization of global governance. Drezner (2008) writes about them in terms of the broader topic of national influence.

On the economic and financial level, some observers of SWFs, such as Summers (2007a), Cox (2007a), and Keller (2009), would address some of the issues of influence on market dynamics raised above by encouraging the funds to conduct their investment activities via mandates granted to intermediaries. Many SWFs in fact do so to a substantial degree. As discussed further in chapter 4, this type of practice, even if it were universal (which it is not), offers no guarantee against conflicts of interest and the exploitation of inside information. The presence and extent of any conflict depends on how much at arm's length the contract is between the SWF and the holder of the mandate. If the contract involves the placement of

---

32. Mezzacapo (2009) lists a number of concerns about SWFs in home and host countries that fall in the categories employed here. The category of conflicts of interest includes issues of corporate governance and strategic investments as well as taxpayers' reactions in home countries and other shareholders' reactions in host countries.

33. For this particular conflict to arise the foreign government does not have to be the owner of a firm or investor. It would naturally, in the first instance unless constrained by prior understandings, be inclined to favor the home-country defendant over the host-country regulator. On the other hand, Linda Chatman Thomsen, then-director of the SEC Division of Enforcement, details the extensive cooperation between the SEC and foreign regulators. See Linda Chatman Thomsen, "Sovereign Wealth Funds and Public Disclosure," testimony before the US-China Economic and Security Review Commission, February 7, 2008.

funds with the choice of investment left entirely up to the manager, no inside information is transmitted either way. If it involves the placement of funds in a particular type of investment, the fund manager knows that the country is interested in that type of investment, say a particular commodity such as gold. The manager has the opportunity to front-run the investment or other investments by the country, in particular if its SWF is large enough to move markets via its investment decisions. If the arrangement involves active participation of the SWF in the management of the investments in the hedge fund, private equity firm, or investment bank, then the potential for an exchange of inside information is two-way. These examples are not meant to suggest that SWFs are unique in presenting this type of potential conflict of interest; they simply point to potential conflicts and to the fact that the use of mandates and outside managers does not make them go away.

Consider next SWF investments in financial sector institutions. In most countries, financial institutions, particularly banks, are treated differently and are subject to special regulatory regimes, in part because their activities are viewed as those of a quasi-public utility, and in part because financial institutions have special privileges in terms of access to discount windows, deposit insurance, and the payments systems.[34] The basic question is whether foreign government ownership, even if indirect or noncontrolling, is compatible with this special status.

To be sure, even the United States with its philosophical preference for reliance on the private sector has financial institutions in the public sector: the farm credit administration, home loan bank system, several so-called government-sponsored entities, and, at present, large stakes in what were once private-sector institutions. One can debate whether these institutions and their management are effective, efficient, or create moral hazard; what cannot be debated is that the United States indeed has them. However, in contrast to influence and control exercised by foreign governments, these financial institutions are subject to influence and control by the US government. Their operations are reasonably transparent. Most important, they are subject to US political processes and preferences. This would not be true for a financial institution that was controlled by a foreign government or in which the foreign government (via its SWF or some other investment vehicle) had a substantial stake.[35] Of course, the institution, its board members, and its shareholders would be subject to whatever regulations and supervision apply to all such financial institutions.

---

34. In the wake of the 2007–09 global financial crisis, the US financial regulatory framework has been reexamined and its perimeter is expected to be extended. This fact serves to reinforce the tensions and conflicts discussed.

35. In fact, since the early 1980s the Federal Reserve has followed a policy of not allowing foreign governments to control US-chartered banks (depository institutions) except in very special, and normally temporary, circumstances.

The basic question even in the case of only a large stake that is not associated with board membership is whether the shareholder and its government will exercise what I have called undue influence over the financial institution in its business and investment decisions. This is a vague term, and presumably all shareholders following the principles of shareholder democracy seek to influence the decisions of the entities in which they have a stake. Nevertheless, this is a potential problem, and it is more of a problem than in the case of a bricks-and-mortar investment in the United States, or any other country, because it is easier to loot a bank or abruptly divert its financial activities than to do so with other types of investments. Regulators around the world are not well equipped to supervise behavior, but I have suggested in the US case that perhaps they should be given the authority and should start to develop procedures for doing so.[36]

Can I provide a concrete example in this area? Yes, and I do not have to go far. After the November 27, 2007 announcement of the $7.5 billion investment by ADIA in Citigroup, the *Wall Street Journal* on January 11, 2008 reported that the new investors had let the new management of Citigroup know that they would not be pleased if Citigroup were to seek to raise additional capital elsewhere and dilute ADIA's stake. The report may not have been accurate, and even if it were, ADIA would not have been the first shareholder to voice these concerns. Besides, Citigroup appears to have ignored ADIA's reported preferences. However, the issue became more complicated as Citigroup's financial situation deteriorated further, ADIA filed a claim on Citigroup in mid-December 2009 for fraudulent misrepresentations, and the US government acquired a stake in the institution. One of the complications was that more governments became involved in the Citigroup case, such as the government of Mexico, where Citigroup owns Banamex. This tale illustrates a potential conflict between a regulated US financial institution and a foreign government investor, and more importantly between a regulated US financial institution, a foreign government investor, and the supervisors of the US institution.

A slightly different example, but one that also speaks to the issue of behavior, is the controversy over the "mystery" Middle Eastern investor in UBS in late 2007. Under US laws and regulations, there is no requirement that those who purchase small stakes in US corporations of less than 5 percent disclose their stakes. However, the spirit of the laws, regulations, and common practices has dictated that investors taking significant if small stakes normally disclose their actions, with the highly relevant exception of when a potential hostile takeover is involved.

---

36. See Edwin M. Truman, Sovereign Wealth Fund Acquisitions and Other Foreign Government Investments in the United States, testimony before the US Senate Committee on Banking, Housing, and Urban Affairs, November 14, 2007, available at www.piie.com (accessed on July 12, 2010).

A further example involves China and the CIC's ownership control of most major Chinese banks through the Central Huijin Investment Company. When these banks sought to open offices in the United States, their owner became a bank holding company under US banking law and subject to the supervision of the Federal Reserve. Although the conflict between the legal structures in the United States and China (and its SWF) was resolved following years of discussions, it illustrates the issues with respect to SWF investments.

Finally, the possibility arises of countries using their SWFs to co-invest in foreign countries with private or state-owned enterprises of the home country. This use of an SWF was suggested in the *Hindustan Times* on August 18, 2008, in the context of a story on Indian consideration of the establishment of a $5 billion SWF, which stated that "such a fund could help Indian companies grow their global footprints through acquisition and also enable higher return on accumulated foreign exchange reserves, which in India's case is one of the lowest in the world."[37] One of the early investments of China's CIC was in the Hong Kong IPO of the China Railway Group, a state-owned construction company. This type of investment or co-investment by SWFs and state-owned companies or national champions, at a minimum, raises the potential for conflict over subsidies that give the investment or company an international competitive advantage.

Potential conflicts between SWFs and markets, between SWFs and governments, and between governments themselves because of the activities of SWFs are indeed real. They are not unique, but they should not be denied. Both the home countries to SWFs and the hosts to their investments have an interest in minimizing such conflicts.

Concluding Comments

What should we conclude from this review of the principal areas of concern about SWFs? It has focused on (1) mismanagement of the investments; (2) pursuit of political or economic power objectives; (3) exacerbation of financial protectionism; (4) contribution to financial market turmoil and uncertainty; and (5) conflicts of interest between home and host countries. First, these concerns are not entirely fanciful. Critics can point to evidence in each of the five areas. Second, the concerns are almost certainly exaggerated by some critics. Third, some of the concerns are directed not at SWFs but at other forms of government-sponsored foreign investments. Focusing on SWFs may deflect attention from the real locus of concern. Fourth, the concerns in part arise from the opacity of SWFs. This suggests that demystifying these funds should help to make the world safer for them.

---

37. Gaurav Choudhury, "RBI not keen on managing sovereign wealth fund," *Hindustan Times*, August 18, 2008.

4

Possible Policy Responses to Sovereign Wealth Funds

While the previous chapter outlined five areas of concern about sovereign wealth funds, this chapter considers a range of policies that might be adopted or adapted to address these concerns. Most proposals fall under the heading of regulation by the recipient country either in a comprehensive or a limited form.

It is useful to consider, first, what regulation of SWFs would involve. In principle, regulation could be imposed in the jurisdiction receiving SWF investments, by the home country, or by both. In practice, the focus is on host-country regulation though funds are subject to the laws and regulations of their home countries. Since there are many jurisdictions receiving SWF investments, many with SWFs of their own, the almost inevitable result of uncoordinated national approaches would be an uneven pattern of regulation for SWFs.

Abstracting from SWFs per se, national financial regulatory regimes focus either on domestic financial institutions and their activities or on investment from outside the country, although there are overlaps. In its domestic focus, regulation aims to strike a balance between promoting the safety and soundness of the institutional providers of funds and financing and protecting the integrity of markets and the recipients of funds—the consumers of financial services. Moral hazard considerations are involved on both sides of the balance. In its external focus, regulation aims to protect the recipient country and, in some cases, its indigenous institutions.[1]

---

1. See Rose (2008) for a full treatment of this strand of the regulatory literature as it might be applied to SWFs.

From this framing of the general focus of financial regulation, it follows that bank-like regulation does not apply to SWFs except to the extent that the SWFs invest in banks and those investments are not otherwise covered by existing regulations. Setting bank-like regulation aside, and in light of the five basic concerns about SWFs discussed in the previous chapter, consideration can be given to four possible approaches to the regulation of SWFs: comprehensive regulation of all their activities, prohibitions of specific investments, limitations on investment activities, or reciprocal arrangements. My conclusion is that none of these approaches offers much promise in addressing the concerns about SWFs identified in chapter 3. That said, public policy needs to try to address the wide variety of concerns about SWFs, and so this chapter examines the aforementioned approaches to SWF regulation, while the next chapter will outline my preferred approach of establishing an international standard or best practices to promote SWF accountability and transparency.

Comprehensive Regulation

One approach to the regulation of SWFs would make no distinction between foreign and domestic investors and exploit the potential for using existing laws, rules, and regulations to influence, control, or guide all foreign government investments on a national treatment basis. The primary aim would be to address concerns about SWFs' contribution to market turmoil and uncertainty. Countries might examine their competition or regulatory disclosure policies in light of some of the issues that SWFs raise to ensure that those policies remain adequate to the task.[2] In the United States, this would mean looking beyond the on-off switch associated with the Committee on Foreign Investment in the United States (CFIUS) to rules and regulations, for example, of the SEC on share acquisitions, market integrity, corporate governance, and disclosure.[3] The Federal Reserve and other bank regulators, as well as other US regulatory and supervisory agencies, have mandates covering banking and finance as well as strategic sectors, such as energy, or market competition.[4]

---

2. Greene and Yeager (2008) examine this approach.

3. SWFs are subject to the requirement to disclose their intentions if they hold more than 5 percent of a registered class of securities and to disclose changes in their holdings if they hold more than 10 percent. They are required to disclose their portfolios to the SEC if they manage more than $100 million of SEC-registered securities. Some of these requirements can be avoided depending on how an SWF structures its US investment vehicle. See Linda Chatman Thomsen, "Sovereign Wealth Funds and Public Disclosure," testimony before the US-China Economic and Security Review Commission, February 7, 2008.

4. In 1988, the UK Monopoly and Mergers Commission, in the interest of fostering competition, required Kuwait's SWF to reduce its stake in British Petroleum from 20 percent to less than 10 percent.

National treatment is a concept of which economists are fond, precisely because it is nondiscriminatory in its effects. But there are many exceptions in practice. This reality is illustrated in the United States in the tax treatment of SWFs. A study by the Joint Committee on Taxation of the US Congress (2008) concluded that, with a few minor exceptions (most of which could be avoided through the use of well-designed investment vehicles), SWFs receive no more favorable treatment on their portfolio and nonportfolio investments in the United States than other foreign investors, which are in some respects treated better than domestic investors. (Oversimplifying only a bit, foreign direct investment is taxed like other forms of commercial activities, subject to the effects of tax treaties, and other investments essentially are untaxed.) Thus, the objections raised by critics such as Fleischer (2008, 2009) to the taxation of SWFs are essentially objections about the way the United States taxes foreign (primarily portfolio) investments. They have little to do with SWFs per se.

National treatment aside, the regulation of SWFs could be approached in a manner similar to other forms of regulation of foreign investment. Presumably the aim would be to address concerns about countries using their SWFs to pursue national political or economic objectives. The approach might yield some benefits in limiting market turmoil and uncertainty, but the result could be to exacerbate conflicts between countries—the fifth column.

One challenge in this type of comprehensive approach is that it would have to be broadly applied internationally, for example via agreement or treaty, so as not to disadvantage those countries within the regime vis-à-vis those outside it. Another challenge would derive from the somewhat amorphous nature of SWFs. If a country or group of countries tried to apply formal regulation to a preferred definition of such funds, the countries with the funds would either avoid the countries entirely or morph their funds into forms that did not fall under the definition (e.g., in the form of de facto investment accounts as part of their reserve holdings). A case can be made for a comprehensive approach to government-controlled foreign investments starting with foreign exchange reserves and ending with investments by government-controlled entities, but that approach would suffer from two challenges.[5] First, in the current environment of antiglobalization such a regime either might be so restrictive as to be counterproductive or might fail to attract sufficient support for ratification. Second, to the extent that the regime prohibited certain types of investments, it would be necessary either to force a large amount of disinvestment or to grandfather that investment—and either treatment would be problematic politically, economically, and financially. Neverthe-

---

5. I proposed such a broad approach in Truman (2007). Mattoo and Subramanian (2008) have suggested involving the World Trade Organization in the establishment of a standard for SWFs. See chapter 7.

less, a broad, comprehensive approach to government-controlled investments is an appropriate long-term goal.

Such a comprehensive regime for SWFs might apply only to controlling investments and not to "passive investments" as that term is used in the regulations issued by the US Department of the Treasury (2008b) for the CFIUS. However, no bright line is established by those regulations to distinguish controlling from passive investments.

The CFIUS regime was established formally under section 721 of the Defense Production Act of 1950 through the Exon-Florio amendment in the Omnibus Trade and Competitiveness Act of 1988, and most recently was further strengthened and codified by the Foreign Investment and National Security Act (FINSA) of 2007.[6] It applies to all foreign investments in the United States, establishes procedures for the review of such investments, and gives the president power to disapprove of such investments when they involve control and are deemed to threaten to impair US national security (Graham and Krugman 1995, Graham and Marchick 2006). This special regime distinguishes between domestic and foreign investors and applies in principle to both government and nongovernment investments, but only where control is involved. What is meant by national security is not defined in the legislation, but the US Treasury has issued guidance concerning the types of transactions that have presented general national security considerations. Critics of the US regime who tend to favor a form of negative-list approach (Demarolle 2008, 27), as discussed below, argue that the regime provides the US authorities with extremely broad latitude to determine whether a planned foreign investment should be subjected or not to the CFIUS procedure. Supporters argue that the real world is neither black nor white.

One can imagine a tighter regime applying to all foreign investments in a country or to all foreign government investments, controlling and noncontrolling. It has been suggested that each dollar of foreign-government-owned investment in the United States—direct investment of any size, purchases of stock, purchase of bonds, US treasury securities—on a case-by-case basis should be subjected to a range of tests including the current state of US relations with the home country of the entity or person making the investment and whether the country offers reciprocal treatment.[7]

Such a regime would be technically impossible to implement without dramatic changes in today's globalized financial system that would transform the system as we know it. The regime in effect would require the reimposition of comprehensive exchange and capital controls that have been largely dismantled, except in a few developing countries, since the end of World War II. At the extreme, funds of any type could not flow

---

6. The CFIUS as an informal interagency committee was established in 1975.

7. See the testimony of Gal Luft and the exchanges on pages 64–65 in US House of Representatives Committee on Foreign Relations (2008).

unless their flow received prior approval, presumably after their origins were traced. Given the ambiguity in many countries between governments and the private sector, a tight regime of foreign investment control would have to drop that distinction. Moreover, the introduction of an overtly political test into the approval process, at least in the United States, fails to recognize that the warmth of US relations with a country changes from decade to decade, if not month to month, raising again the grandfathering issue.

A comprehensive approach to the regulation of SWFs does not appear to be in the cards and, in any case, would only address one or two of the concerns about them—the potential pursuit of national political or economic power objectives and, perhaps indirectly, concerns about market turmoil and uncertainty.

Prohibition of Specific Investments

For some observers, a more promising approach than a comprehensive regulatory regime applying to foreign investments, or to foreign investments by governmental entities such as SWFs, is to establish a list of sectors in which SWFs, or foreign government entities more generally, are not allowed to invest—that is, a negative list of sectors in which such holdings would not be permitted.[8] This would be a more targeted approach to addressing concerns about the political objectives of SWF investments. Such a de facto "safe harbor" approach roughly corresponds to the current regime for foreign investment in many OECD countries today, including France and also Russia, but it could be expanded and codified.[9] Marchick and Slaughter (2008) argue in the case of foreign investment in general that countries should avoid sector-based lists for determining investment reviews or only use them as a second-best alternative. Against the possible benefit to foreign investors of increased certainty in treatment, they stress the practical problems involved in sensibly creating and applying these lists.

An open invitation to countries to rule out investments by SWFs in certain sectors, however, almost certainly would produce a very long list of prohibited sectors in many countries, in particular if the use of lists ruled

---

8. Advocates include the editorial page of the *Financial Times* (October 22, 2007) and George Kleinfeld, "Foreign State Funds Should Be Offered Shelter," *Financial Times*, November 28, 2007. Kleinfeld, a Washington lawyer, was admirably motivated to lower the cost to SWFs investing in the United States by offering a safe harbor for SWF investments in other sectors.

9. Some OECD countries, such as France, follow a modified version of the negative-list approach; foreign investments in the 11 sectors on the French list are subjected to prior authorization from the minister for the economy. Another modification is for the host government to own, or to acquire defensively, golden shares in the relevant firms in strategic industries, which would allow the government to control key decisions of the firm regardless of the other investors.

out the possibility of any form of investment review. If the lists did not rule out reviews, then the utility of the lists would be reduced. Moreover, there could be knock-on effects in other countries considering their own investment regimes, which would tend to either create a crazy quilt of de facto regulation or be used by local interests to expand national lists. For the United States at least, where foreign investment rivals foreign trade for lack of public support and understanding, such an approach would be problematic (see chapter 3). Graham and Marchick (2006, 148–49) reported that in 2003 the US Department of Homeland Security identified 12 sectors that it considered critical infrastructure: agriculture and food, water, public health, emergency services, the defense industry, telecommunications, energy, transportation, banking and finance, chemicals, postal services and shipping, and information technology. They note that those industries in 2002 accounted for 24.4 percent of US nonfarm civilian workers. One can imagine that a list of prohibited sectors to SWF investments could be much longer. The FINSA requires CFIUS to consider and report on the implication of foreign investments in critical infrastructure and technologies, but the application of those tests is substantially narrower than an outright prohibition and is limited by the standard that the investment must threaten to impair US national security.

Leaving aside the special features of the US economic and political environment, to be broadly applicable the negative-list approach would have to define what is meant by investment. Would the restriction be on any investment (bonds as well as stocks) of any size regardless of whether control would be involved?

An alternative is a positive-list approach to certain investors. At a conference on foreign investment at Columbia University in October 2008, Manfred Schekulin, director of export and investment policy at the Austrian Ministry of Economics and Labor, thoughtfully mused about a concept of knowing your foreign investor: say "yes" to an investment if the host authorities know and are comfortable with the investor, but perhaps "no" to an investment if the host authorities do not know or are uncomfortable with the investor. This concept is an extension of ideas such as knowing your customer and applying suitability criteria to senior management in financial institutions. However, the nondiscriminatory application of such a concept would be difficult to ensure if it rests on judgments that necessarily would be subjective and might well be biased. For example, we trust those we know and went to school with more than those we do not know or with whom we have had no common experiences.

In addition, it is reasonable to ask why host countries should single out SWFs as a group with respect to the sectors in which they can invest or where they come from while other forms of government investments via state-owned or state-controlled entities would be permitted. Moreover, if the restrictions were broad in terms of the type of investment entity and tight in terms of the scale of the investment, what would be done about the substantial existing international investments by government entities? Grandfathering creates its own competitive distortions.

Finally, under this approach of limiting the sectors in which SWFs could invest, there would be the issue of indirect investments via special-purpose vehicles registered in some Caribbean location or merely via investing in hedge funds, private equity firms, or other types of investment vehicles.

Thus, prohibitions of investments by SWFs in specific sectors would offer limited benefits in addressing the possible national political or economic power motivations of such investments and would be problematic in terms of practicality and effectiveness even in terms of achieving this limited objective.

Limitations on Investment Activities

Short of outright prohibitions on investments by SWFs in some sectors, consideration might be given to imposing limitations on the activities of SWF investors. This approach might be motivated by concerns about the potential for market disruption associated with SWF activities as well as about the exercise of political or economic power. For example, SWFs (individually or as a class) might be (1) limited in the size of their stakes in domestic financial or nonfinancial corporations; (2) prohibited from appointing members to the boards of the corporations; (3) limited to holding nonvoting shares (or prohibited from voting their shares); or (4) required to channel their investments through intermediaries.[10] Indeed, a number of SWFs have voluntarily adopted, or have been persuaded to adopt, these types of limitations in some of their higher-profile investments. However, voluntary restraint is different from unilateral, across-the-board limits.

These types of limitations might appear on their surface to be attractive alternatives to outright prohibitions. However, on closer examination they

---

10. The *Financial Times* in its October 22, 2007 editorial advocated the first proposal. In August 2007 in the *Financial Times* Jeffrey Garten called for a limit of 20 percent on stakes without direct consultation between the home and host governments ("We Need New Rules for Sovereign Funds," *Financial Times*, August 8, 2007). In the context of an SWF code of conduct, Hildebrand (2007) also endorsed this approach, writing that an "SWF code of conduct will have to set the limit for individual stakes at a level significantly below the typical threshold of a controlling minority, let alone an absolute majority." Recall from chapter 3 that a number of SWFs already limit their stakes, but recall also that other SWFs do not. Gilson and Milhaupt (2008) advocated the third proposal; they argue that transforming voting into nonvoting shares when they are held by an SWF would separate the economic profit motive from the strategic or political motive. Buiter (2007) made a similar proposal directed at "the risk of political extortion by a foreign state-owned investor," in effect addressing the conflict-of-interest concern identified in chapter 3. In July 2007 in the *Financial Times,* Summers (2007a) advocated the use of intermediaries, as did Stuart Eizenstat and Alan Larson in the *Wall Street Journal* later that year ("The Sovereign Wealth Explosion," November 1, 2007, A19).

are subject to many of the same technical implementation issues as more draconian approaches.

First, it is not at all clear that one can separate the motives of shareholders neatly into the economic and the strategic as suggested by Gilson and Milhaupt (2008). Moreover, large shareholders have many other means of influencing the management of the companies in which they invest aside from voting their shares. It is a foolish management of a corporation that does not at least listen to an important shareholder even if that shareholder holds less than, say, 5 percent of the shares of the corporation.

Second, disenfranchising shareholders is inconsistent with most notions of shareholder democracy and its associated benefits in terms of economic efficiency. Moreover, if a country is going to disenfranchise SWFs as voting shareholders, is it going to treat domestic governmental entities, such as pension SWFs, the same way? Whether it does so or not, the country can expect that other countries almost certainly would retaliate. That retaliation would be against a broader definition of SWFs, including government pension funds. In the US case, state and local government pension funds held more than $400 billion in foreign assets at the end of 2009. Even if retaliation against US SWFs were a politically acceptable cost in the United States, it would be a high price to pay in terms of reduced opportunities for diversification.

Lowery (2008) endorsed a more sensible approach: either an SWF should choose voluntarily not to vote its shares or it should disclose how it votes, as is now done voluntarily by some UK institutional investors and is required by the SEC for US mutual funds.[11] The objective of the SEC rule for mutual funds is to address concerns about conflicts of interest and, as noted earlier, similar concerns arise with respect to SWFs. It is an open question whether SWFs would face a formal SEC compliance requirement in this area. Keller (2009) proposes legislation to impose a compliance procedure that would involve a presidential determination with respect to accepting a process agreed upon by the SEC and the SWF. Formally singling out SWFs by unilaterally imposing such a requirement would likely be perceived as protectionist by their home countries.[12]

As for the required use of intermediaries (Summers 2007a, Keller 2009, Cox 2007a), this would be a difficult requirement to enforce.[13] Moreover,

---

11. A similar approach was under consideration in the European Union prior to the 2007–09 global financial crisis (Mezzacapo 2009), and the crisis has intensified pressures to move in this direction for hedge funds, private equity firms, and, by extension, SWFs.

12. As discussed in chapter 6, the Santiago Principles call for the SWFs voluntarily to disclose publicly their approach to voting their shares of publicly listed companies.

13. Keller (2009) suggests that in the interests of minimizing costs, the requirement be associated with an ownership threshold, which would add an additional level of complexity and the potential for being viewed as protectionist, in particular if the United States applied the requirement unilaterally.

unless there were complete transparency about the nature of the contractual arrangements, and those contracts ensured arm's-length investment decisions without advance direction or limitations (and vice versa), most of the same concerns about SWF investments would remain. Additional concerns would be created because of the potential use of offshore intermediaries and entities such as hedge funds and private equity funds. Finally, since governments have investment vehicles other than SWFs, ranging from their reserves to their government-owned or -controlled banks and nonfinancial corporations, little would be accomplished by forcing investments into other channels.

A variation on this proposal is one made by Aizenman and Glick (2007) to encourage SWFs to invest in well-diversified index instruments. They note the advantages to the funds of this investment strategy, suggesting that large funds are rarely likely to beat the market as a whole, in particular the global market. On the other hand, there is a large difference between encouragement and a requirement that SWFs invest only in this manner. A requirement would not only be discriminatory to the SWFs, but would increase the probability of regulatory arbitrage, given that some countries already invest a portion of their foreign exchange reserves in equities.

My conclusion is that the approach of establishing limitations on SWFs in their investment activities in order to protect the integrity of markets, or to limit the pursuit of political or economic power objectives, offers limited benefits and would be difficult to apply.

Reciprocal Arrangements

A final possible policy response to SWFs is to insist on reciprocal treatment. A country or group of countries might require countries with SWFs to grant reciprocal treatment to investments from the countries in which the SWF wants to invest, including, but presumably not limited to, investments by SWFs of the host country. In terms of concerns about SWFs, the threat of financial protectionism against SWFs would be turned around to promote protectionism.

The Commission of the European Communities (2008) linked its own openness to foreign investment and the principles of its internal market with respect to SWFs and other foreign investors to its efforts to open third-country markets to EU investors—implicit use of leverage by example. Gerard Lyons (2007) has advocated a more aggressive pursuit of a level playing field with countries whose SWFs, for example, want to invest in Western financial institutions, but he would stop short of erecting barriers to SWF investments if those efforts failed. The commission, no doubt, was responding to sentiments previously expressed by European leaders such as Luxembourg Prime Minister and Euro Group President

Jean-Claude Juncker when he said, "Countries that protect their own markets cannot expect to be allowed to make unimpeded investments in Europe."[14] Jeffrey Garten argued that reciprocity should be required for all countries with SWFs that want to invest in the United States or Europe.[15] If the funding of the SWF involved monopolistic pricing practices—such as petroleum or other policy distortions such as exchange rate policy—Garten would use approval of SWF investments as leverage over those policies. Garten's argument illustrates the fact that the nature of any formal reciprocity requirement would have to be specified. Would the reciprocal treatment be for the SWFs of the countries receiving SWF investments from other countries, or would it involve a broader reciprocity for all investments from the open host country into another country whose SWF was investing in the country in question? The former would be consistent with normal reciprocity agreements, but that does not seem to be the motivation of most advocates. They want the home country to be open to investment from the host country whether by a government-owned or -controlled entity such as an SWF or by a private investor.

In general, reciprocity should be discouraged as a tool of international financial diplomacy where its use currently is not absent but is less common than in the trade area. International standards should be based on national treatment as much as possible. All potential host countries should welcome foreign investment; in general, inflows of foreign capital provide additional net saving to increase investment, which produces other economic benefits, though not entirely without the potential for subsequent macroeconomic problems and controversies. Given that the forms of investments by SWFs can be many and varied, and given that restrictions on foreign investments in many countries today are many and varied, it would be next to impossible to administer a broad program of country-by-country and category-by-category reciprocity for countries with SWFs.

On the other hand, countries with SWFs can make a strong case for a level playing field on international investment as well as other dimensions of international finance such as governance of the major international economic and financial institutions. For decades, the traditional industrial countries have preached doctrines of open markets and receptivity to capital flows, particularly in the form of foreign direct investment. Given the substantial recent, and likely ongoing, transfer of relative wealth from industrial countries to emerging-market economies, even if this process slows from the pace of 2002–07, the shoe now is on the other foot on openness, with the important qualification that many of the new breed of foreign investors are governments. Hypocrisy in international

---

14. Reported in *Handelsblatt*, October 19, 2007.

15. Jeffrey Garten, "We Need New Rules for Sovereign Funds," *Financial Times*, August 8, 2007.

finance is no more attractive than in other areas of human and sovereign interaction.

Establishment of a standard of reciprocity as the quid pro quo for SWF investment may be an attractive political response to public opinion. This is the argument made by Demarolle (2008) in the French and European context. He rejects a special regime for SWF investments, but favors a dialogue with countries with SWFs founded on the principle of reciprocity. The dialogue would help open doors to investments by companies in host countries to SWF investments in the home countries of the SWFs, such as China and Russia, and thereby break down what Demarolle sees as an unsatisfactory asymmetry. Demarolle's aim is to make progress. He argues that the principle of reciprocity does not necessarily mean identical treatment.

However, establishment of a reciprocity standard for SWF investment would do little to address the concerns about SWFs summarized in chapter 3. In fact, few of the remedies outlined in this chapter promise much on that score.

To summarize, most of the proposed policies regarding SWFs are intended to deal with the concern in countries receiving SWF investments about the pursuit of political and economic power objectives by the countries with the funds: comprehensive regulation, prohibitions on specific SWF investments, or limitations of various types on the form or conditions of investment. In general, these mechanisms of comprehensive regulation would be costly and ineffective. Some of them could prove to be deleterious to the host country as well as to the global financial system. One exception might be comprehensive approaches that are applied on a national treatment basis, but in those cases issues arise regarding the cost of additional regulation.

It could be argued that some of the proposed limits on SWF investments, such as the size of stakes and voting rights, would limit the potential for market turmoil and uncertainty associated with the activities of SWFs. But that is a stretch. Moreover, by potentially driving the funds into less transparent channels of investment, they also might be counterproductive in terms of this concern. The issue of regulatory arbitrage is common to most approaches to SWF regulation in part because of the difficulty in precisely defining these pools of official capital.

A formal or informal reciprocity requirement on countries with SWFs is difficult to square with any of the concerns SWFs raise. It is better viewed as fanning the flames of financial protectionism. If the result were tit-for-tat escalation, the consequences for financial markets and their turbulence would be magnified beyond the mere denial of a few billion dollars of capital inflows.

Along the same lines, unless carefully negotiated and established in a multinational context, including a number of countries that are both home and host to SWFs, the approaches summarized in this chapter would tend to increase conflicts of interest rather than reduce them, with the possible technical exception of an outright prohibition.

Finally, none of the approaches discussed in this chapter bear directly on the issue of mismanagement of investments by the home country. Where they are at all relevant, such as regarding limitations on such investments, one could argue that they tend to exacerbate the underlying issues by discouraging the home country from investing using normal commercial structures.

Nevertheless, SWFs are here to stay, and they raise a wide variety of concerns. Public policy has an obligation to try to address these concerns. Starting in 2007, I argued that the best combined approach to SWFs was via the establishment of an international standard or set of best practices to promote SWF accountability and transparency. The next chapter outlines my preferred approach.

5

Accountability and Transparency: The Sovereign Wealth Fund Scoreboard

As summarized at the end of chapter 4, most of the suggested approaches to address the five concerns about sovereign wealth funds discussed in chapter 3 are at best deficient and at worst counterproductive. In 2007, when I first began to think and write about making the world safer for SWFs, I proposed a collective effort to develop an internationally agreed-upon standard for SWFs (Truman 2007).[1]

I suggested, unrealistically but with good intentions, that the standard should apply to the gamut of international investment activities of governments, starting with traditional foreign exchange reserves, covering SWFs of all types, and including pension funds, investment holding companies, and miscellaneous international assets. My principal short-run focus, however, was SWFs. In making this suggestion, I was motivated and encouraged by similar international efforts to enhance transparency and accountability, specifically in the context of the Asian financial crises in the late 1990s (see box 5.1).

In the context of SWFs and the concerns summarized in chapter 3—mismanagement of SWF investments, pursuit of political or economic power objectives, financial protectionism in anticipation of or in response to the pursuit by SWFs of those objectives, financial market turmoil and uncertainty, and conflicts of interest—transparency primarily is a tool to

---

1. Some characterize the use of agreed-upon international standards as a "soft law" approach to such issues (Rose 2008).

Box 5.1 International transparency standards—Some history

In the wake of the Asian financial crises in the late 1990s, a group of systemically significant economies formed the Group of 22 (G-22) in a collective effort to assemble the lessons from those crises. The G-22, which turned out to be the precursor of the Group of Twenty (G-20), sponsored three working groups, one of which focused on the critical topic of enhancing transparency and accountability.[1]

In its report released in October 1998, the Working Group on Transparency and Accountability concluded that "a lack of transparency and accountability exacerbated financial weaknesses at the firm and national levels and complicated efforts to resolve the ensuing crisis" (Group of 22, 1998). The report observed, "Transparency contributes to the efficient allocation of resources by ensuring that market participants have sufficient information to identify risks and to distinguish one firm's, or one country's, circumstances from another's. Moreover, transparency helps to inform market expectations, thereby helping to stabilize markets during periods of uncertainty and also contributing to the effectiveness of announced policies." The report also said, "Accountability refers to the need to justify and accept responsibility for decisions taken. Accountability imposes discipline on decision-makers, thereby helping to improve the quality of decisions taken. Transparency helps to promote accountability by obliging decision-makers to make their decisions and the reasoning behind them known."

The working group also gave a further boost to the development of the IMF's Special Data Dissemination Standard (SDDS) and General Data Dissemination System, including the establishment of the Reserves Template (IMF 2000) as part of the SDDS. The working group recommended enhancement of various data collection and publication systems as well as establishment of a working party including private-sector representatives "to examine the modalities of compiling and publishing data on the international exposures of investment banks, hedge funds, and other institutional investors." This last recommendation did not produce any specific results, but the underlying issues continued to inform debates about the structure and functioning of the international financial architecture and are very much a part of the discussion of lessons to be learned and applied in the aftermath of the global economic and financial crisis of 2007–09.

---

1. The mandates of the other two working groups were on strengthening financial systems and managing international financial crises.

enhance accountability. However, transparency and accountability can also be treated as separate, but related, concepts. As part of my research on SWFs, I considered what would be appropriate content for such an international standard. In the process, I developed a scoreboard for SWFs that the Peterson Institute for International Economics released in October

2007.[2] I subsequently revised the scoreboard and expanded the coverage of SWFs, and the results were released in April 2008 (Truman 2008a).[3]

This chapter starts with a further update and revision of the scoreboard for SWFs along with a comparison of these 2009 results with those for 2007 and 2008. (Further details about the scoreboard are provided in appendix 5A.) Next, the new scoreboard results are compared with some other indices and indicators. I then address some of the issues that have been raised about this approach to SWF accountability. The chapter concludes with some observations on how an agreed-upon international standard for SWFs will assist in addressing the five principal concerns about such investment vehicles.

The Scoreboard

Table 5.1 presents the results of my latest assessment of the accountability and transparency of 53 SWFs of 37 countries. The funds include 40 of the nonpension SWFs listed in table 2.1 along with the four pension reserve SWFs and nine other pension SWFs.[4] With Doug Dowson and Daniel Xie, I have scored each fund on 33 elements based on systematic, regularly available, public information.[5] We asked simple questions that can be answered

---

2. The published version is Truman (2008c).

3. See also Edwin M. Truman, " Sovereign Wealth Funds: New Challenges for a Changing Landscape," testimony before the Subcommittee on Domestic and International Monetary Policy, Trade and Technology, Financial Services Committee, US House of Representatives, September 10, 2008, available at www.piie.com (accessed on July 12, 2010).

4. We scored 20 of the 23 SWFs listed in table 2.1 with estimated total assets of more than $50 billion. The exceptions were Libya's SWF, for which we had insufficient information; the holdings of the Saudi Arabian Monetary Agency (SAMA) which does not have an identifiable structure independent from the central bank; and Queensland's Investment Corporation, which is a government-owned investment management firm. We treated the two Russian SWFs as one observation, leaving a total of 19 large SWFs, including 11 nonpension SWFs and eight pension SWFs. In addition to the three large nonpension entities listed in table 2.1, we did not score 26 other smaller nonpension entities, as explained in the footnotes in table 2.1, because they are not independent investment pools, are invested exclusively domestically, were too new, and/or insufficient information was available. The scoreboard covers almost 90 percent of the total assets listed in table 2.1 and 85 percent of the international assets, with SAMA accounting for most of the difference.

5. For some of our facts, we relied on independent, published documents, such as those of the IMF or World Bank. However, in general, we required that the SWF produce an ongoing flow of systematic information. Consequently, more is known about some SWFs than is reflected in our scoring, but that information is anecdotal and occasional rather than systematic and regular. For the scoreboard, it is not sufficient that an individual SWF provides information in ad hoc interviews with the press. To be fair, some SWFs state that they are willing to respond to freedom of information or less formal requests for information. One example is the Alberta Heritage Savings Trust Fund, and another is the State Oil Fund of the Republic of Azerbaijan. Although we have tried to be rigorous and systematic in our evaluation of each fund, some degree of subjectivity necessarily is present in our procedure.

Table 5.1   Sovereign wealth fund scoreboard (percent of maximum possible points)

Country	Fund[a]	Structure	Governance	Accountability and transparency	Behavior	Total
Norway	Government Pension Fund-Global	100	100	100	75	97
United States	California Public Employees' Retirement System (P)	88	100	96	100	95
New Zealand	Superannuation Fund (PR)	88	100	100	75	94
Canada	Canada Pension Plan (P)	88	100	96	75	92
United States	Alaska Permanent Fund	94	86	100	75	92
	Wyoming Permanent Mineral Trust Fund	94	93	86	100	91
Canada	Caisse de dépôt et placement du Québec (P)	88	100	89	75	89
France	Fonds de réserve pour les retraites (P)	88	100	89	75	89
Ireland	National Pensions Reserve Fund (PR)	88	100	86	63	86
Netherlands	Stichting Pensioenfonds ABP (P)	88	86	86	75	85
Timor-Leste	Petroleum Fund	100	43	100	75	85
Japan	Government Pension Investment Fund (P)	88	93	80	75	84
Canada	Ontario Teachers' Pension Plan (P)	88	86	89	50	83
Trinidad and Tobago	Heritage and Stabilization Fund	100	64	93	50	83
Australia	Future Fund (PR)	88	86	75	75	80
United States	New Mexico Severance Tax Permanent Fund	94	50	89	75	80
Thailand	Government Pension Fund (P)	88	86	88	13	78
Azerbaijan	State Oil Fund	94	57	89	25	76
Canada	Alberta Heritage Savings Trust Fund	94	57	79	50	74
Singapore	Temasek Holdings	88	79	68	50	73
Chile	Economic and Social Stabilization Fund	94	57	86	0	71
China	National Social Security Fund (P)	81	43	82	50	70
Hong Kong	Exchange Fund	88	43	79	50	70
Chile	Pension Reserve Fund (PR)	81	57	86	0	68
United States	Alabama Trust Fund	94	57	64	50	68
Kazakhstan	National Fund	94	57	64	25	65
Singapore	Government of Singapore Investment Corporation	81	71	61	38	65
Kuwait	Kuwait Investment Authority	88	86	48	25	63
Korea	Korea Investment Corporation	75	71	45	63	60
United Arab Emirates	Mubadala Development Company	63	57	68	25	59
China	China Investment Corporation	75	50	59	25	57

Botswana	Pula Fund	69	57	57	25	56
United Arab Emirates	Dubai International Capital	75	86	36	25	55
Russia	Reserve Fund and National Wealth Fund	81	29	50	25	50
São Tomé and Príncipe	National Oil Account	100	57	29	0	48
Malaysia	Khazanah Nasional	56	50	46	0	44
Mexico	Oil Income Stabilization Fund	81	14	43	25	44
Kiribati	Revenue Equalization Reserve Fund	81	57	7	0	35
Vietnam	State Capital Investment Corporation	81	57	7	0	35
Bahrain	Mumtalakat Holding Company	38	14	43	0	30
Algeria	Revenue Regulation Fund	69	29	14	0	29
Iran	Oil Stabilization Fund	63	29	18	0	29
Nigeria	Excess Crude Account	63	36	14	0	29
Venezuela	Macroeconomic Stabilization Fund	69	14	18	0	27
	National Development Fund	50	14	27	0	27
United Arab Emirates	International Petroleum Investment Company	44	29	21	0	26
Oman	State General Reserve Fund	63	18	18	0	23
Brunei Darussalam	Brunei Investment Agency	44	0	25	0	21
United Arab Emirates	Investment Corporation of Dubai	44	7	21	0	21
Sudan	Oil Revenue Stabilization Account	50	0	14	0	18
Qatar	Qatar Investment Authority	47	14	2	0	15
United Arab Emirates	Istithmar World	31	21	7	0	15
	Abu Dhabi Investment Authority	25	14	4	0	11
	Nonpension total[b]	73	45	47	24	50
	Pension total[b]	87	87	88	62	84
	SWF total[b]	76	56	57	33	59
Memorandum						
United Kingdom	Terra Firma	100	73	79	50	75
United States	Harvard University Endowment	100	69	66	50	69
	TIAA-CREF	100	88	86	75	84
	Blackstone	100	54	75	50	70
	Total[b]	100	71	76	56	74

a. Pension funds (P) and reserve pension funds (PR) shown in italics.
b. For each category the value under total represents the average for all funds.

either yes or no. A "yes" receives a point, but we allow for partial credit. A "no" receives no credit. At least one SWF must receive a positive score on each element for that element to be included; normally several do.[6]

We group the elements in four categories: (1) structure of the fund, including its objectives, links to the government's fiscal policy, and whether the fund is independent from the countries' international reserves; (2) governance of the fund, including the roles of the government, the board of the fund and its managers, and whether the fund follows guidelines for corporate responsibility; (3) accountability and transparency of the fund in its investment strategy, investment activities, reporting, and audits; and (4) behavior of the fund in managing its portfolio and its risk management policies, including the use of leverage and derivatives. Table 5.1 provides overall scores for each fund and for each category. The scores are presented as a percentage of the maximum possible points—33 for the total and in each of the four categories (8, 7, 14, and 4, respectively).

The average score is 59 for all the SWFs scored, and 50 for the nonpension SWFs alone.[7] The median score is 64 for all funds, and 55 for the nonpension SWFs alone. Weighted by actual or estimated foreign assets (from table 2.1), the average is 58 for all funds, and 50 for the nonpension SWFs; the averages are slightly higher when weighted by total assets.

The results presented in table 5.1 point to a number of important summary observations.

First, all SWFs are not the same. Nor is there one cluster of "good" funds and another cluster of "bad" funds. It is remarkable how even knowledgeable researchers, such as Bortolotti et al. (2009), assert that all SWFs lack transparency.[8] The overall scores range from 97 to 11 out of a possible 100. The rating of each fund can be improved. The distribution of scores is quite even, with the largest number of funds (10) in the 80s and the next largest number of funds (nine) in the 20s.

---

6. In the 2007 edition of the scoreboard, we included 33 SWFs of 28 countries that we scored on 25 elements. In the 2008 edition, we included 46 SWFs of 35 countries that we scored on 33 elements. For this edition we have added seven funds and two more countries and again we have scored them on 33 elements; however, we dropped four elements from the 2008 edition (one of which had been in the 2007 edition) because we felt they were more prescriptive than descriptive, and we added four elements from the Santiago Principles discussed in the next chapter. See appendix 5A for details.

7. This average can be thought of as a weighted average of the four categories, where the weights are the number of questions in each category relative to the total. The simple average of the scores in the four categories comes out at three points lower for the two groups of funds individually and, thus, for the total of all SWFs. However, the simple correlation of the two methods of scoring is 0.98.

8. In the words of Bortolotti et al. (2009, 10), "Aside from a few notable exceptions (principally the Norwegian pension and oil stabilization funds), SWFs have been extremely reluctant to disclose any information about their investment policies and returns."

Second, the SWFs are in three broad groups: 14 funds with scores above 80, 14 funds with scores at or below 30, and 25 funds in a middle group. The top group includes funds of two developing countries, Timor-Leste and Trinidad and Tobago, as well as nine pension and three nonpension SWFs from industrial countries.

The middle group includes funds of nonindustrial countries as diverse as Russia, Mexico, Kuwait, and Singapore. Singapore's two funds have close to identical overall scores, but their scores differ on several individual elements. This group also includes Australia's Future Fund and the SWF of the province of Alberta, Canada, though both score above the mean and median for SWFs as a whole.

The bottom group includes four funds from the United Arab Emirates, two from Dubai, and two from Abu Dhabi, one of which is the Abu Dhabi Investment Authority, which scores at the bottom using data from 2009.[9] (However, see box 5.2, which updates the ADIA's scores based on its 2009 annual report published in March 2010.) The ADIA reportedly has an excellent reputation in financial markets and participated in the International Working Group of SWFs that drew up the Santiago Principles. The lowest-ranking SWF from Dubai is Istithmar World, which has been rumored to be in the process of liquidation. Its difficulties are associated in large part with commercial real estate and preceded the problems of its parent Dubai World.

Third, although each of the 13 representative pension SWFs scores 68 or higher, that group of 24 funds also includes nine nonpension SWFs. Thus, it is not unreasonable to hold nonpension SWFs to the standard of accountability of pension funds. Chile's pension and nonpension SWFs are both in the group scoring 68 or better. On the other hand, China's National Social Security Fund is there, but the CIC is somewhat lower at 57.

Fourth, of the 15 nonpension SWFs listed in table 2.1 that have estimated assets of more than $50 billion, we scored 12 of them with $2.6 trillion in estimated total assets and $2.3 trillion in estimated foreign assets of nonpension SWFs, more than 70 percent of the respective totals listed in the table.[10] Norway's SWF is in the top group. The bottom group includes

---

9. A sister organization to the ADIA is the Abu Dhabi Investment Council (ADIC), which was established in 2007. It invests primarily, but not exclusively, in the Abu Dhabi economy, particularly in financial institutions. The Investment Company Institute reports that the ADIA receives 70 percent of Abu Dhabi's fiscal surplus and the ADIC receives 30 percent (www.swfinstitute.org/fund/adia.php [accessed on April 26, 2010]). We do not rate the ADIC on the scoreboard presented here, but in the 2007 and 2008 versions of the scoreboard, we rated it the same as the ADIA because at the time we could not distinguish the ADIA from the ADIC.

10. Excluded SWFs are those of Libya (because we did not have enough information to score the fund), the Queensland Investment Corporation (which is more of a public investment management firm), and in effect one of the Russian SWFs, which we scored as a single entity.

four funds, two in the United Arab Emirates (one each from Abu Dhabi and Dubai), and one each from Algeria and Qatar. The remaining seven are in the middle group. The simple average score for these funds is 52, slightly below the mean and median for all nonpension SWFs.

Fifth, we also scored, for purposes of comparison, four non-SWF investment entities listed as memo items at the bottom of table 2.1. They are the Teachers Insurance and Annuity Association—College Retirement Equities Fund (TIAA-CREF), a private-sector retirement fund that is similar in many respects to public-sector pension funds; the Harvard University Endowment, which managed a portfolio of $26 billion as of June 30, 2009, down from $37 billion a year earlier, on principles of long-term capital preservation and current-period return that are similar to those that motivate some SWFs; the publicly traded Blackstone Corporation, which specializes in private equity investment; and Terra Firma, a UK private equity firm that is not publicly traded. The average score for the four comparators is 74. TIAA-CREF's score (84) is equal to the average for the 13 pension SWFs that we scored, though seven of them score higher. The Harvard Endowment scores somewhat lower at 69 but above the means for nonpension and all SWFs that we scored. Blackstone scores about the same, and Terra Firma a bit higher. Thus, the highest-scoring SWFs do as well as these other four investment entities and vice versa. Moreover, based on this comparison, it is reasonable to expect the majority of the SWFs to score higher in the future. In these cases, the private sector is creating a higher bar for the public sector.

Sixth, the difference in scores among different SWFs from the same country, mentioned above, is not unique to China or Singapore. The scores for the four Canadian funds range from 74 to 92, and the scores for the five US funds range from 68 to 95. It also should be noted that despite the low scores for many of the funds from the United Arab Emirates, one SWF from Abu Dhabi (Mubadala Development Company) scores at the mean for all nonpension SWFs, and one from Dubai (Dubai International Capital) scores only slightly lower. This lack of intracountry uniformity suggests that the influence of the particular government owner of an SWF is not the only determinant of how a fund scores on the SWF scoreboard. It is one influence, but the history and nature of the fund's operations are also relevant.

Seventh, there is a strong correlation of 0.959 between the total scores for the 53 SWFs and the category of accountability and transparency. Many commentators like to stress the *transparency* of SWFs, but in my view the central issue is their *accountability* to their own citizens (as direct or indirect owners of the assets), to citizens (including government officials) in the countries in which they invest, and to participants in financial markets. Transparency is only a means to this end. Moreover, the grouping of scores is essentially identical if one examines only the category of accountability and transparency.[11]

Table 5.2 presents a summary analysis of the SWF scoreboard results comparing various groups of funds. It shows the number of funds in each group, the overall average and standard deviation for the group, and the *t*-test statistic of whether the means are significantly different. Confirming the visual inspection of table 5.1, the means for pension and nonpension SWFs are significantly different at the 1 percent level. Relevant to the discussion in chapter 6 on the Santiago Principles, the average for the 22 SWFs that participated in that process, and are now part of the International Forum of Sovereign Wealth Funds (IFSWF), is also significantly different from the 21 other nonpension SWFs.[12] The mean score for nonpension SWFs of OECD countries is significantly different from that for those not owned by OECD countries.[13] The average for funds of non-OECD

---

11. Eighteen SWFs score 86 or higher in the accountability and transparency category alone. They include a few that score relatively higher than on the SWF scoreboard as a whole, such as Azerbaijan's State Oil Fund and Chile's two funds. On the other hand, Japan's Government Pension Investment Fund scores relatively lower at only 80 in the accountability and transparency category alone. Within this category, 16 funds score 29 or lower. They include 13 of the 14 lowest-scoring funds on the SWF scoreboard as a whole. The exception is Bahrain's Mumtalakat Holding Company, which has a relatively higher score in this category than for the SWF scoreboard as a whole. On the other hand, São Tomé and Príncipe's National Oil Account and the SWFs of Kiribati and Vietnam score relatively lower.

12. In this comparison, we include the three pension reserve SWFs because they are members of the IFSWF and included in the definition of SWFs that that group uses.

13. This result holds if the funds of Chile, Korea, and Mexico are included in the non-OECD group.

Table 5.2   Summary analysis of sovereign wealth fund scoreboard
(tests of significant differences)

Comparison	Number	Mean score	Standard deviation	t-test statistic
Pension SWFs	13	84	8.5	4.8**
Nonpension SWFs	40	50	24.9	
Nonpension SWFs[a]				
IFSWF[b]	23	63	24.4	3.0**
Non-IFSWF	21	42	22.4	
OECD[c]	13	78	15.3	5.0**
Non-OECD	31	43	22.0	
Non-OECD SWFs				
Middle East	11	31	18.6	2.8*
Non-Middle East[c]	24	51	20.4	
Non-Middle East SWFs[c]				
Asian	10	57	19.0	1.2
Non-Asian	14	47	21.0	

* = significant at 5 percent level; ** = significant at 1 percent level.
a. Including Australian Future Fund, Chilean Pension Reserve Fund, Irish National Pensions Reserve Fund, and New Zealand Superannuation Fund.
b. SWF members of the International Forum of Sovereign Wealth Funds (IFSWF); see chapter 6.
c. Including SWFs of Chile, Korea, and Mexico.

countries in the Middle East is significantly different from that of funds of other non-OECD countries, but only at the 5 percent level, which bears out some of the conventional wisdom. Finally, there is no significant difference between the average for funds of Asian countries and those from non–Middle East, non-OECD countries.

Figure 5.1 presents a different type of comparison: between the SWF scoreboard and the log of SWF assets under management for the 30 SWFs with assets of more than $10 billion. The results reject the oft-heard assertion that the larger the SWF, the less transparent it is, at least on the basis of the SWF scoreboard. In fact, the relationship is slightly positive, but not significant. Visual inspection confirms that it holds for the smallest funds as a group, for the largest funds, and for the group in the middle. The relationship is anchored by the SWF scoreboard result for the ADIA in the lower right-hand corner. Substituting the 2010 score for the ADIA (see box 5.2) increases the positive slope, but it is still not significant. Eliminating Norway at the upper right-hand corner also would not change the basic nonresult.

Elements of the Scoreboard

Tables 5.3 to 5.6 present the scoreboard results for each element in each of the four categories in turn: structure, governance, accountability and

Figure 5.1 Sovereign wealth fund scoreboard and fund asset size

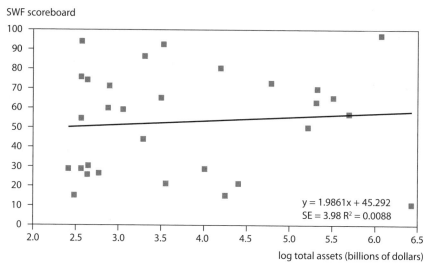

SWF scoreboard

$$y = 1.9861x + 45.292$$
$$SE = 3.98 \; R^2 = 0.0088$$

log total assets (billions of dollars)

Source: Table 2.1 for total assets.

transparency, and behavior. The score for each element is the sum of the scores across SWFs as a percentage of the maximum possible score, which is 53, the total number of funds. From the summary in table 5.1, SWFs as a group score highest on the eight elements in the structure category. The pension SWFs score equally well on seven elements in the governance category and the 14 elements in the accountability and transparency category, but less well on the four elements grouped under behavior. The nonpension SWFs score about the same in the governance and accountability categories, but decidedly less well under behavior.

Structure

The structure category (table 5.3) covers the basic organization of each SWF. An SWF's high score on the elements in this category provides confidence to the citizens of the home country and of countries where the fund may invest that the fund's organization is transparent. This is a first step in facilitating the process of holding the government and the fund accountable. On average, all SWFs that we have scored achieve a reasonably respectable 76, nonpension SWFs 73, and pension SWFs 87. Overall, the majority of funds comply with each element in this category in that the combined score is greater than 50, including some partial scores (see appendix 5A). The coefficient of variation (the mean divided by the standard deviation, a measure of dispersion, across the eight elements) is the smallest of any category at 0.174.

Table 5.3 Structure component (percent of maximum possible points)

Element	Nonpension	Pension	Total
Objective stated	95	100	96
Legal framework	83	100	87
Changing the structure	73	96	78
Investment strategy	67	96	74
Fiscal treatment			
Source of funding	88	100	91
Use of fund earnings	56	100	67
Integrated with fiscal and monetary policies[a]	61	50	58
Separate from international reserves[a]	64	50	60
Total	73	87	76

a. These items do not apply to pension funds, and we assign a neutral half point.

One might think that all SWFs would have a clearly defined objective, but this is not the case. Although the highest level of compliance is with this element, only 95 percent of the maximum of 53 points (one for each fund) is recorded because the statements of objectives for four SWFs are rather vague.[14] The vast majority of SWFs also have clear legal frameworks, but our assessment of the public record is that seven do not.

Another relevant feature is whether there is a formal procedure to change the SWF's structure, which there is for about three-quarters of the funds. It is unrealistic to think that, once established, a fund's structure should be immutable to political forces or changing circumstances. An immutable structure is an invitation either to illegal activity or to overturning the structure completely. The process of changing the structure is more straightforward and less subject to caprice if it is initially grounded in law. Norway has altered the structure and orientation of its SWF several times since it was first established in 1990, but a number of SWFs have collapsed or have been liquidated in part because their structures and requirements were excessively rigid.

The structure category includes whether the SWF has a clearly stated overall investment strategy. Most funds do, but for nine no such statement is publicly available, and for another 10 the public statement is imprecise. On the other hand, to require that SWFs state formally that investment decisions are based solely on economic grounds rather than political, foreign policy, or noncommercial considerations—as was suggested by Kimmitt (2008) and echoed by other US Treasury officials (Lowery 2008)—is an empty statement because such a commitment would be

---

14. In this 2009 version of the SWF scoreboard, the funds are the Abu Dhabi Investment Authority, Oman's State General Reserve Fund, Sudan's Oil Revenue Stabilization Account, and Venezuela's National Development Fund (Funden).

very difficult to translate into an operational test. Instead of relying on empty policy statements, it is more informative to examine the overall structure of the fund, its governance, and other aspects of its activities, as the SWF scoreboard does.

Fiscal treatment is central to maintaining the macroeconomic stability of a country with an SWF. This involves several elements, including how an SWF receives its funding, when and under what circumstances its principal and earnings are available to the government, and whether these flows are integrated with the budget. As detailed in IMF (2007c), for example, basic principles of good public finance aim at limiting the procyclical influence of an SWF on its country's fiscal policy. It follows that an SWF should not be used as a second budget, any nonadministrative expenditures by a country's SWF should be integrated with the overall budget of the government, and the government should avoid explicitly and, if possible, implicitly borrowing against resources building up in the SWF. In addition, clear rules and principles in this area help to limit the potential scope for corruption in the management of the SWF.

While the majority of SWFs clearly specify the source of their funding, this is not always the case: compliance is only 88 percent for the nonpension SWFs. In the lead-up to the formulation and adoption of the Santiago Principles for SWFs, representatives of the US Treasury argued that where and how a fund obtains its foreign exchange should determine whether it should be subject to such principles, for example, including funds financed either from foreign exchange market intervention or earnings from natural resource exports, but excluding those financed from other sources such as fiscal revenues or pension contributions.[15] This approach is too narrow, however; the public policy issues raised by SWFs are present wherever such a fund obtains its resources.

Compliance in clearly indicating how the earnings and principal of an SWF are to be used is substantially lower than compliance regarding the SWF's indicating its source of funding. A majority of funds have clear rules about how they are to interact with the government budget. In a number of cases, those rules or guidelines are not rigorously followed, as in the case, for example, of Norway and its Government Pension Fund-Global, which has tended to provide more financing to the Norwegian government than is called for in its guidelines.[16] As detailed in the 2009 IMF Article IV review of the Norwegian economy (IMF 2010, 23), "The experience of recent years suggests that fiscal loosening during downturns tends to be much more aggressive than the corresponding tightening during good

---

15. David H. McCormick, testimony before the Joint Economic Committee, February 13, 2008.

16. This issue does not normally arise for pension SWFs. For that reason, we have scored them with a neutral half a point in order not to bias the relative overall scores of pension and nonpension SWFs.

times, implying a slight expansionary bias relative to the 4-percent target" draw on the SWF's capital on average over the business cycle.[17] The last element in the structure category is whether the resources in the SWF are separate from the country's international reserves. Only about two-thirds of the nonpension funds have this feature.[18] A lack of separation between an SWF and the country's international reserves creates ambiguity about the investment activities and objectives of the SWF as well as about the management and quality of the government's international reserves. Such lack of separation also is inconsistent with the spirit, if not the letter, of the IMF's *Guidelines for Foreign Exchange Reserve Management* (IMF 2004). On the other hand, in the wake of the 2007–09 global economic and financial crisis fewer countries may feel that their reserves are excessive. Therefore, in establishing new SWFs countries might be reluctant to segregate their reserves from such funds.

Governance

The governance category (table 5.4) covers the respective roles of the government, governing bodies, and SWF managers in the operations of a fund and also the use of corporate governance and ethical guidelines as part of those activities. Compliance with the elements in this category is far from complete or uniform. On average, all SWFs score only 56 and nonpension funds score 45, but the pension funds score a more respectable 87. However, the dispersion of results on the seven elements as measured by the coefficient of variation of 0.468 is the highest of any category, by a small margin.

In the context of establishing a sound governance structure, full compliance with the first four elements—clear roles of government, a governing body or bodies, and managers, and whether the managers alone make investment decisions—would indicate that the SWF operates at arm's length from the government, presumably with an appropriate set of checks and balances. These checks and balances are the central focus of the next category (accountability and transparency). Unfortunately, for nine of the 40 nonpension funds, the role of government is not defined at all, and for another six that role is ambiguous, producing a score of 70.

The role of the governing body or bodies that set the actual strategy and policies for the SWF should also be clearly defined. This is not the case for eight of the nonpension funds.

---

17. Compared with the 4 percent norm, the average structural nonoil fiscal deficit as a percent of the SWF's capital was 5 percent in 2004–05, 3.5 percent in 2006–08, and a projected 5.7 percent for 2009 and 2010.

18. Again, this issue does not normally arise for pension SWFs, so we have scored them with a neutral half a point in order not to bias the relative overall scores of pension and nonpension SWFs.

Table 5.4 Governance component (percent of maximum possible points)

Element	Nonpension	Pension	Total
Role of government	70	100	77
Role of governing body	81	100	86
Role of managers	74	100	80
Decisions made by managers	45	92	57
Internal ethical standards	24	62	33
Guidelines for corporate responsibility	13	85	30
Ethical investment guidelines	10	73	25
Total	45	87	56

For nine funds, the role of managers also is not defined, and again for another three their role is ambiguous, for a score of 74. In less than about half of the nonpension SWFs, actual investment decisions may not be made exclusively by managers but instead by the government or a government-controlled board. Similarly, for China's pension SWF (the National Social Security Fund) the managers are not solely responsible for investment decisions. This is a crucial element if the activities of SWFs are to be conducted at arm's length from the government.

Of the dozen largest nonpension SWFs that we scored, five report that their investment decisions are made exclusively by investment managers. They are those of Australia, Kuwait, Norway, and the two Singapore funds. When we constructed this edition of the SWF scoreboard, we could find no such statements for the seven other funds (those of Algeria, the CIC, Hong Kong, Qatar, Russia, the Abu Dhabi Investment Authority, and the Investment Company of Dubai).

Only about a quarter of nonpension SWFs have publicly stated standards for the internal ethics of the fund's professional staff. Such standards are one of the most obvious ways to signal a fund's concern about a wide range of destructive practices, including corruption. Most of the pension SWFs we looked at have such standards, but those we scored from the province of Ontario, Canada, Chile, China, the Netherlands, and Thailand do not.

Only a few SWFs (30 percent overall) make a public statement about adhering to guidelines for corporate social responsibility such as those developed under the auspices of the OECD (2000). They include three nonpension SWFs (Norway's Government Pension Fund-Global, Dubai International Capital, and the Alaska Permanent Fund) and four other such funds that make a general statement about exercising corporate responsibility. Eleven of 13 pension SWFs clearly state that they adhere to guidelines of corporate responsibility.

A more controversial element in this category concerns the adoption of ethical investment guidelines in the operation of SWFs. In a world of endowments of nonprofit organizations such guidelines are often described as "socially responsible investing," but more may be involved as well, such as active promotion of clean energy, as in the case of the Norwegian SWF, or sustainable development, which no SWF currently promotes.[19] It could reasonably be argued that the objectives of an SWF should be merely to implement its investment strategy and maximize financial returns subject to whatever risk management constraints have been established. In this case, the fund's ethical investment guidelines would involve ignoring so-called ethical considerations per se. However, in some cases, an SWF may implicitly limit its investments in certain instruments, entities, activities, or countries without a clearly articulated set of guidelines. The SWF scorecard says it is better to have stated guidelines even if others do not agree with the policy. At least four nonpension SWFs have adopted such guidelines.[20] Those who think that such a requirement is onerous should note that the pension SWFs score 73 on having a policy with respect to ethical investments.[21] A recent study found that 21 percent of US colleges and universities follow some form of social investment policy (NACUBO and Commonfund 2010).

Accountability and Transparency

Accountability to the citizens of the home country of an SWF and to the citizens and government of the countries in which it invests, as well as to participants in financial markets more generally, should be the principal motivating objective of SWF best practices. Transparency about the fund's structure and operations is a means toward this broader end. Consequently, the elements included in this category are crucial to the overall compliance of an SWF with generally accepted standards. Table 5.5 provides a summary of compliance on the 14 elements in this category. Average overall compliance is about 57 (with a high of 79 on one element and a low of 36 on another), but compliance by nonpension funds is less than 50 (with a high of 73 and a low of 26), while compliance by pension funds comes in at 88 (with perfect scores on five elements). Overall, the dispersion of results for these 14 elements is quite low, with a coefficient of variation of 0.233.

The four elements in the subcategory of investment strategy implementation are designed to clarify how each SWF conducts its strategy. The first element is whether the fund publishes the broad categories of assets in

---

19. An example of such guidelines is the UN Principles for Responsible Investing.

20. They are Norway's Government Pension Fund-Global, Kuwait Investment Authority, Dubai International Capital, and Wyoming's Permanent Mineral Trust Fund. The Kuwait Investment Authority limits investments in certain countries.

21. The exceptions are Australia's Future Fund, Chile's Pension Reserve Fund, China's National Social Security Fund, and (with only partial credit) Japan's Government Pension Investment Fund.

Table 5.5 Accountability and transparency component
(percent of maximum possible points)

Element	Nonpension	Pension	Total
Investment strategy implementation			
Categories of investments	67	100	75
Use of benchmarks	44	100	58
Use of credit ratings	40	85	51
Mandates published	45	88	56
Investment activities			
Size of fund	73	100	79
Returns of fund	51	100	63
Location of investments	41	58	45
Specific investments	26	69	36
Currency composition	30	62	38
Reports			
Annual reports	59	100	69
Quarterly reports	34	85	46
Audits			
Regular audits	60	96	69
Audits published	40	92	53
Audits independent	56	96	66
Total	47	88	57

which it invests, such as stocks, bonds, real estate, alternative investments, and foreign exchange. This is universally the case for the sample of pension SWFs. About 20 percent of the nonpension SWFs provide no information on the categories of assets in which they invest; about another 20 percent release some information; and almost 60 percent match the pension SWFs.

Each of the pension SWFs, but less than half of the nonpension SWFs, reports the use of benchmarks in whole or in part to guide its investments. Credit ratings play a similar role: 11 of the 13 pension SWFs use them systematically, sometimes imposed by law or regulation, and somewhat more than a third of nonpension SWFs do so. It could be argued that these two elements are largely descriptive of the investment and risk management practices of SWFs, but they provide some concrete, if indirect, evidence of professionalism in the funds' operations. Of course, the extent of the use of benchmarks and credit ratings depends in part on the nature of the SWFs' overall investment strategy.

The same cannot be said for the last element in this subcategory: whether the SWF identifies holders of individual investment mandates. Through this type of disclosure, the public both inside and outside the country can check on the records, quality, and reliability of those intermediaries. Disclosure also limits the scope for sweetheart arrangements and corruption. Eleven of the 13 pension funds provide this information, and a 12th does in part. The nonpension funds score less than 50 as a group, but 20 of them do provide this information or state that they do not grant mandates.

Investment activities are the next subcategory under accountability and transparency. Average compliance with the five elements included in this subcategory ranges from high to quite low. First is whether the SWF makes public its size. One might think it is obviously appropriate and necessary to do so, but eight nonpension funds do not, and another six provide only partial information, resulting in an overall score of only 79, and 73 for the nonpension SWFs alone.

What is the rationale for such nondisclosure? Some argue, as with a country's foreign exchange reserves, that the size of an SWF is a state secret. But that approach to reserve management went out of fashion more than a decade ago in the wake of the Tequila crisis and the Asian financial crisis. The adoption of the reserve template as part of the IMF's Special Data Dissemination Standard (Kester 2001) codified this change. A related argument is that if a country's enemies know the size of its asset holdings, including in its SWF, the country might be more vulnerable to military attack. However, as in the case of Kuwait following the 1990–91 Gulf War, the foreign assets of an SWF are not within the country.[22] The most plausible argument is that the citizens of the country, knowing how large the assets of the SWF are, will mobilize politically to obtain immediate access to them. A less respectable version of this argument, which applies as well to the next element (disclosing the SWF's returns), is that public release of the SWF's investment record would embarrass the authorities. This is a political issue in many jurisdictions, as those involved with the Alaska Permanent Fund and Wyoming's Permanent Mineral Trust Fund have testified (Cowper 2007, Lummis 2007), but nondisclosure as a strategy to deal with such pressures is likely to exacerbate them over the long term. About half of nonpension SWFs do not disclose their annual returns or their disclosure is incomplete, but half also provide some or substantial overall information.

Only a dozen nonpension and four pension SWFs fully disclose the geographic location of their foreign assets. Four nonpension SWFs disclose the specific assets in their portfolios, though several others provide some information on key investments. A majority of pension SWFs comply with this element.

One of the issues with respect to the potential role of SWFs contributing to financial market turbulence and uncertainty is their effect on exchange rates as they convert foreign exchange, predominantly held in dollar assets but also disproportionately in euro assets, into a portfolio of

---

22. The Kuwait Investment Authority operates under prohibitions and penalties for public disclosure of information, but it nevertheless now makes public the size of its General Reserve Fund, which is invested primarily in Kuwait, and its much larger Future Generation Fund, which is invested primarily outside the country. Overall, the Kuwait Investment Authority is at 63 on the scoreboard—slightly above the median and the mean score for all nonpension SWFs.

assets more diversified with respect to currency composition. A simple way to address this concern is to publish information on the currency composition of countries' SWF assets, as more than two dozen countries do with respect to their foreign exchange assets. Surprisingly, nine of the 40 nonpension SWFs disclose in detail the currency composition of their portfolios and another seven provide some information; eight pension SWFs do so. But, why don't all SWFs follow the example of the few? One answer is that the practices of each SWF evolved in isolation and many funds until recently were unaware of the practices of others.[23] Annual reports, in principle, should contain much of the information covered by the elements in the subcategories of investment strategy implementation and investment activities in the scoreboard. However, 11 nonpension SWFs do not issue annual reports at all and only 18 funds issue reasonably complete reports to the public, producing a combined score of 59.

About two-thirds of the SWFs that issue complete annual reports also issue quarterly reports on their operations. Views differ on the desirability of quarterly financial reporting. Some argue that it promotes too much focus on short-term returns. The principal argument for quarterly reporting by an SWF is transparency. The fund should be able to withstand the influence of excessive short-term emphasis given that it is not subject to the disciplines of the financial market, but rather only to those of the political market. A fund also should be able to do so without tipping its hand about implementing its investment strategy. Reports are normally issued with a lag of a month or two. Not surprisingly, each of the 13 pension SWFs issues an annual report, and only one does not issue any quarterly report (Canada's Caisse de Dépôt et Placement du Québec). Two others issue only partial quarterly reports.

The final group of elements in this category focuses on audits. Regular audits, preferably independent and published, are a central element of accountability and transparency. For this reason, the scoreboard includes a maximum of three points in this area: Is the fund audited? Is the audit published? Are the auditors independent of the fund and its management?

Fifteen nonpension SWFs are not subject to audit as far as can be ascertained from the public record, and for two others the audit appears to be less than complete. As a result, nonpension SWFs score a combined 60 on this element while the pension SWFs score 96. For seven nonpension funds where there is some type of audit, it is not published at all, producing a score of only 40. Twenty-two nonpension SWFs report that they are independently audited, for a score of 66, including Norway's Government Pension Fund-Global, which shifted to a fully independent audit in 2008. If the auditing is internal, it takes away some of the objectivity.

---

23. See the discussion of table 5.9.

However, we allow full credit if it is done by a separately constituted government auditing authority. Almost all pension SWFs have full scores on these three elements.

Behavior

The last category focuses on the investment behavior of the funds (table 5.6). It combines aspects of risk management with features that may be of concern to market participants because of the potentially large scale of SWF investment activities. Overall compliance averages 33; the nonpension funds score 24, and the pension funds score 62. In this category with the fewest elements, the coefficient of variation is 0.464, essentially the same as for the governance category.

The first element is whether an SWF has a publicly stated risk management policy. Almost all of the pension SWFs do; the exceptions are Chile's Pension Reserve Fund and Thailand's Government Pension Fund. On the other hand, only 11 of the 40 nonpension SWFs do the same, including those in China, Korea, Singapore, Timor-Leste, and Norway, as well as most of the US SWFs.

An aspect of risk management policy is whether a fund has a policy on the use of leverage, which four of the nonpension SWFs and half of the pension SWFs do. It should be noted again that having a policy of limiting the use of leverage is not the same as having no involvement with leverage, as is claimed by some who depict the activities of SWFs as benign and long-term in orientation. Several funds do take on leverage.

A similar question is whether a fund has a publicly stated policy on the use of derivatives, which is the case for a larger proportion (more than a third) of nonpension, and almost all pension, SWFs. Most, but not all, funds that have a policy on the use of derivatives—12 of 15 nonpension SWFs and 11 of 12 pension SWFs—say that derivatives are used primarily for hedging.

The final element of this category and the scoreboard is whether the fund has a rule or guideline for how it adjusts its portfolio. Six nonpension SWFs do so in some form, producing a score of 14. For example, Norway's Government Pension Fund-Global states that it uses new inflows of resources to make adjustments in its portfolio in light of market changes that move the portfolio away from its benchmarks—in other words, a policy of portfolio rebalancing. New Mexico's Severance Tax Permanent Fund and Wyoming's Permanent Mineral Trust Fund follow similar guidelines, and the Korea Investment Corporation uses something close. Interestingly, a larger proportion of the pension SWFs have guidelines that are a matter of public record.

This review of the various elements of the SWF scoreboard points to two broad conclusions. First, there is a diversity of compliance. This almost certainly reflects the diversity of political and cultural origins of the

Table 5.6   Behavior component (percent of maximum possible points)

Element	Nonpension	Pension	Total
Risk management policy	30	85	43
Policy on leverage	16	38	22
Policy on derivatives	38	88	50
Portfolio adjustment	14	35	19
Total	24	62	33

various funds. Second, the pension SWFs reviewed have a higher level of compliance with each element. This suggests that there is a more fully developed implicit global standard for pension funds. This record suggests that in the future nonpension funds may conform to a greater degree with the elements of the SWF scoreboard presented here.

Evidence of Progress

Tables 5.7 to 5.9 address the question of whether there has been any change, which I would interpret as progress, over the past three years in how SWFs score on the elements included in the SWF scoreboard. Tables 5.7 and 5.8 provide a perspective on the evolution of the individual funds and table 5.9 of the elements in the scoreboard.[24]

The top part of table 5.7 focuses on the 33 funds that have been scored three times. They were scored on a different number of elements each time, but that does not introduce much of a bias in relative performance, as can be seen by comparing tables 5.7 and 5.8. The latter provides scores for the funds on the 24 elements that have been included in all three scoreboards. In the bottom of tables 5.7 and 5.8, results are presented for the 13 funds that have been scored twice.

Without controlling for the slightly different list of elements, the average improvement in table 5.7 for the funds that have been scored three times since they were first scored in 2007 is 12 points. The average improvement

---

24. In general, the evolution of the scores reflects changes instituted by the SWFs themselves. For a few funds, the evolution reflects our obtaining more complete information. In that latter respect, one could argue that progress by the funds has been exaggerated. However, in most cases, the funds themselves responded to earlier editions of the scoreboard and pointed us to or provided additional public information. I would regard this as a measure of progress in that the funds took the responsibility. In a very few cases, managers of the fund have shared with us some of the information that we think should be available regularly and publicly but is available only to those who ask. An example is the Alberta Heritage Savings Trust Fund. However, this approach is hardly consistent with the overall purpose of our exercise and receives no credit. The Alberta fund, maybe partly as a result, scores above the mean and median for all SWFs at 74, but not as well as other Canadian entities.

Table 5.7　Comparison of sovereign wealth fund scoreboards (all elements)

Country	Fund[a]	Score 2009	Change in percentage points 2008–09	Change in percentage points 2007–09	Percent change in percentage points 2007–09
Funds scored three times					
Norway	Government Pension Fund-Global	97	5	5	5
United States	*California Public Employees' Retirement System (P)*	95	8	14	18
New Zealand	*Superannuation Fund (PR)*	94	3	4	4
United States	Alaska Permanent Fund	92	0	22	32
Timor-Leste	Petroleum Fund	85	5	–2	–2
Trinidad and Tobago	Heritage and Stabilization Fund	83	30	34	70
Australia	*Future Fund (PR)*	80	5	18	30
Azerbaijan	State Oil Fund	76	–2	10	15
Canada	Alberta Heritage Savings Trust Fund	74	1	2	–2
Singapore	Temasek Holdings	73	27	19	35
Chile	Economic and Social Stabilization Fund	71	0	9	15
Kazakhstan	National Fund	65	2	7	12
Singapore	Government of Singapore Investment Corporation	65	24	56	624
Kuwait	Kuwait Investment Authority	63	15	15	31
Korea	Korea Investment Corporation	60	9	24	66
United Arab Emirates	Mubadala Development Company	59	45	47	392
China	China Investment Corporation	57	19	33	137
Botswana	Pula Fund	56	1	0	0
Russia	Stabilization Fund of the Russian Federation	50	–1	12	32
São Tomé and Príncipe	National Oil Account	48	0	–1	–1
Malaysia	Khazanah Nasional	44	6	6	16
Mexico	Oil Income Stabilization Fund	44	–3	16	57
Kiribati	Revenue Equalization Reserve Fund	35	6	5	16
Algeria	Revenue Regulation Fund	29	2	11	60
Iran	Oil Stabilization Fund	29	6	7	31
Venezuela	Macroeconomic Stabilization Fund	27	5	5	24
	National Development Fund	27	6	3	10
Oman	State General Reserve Fund	23	3	3	14
Brunei Darussalam	Brunei Investment Agency	21	3	11	112
Sudan	Oil Revenue Stabilization Account	18	–2	–2	–9
Qatar	Qatar Investment Authority	15	6	7	89
United Arab Emirates	Istithmar World	15	3	2	17
	Abu Dhabi Investment Authority	11	3	7	165
Average		54	7	12	64
Funds scored twice					
Canada	*Canada Pension Plan (P)*	92	2		
United States	Wyoming Permanent Mineral Trust Fund	91	2		
Canada	*Caisse de dépôt et placement du Québec (P)*	89	2		
France	*Fonds de réserve pour les retraites (P)*	89	2		
Ireland	*National Pensions Reserve Fund (PR)*	86	5		
Netherlands	*Stichting Pensioenfonds ABP (P)*	85	5		
Japan	*Government Pension Investment Fund (P)*	84	2		
United States	New Mexico Severance Tax Permanent Fund	80	–5		
Thailand	*Government Pension Fund (P)*	78	–2		
Hong Kong	Exchange Fund	70	5		
China	*National Social Security Fund (P)*	70	–2		
Chile	*Pension Reserve Fund (PR)*	68	2		
Nigeria	Excess Crude Account	29	3		
Average		78	1		

a. Pension funds (P) and reserve pension funds (PR) shown in italics.

Table 5.8   Comparison of sovereign wealth fund scoreboards (24 elements)

Country	Fund[a]	Score 2009	Change in percentage points 2008–09	Change in percentage points 2007–09	Percent change in percentage points 2007–09
Funds scored three times					
Norway	Government Pension Fund-Global	97	0	6	7
United States	*California Public Employees' Retirement System (P)*	95	0	11	14
New Zealand	*Superannuation Fund (PR)*	94	0	0	0
United States	Alaska Permanent Fund	92	0	21	30
Timor-Leste	Petroleum Fund	85	4	5	6
Trinidad and Tobago	Heritage and Stabilization Fund	83	25	41	87
Australia	*Future Fund (PR)*	80	4	13	20
Azerbaijan	State Oil Fund	76	2	15	23
Canada	Alberta Heritage Savings Trust Fund	74	0	2	–3
Singapore	Temasek Holdings	73	17	17	30
Chile	Economic and Social Stabilization Fund	71	0	17	28
Kazakhstan	National Fund	65	0	4	7
Singapore	Government of Singapore Investment Corporation	65	23	51	544
Kuwait	Kuwait Investment Authority	63	4	9	19
Korea	Korea Investment Corporation	60	0	18	53
United Arab Emirates	Mubadala Development Company	59	46	50	400
China	China Investment Corporation	57	26	47	225
Botswana	Pula Fund	56	2	–6	–11
Russia	Stabilization Fund of the Russian Federation	50	3	21	59
São Tomé and Príncipe	National Oil Account	48	0	7	16
Malaysia	Khazanah Nasional	44	0	10	29
Mexico	Oil Income Stabilization Fund	44	0	23	79
Kiribati	Revenue Equalization Reserve Fund	35	0	4	13
Algeria	Revenue Regulation Fund	29	2	17	89
Iran	Oil Stabilization Fund	29	0	8	36
Venezuela	Macroeconomic Stabilization Fund	27	2	6	27
	National Development Fund	27	0	3	13
Oman	State General Reserve Fund	23	0	6	30
Brunei Darussalam	Brunei Investment Agency	21	0	15	140
Sudan	Oil Revenue Stabilization Account	18	0	4	20
Qatar	Qatar Investment Authority	15	0	4	50
United Arab Emirates	Istithmar World	15	0	3	23
	Abu Dhabi Investment Authority	11	2	5	125
Average		54	5	14	67
Funds scored twice					
Canada	*Canada Pension Plan (P)*	92	0		
United States	Wyoming Permanent Mineral Trust Fund	91	2		
Canada	*Caisse de dépôt et placement du Québec (P)*	89	0		
France	*Fonds de réserve pour les retraites (P)*	89	0		
Ireland	*National Pensions Reserve Fund (PR)*	86	0		
Netherlands	*Stichting Pensioenfonds ABP (P)*	85	0		
Japan	*Government Pension Investment Fund (P)*	84	0		
United States	New Mexico Severance Tax Permanent Fund	80	2		
Thailand	*Government Pension Fund (P)*	78	0		
China	*National Social Security Fund (P)*	70	0		
Chile	*Pension Reserve Fund (PR)*	68	0		
Hong Kong	Exchange Fund	70	0		
Nigeria	Excess Crude Account	29	0		
Average		78	0		

a. Pension funds (P) and reserve pension funds (PR) shown in italics.

Table 5.9 Comparison of sovereign wealth fund scoreboard elements (24 elements)

Element	Score, 2009	Change in percentage points 2008–09	Change in percentage points 2007–09	Percent change in percentage points 2007–09
Structure				
Objective stated	94	0	6	7
Source of funding	86	3	6	8
Use of fund earnings	58	2	6	12
Integrated with budget	67	3	13	24
Investment strategy	69	7	16	30
Changes in the structure	73	6	33	85
Separate from international reserves	79	0	0	0
Total	75	3	11	23
Governance				
Role of government	71	8	18	34
Guidelines for corporate responsibility	20	0	6	44
Role of managers	74	3	3	4
Ethical investment guidelines	12	0	3	33
Total	44	3	8	29
Accountability and transparency				
Published mandates	52	3	35	209
Returns of fund	55	10	22	66
Published audits	45	12	21	88
Annual reports	64	9	20	47
Independent audits	65	6	20	43
Categories of investments	63	12	20	46
Regular audits	70	6	15	28
Location of investments	40	8	15	61
Specific investments	25	2	14	136
Quarterly reports	41	5	10	32
Currency composition	35	5	9	35
Size of fund	76	3	8	11
Total	53	7	17	67
Behavior				
Portfolio adjustment	14	6	9	200
Overall total	56	5	14	53

in the core set of 24 elements is 14 points—table 5.8—but each of the 24 elements is worth an additional 1.13 points.

The SWFs that have shown the largest increases in scores come from a variety of countries. The list is led by Singapore's GIC, the Mubadala Development Company of the United Arab Emirates (Abu Dhabi), Trinidad and Tobago's Heritage and Stabilization Fund, the CIC (which took over the Central Huijin Investment Company, which we scored in 2007), and the Korean Investment Corporation. The score of the Alaska Permanent Fund also increased by more than 20 points. Table 5.8 shows that on a consistent set of questions the list of funds showing substantial improvements is essentially the same, and is identical for the four funds with the largest increases in scores.

Among the funds that scored 80 or higher in the latest edition of the SWF scoreboard are several that have improved their scores since 2007, including Australia's Future Fund, the California Public Employees' Retirement System (CalPERS), and even the top-scoring Government Pension Fund-Global of Norway. This illustrates the earlier point that every fund can improve.

The bottom portion of table 5.7 shows less improvement in part because nine of the 13 funds are pension SWFs that were incorporated into the second edition scoreboard exercise to provide more of a comparison with the nonpension SWFs. Generally the pension funds score higher, providing less scope for improvement, notwithstanding the results for CalPERS and the Australian Future Fund shown in the top panel.[25] Similarly, the seven funds added in the latest edition of the scoreboard have an average score of 49, less than the averages for the other two groups.[26] The bottom portion of table 5.8 shows that there was very little overall improvement in the scores of the 13 funds that were scored only twice.

Turning to the areas of increased compliance or adherence to the scoreboard as it was originally constructed, table 5.9 focuses on the 24 elements in the 2007 edition that are in the latest edition and how the performance of the original 33 funds has evolved on those elements. As noted in connection with the discussion of table 5.8 and the record of the 33 funds, the increase in scores is significant if not overwhelming.

Focusing on the two-year change in 2007–09, increases were recorded in every element, with the exception of treating the SWF separately from the home country's international reserves. The governments have made substantial changes in other elements included in the structure category, in particular with respect to provisions for changing that structure, articulating an overall investment strategy, and integrating the SWF's operations with the budget. There has been an accompanying increase in clarifying the role of government in the management of the funds.

The most dramatic changes have been in the area of accountability and transparency, where for six elements the change has been more than 20 percentage points. Even in the area of portfolio adjustment there have been some improvements.

---

25. An inspection of table 5.8 reveals that the small improvement shown for New Zealand's Superannuation Fund reflects changes in the list of elements between 2007 and 2009 rather than a change with respect to the core 24 elements.

26. The added group of funds includes the lowest-scoring Dubai International Capital at 21 and the highest scoring Ontario Teachers' Pension Fund at 83.

Why have these changes occurred? As noted earlier, the activities of the funds have increased in salience in their home countries. The authorities appear to have responded with an increase in overall accountability and transparency. In addition, during this period the international profile of SWFs increased and the Santiago Principles were developed. The authorities appear to have responded to these developments. Finally, I know from personal contacts that the authorities responsible for a number of the funds have reacted to the publication of the first two editions of the SWF scoreboard in late 2007 and early 2008.

Comparison with Other Indices and Indicators

In the next chapter, I compare the results of the SWF scoreboard presented here with the international standard for SWFs that was agreed upon by the IWG in September 2008—what are known as the Santiago Principles or Generally Accepted Principles and Practices of SWFs. However, the Santiago Principles have just begun to influence the behavior of the authorities of countries with SWFs. Meanwhile, the results of one other measure of SWF practices, the Linaburg-Maduell Transparency Index, can be compared with the scoreboard I have developed. In addition, it is useful to compare the results of the scoreboard with other indicators of the national environments in which SWFs operate.

The Linaburg-Maduell Transparency Index is produced by the Sovereign Wealth Fund Institute and scores SWFs on 10 principles (Linaburg and Maduell 2010). Each fund receives a score of either one or zero on each principle with a minimum overall score of one. The developers list the principles but do not provide substantial information about how their principles are applied. Indeed, they state on their website, "There are different levels of depth in regard to each principle, judgment of these principles is left to the discretion of the Sovereign Wealth Fund Institute."[27] Seven of the 10 principles overlap, in whole or in part, with about half of the elements in the scoreboard presented in this chapter.[28] There is no overlap with three principles.[29]

---

27. If a background or technical paper on the Linaburg-Maduell index exists, it has not been released to the general public. The index is at www.swfinstitute.org/research/transparency index.php (accessed on April 26, 2010).

28. In some cases the overlap appears to be very clear with one or more of the elements in the scoreboard. In other cases, it is less clear. And in some cases, Linaburg and Maduell include in a principle an aspect that is not captured by any of the elements in the scoreboard. For example, total management compensation is included in a principle along with total portfolio market value and returns.

29. The three other Linaburg-Maduell principles are whether the fund manages its own website, whether it provides an address and contact information, and whether, if applicable,

Figure 5.2   Sovereign wealth fund scoreboard and the Linaburg-Maduell index

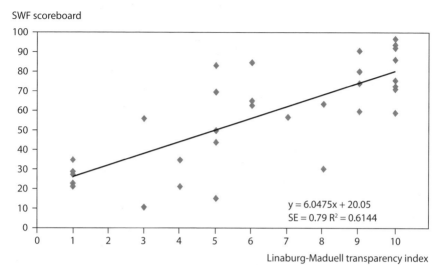

SWF scoreboard

$y = 6.0475x + 20.05$
$SE = 0.79\ R^2 = 0.6144$

Linaburg-Maduell transparency index

Source: Linaburg and Maduell (2010) for transparency index.

As of the fourth quarter of 2009, Linaburg and Maduell rated 44 funds, of which 36 are covered in the SWF scoreboard.[30] Figure 5.2 is a scatter diagram of the two sets of scores. The results are broadly similar, with a significant, positive correlation of 0.61, but there are some prominent outliers.

Linaburg and Maduell rate as perfect 10s eight SWFs that are included in the SWF scoreboard. The average score for those eight funds on the scoreboard is 81, with a standard deviation of 13 points. The scores range from a high of 97 for Norway's Government Pension Fund-Global to a low of 59 for the Mubadala Development Company in Abu Dhabi. The Korea Investment Company receives a Linaburg-Maduell score of 9 and a 60 on the scoreboard. Bahrain's Mumtalakat Holding Company receives a Linaburg-Maduell score of 8 and a 30 on the scoreboard.

---

it identifies subsidiaries and their contact information. For this and another "if applicable" principle, the user does not know the scoring if the question is not applicable.

30. Three of the additional eight funds—those of Angola, Libya, and Mauritania—are listed in table 2.1. Linaburg and Maduell also rate the Saudi Arabian Monetary Agency, which is listed in table 2.1 but is not generally included as an SWF, and the Saudi Arabian Public Investment Fund, which is understood to invest exclusively in domestic projects. They also rate the China-Africa Development Fund and the investment company of China's State Administration of Foreign Exchange (SAFE); although the investment activities of both raise concerns similar to those raised by SWFs, they generally are not included in the SWF universe. The other two entities rated by Linaburg and Maduell but not in the SWF scoreboard are located in the United Arab Emirates. Three UAE SWFs appear on both lists.

At the other extreme, Linaburg and Maduell rate eight SWFs on the scoreboard as 1. On the SWF scoreboard, their mean score is 31, with a standard deviation of 10 points and scores on the scoreboard ranging from 21 for the Brunei Development Agency to 35 for Kiribati's Revenue Equalization Reserve Fund. The Abu Dhabi Investment Authority is rated at 3 by Linaburg and Maduell but received the lowest score of 11 on the SWF scoreboard as of the end of 2009.[31] Trinidad and Tobago's Heritage and Stabilization Fund receives a score of only 5 from Linaburg and Maduell but 83 on the scoreboard. The Petroleum Fund for Timor-Leste is rated at 6 by Linaburg and Maduell but 85 on the scoreboard.

The Linaburg-Maduell index is self-described as focusing on transparency. The SWF scoreboard focuses on the broader concept of accountability to the general public in the home and host country as well as to markets. This may account for some of the differences. The Linaburg-Maduell judgmental weighting algorithm may also account for the more pronounced differences between the two sets of results.[32]

Figure 5.3 provides another a type of comparison with the results of the SWF scoreboard. It presents a summary of the results assembled in the Hill & Knowlton and Penn Schoen Berland (2010) survey of perceptions of SWFs and their reputation. The reputation variable, shown on the x-axis, is constructed from the sum of answers to three questions about the funds of 18 countries: Does transparency/accountability/good governance apply to the funds of these countries? The SWF scoreboard results are shown on the y-axis, averaging the results for countries with more than one SWF and treating Abu Dhabi and Dubai as separate countries. As depicted in the figure, there is a significant positive relationship between the SWF scoreboard result and the reputation of the SWFs of the countries. However, the relationship is not very tight, and the figure labels some of the outliers. Norway, Kuwait, China, Kazakhstan, and Botswana score better than the average relationship, and Dubai and Qatar score worse.

As has been emphasized throughout this study, SWFs are a collective description of government investment vehicles with diverse objectives in a wide range of countries with different histories and cultures. Nevertheless, in their international investments they are part of one global financial system and each feels pressure to conform to evolving global norms. We examined the statistical relationship between several representations

---

31. Both the SWF scoreboard and the Linaburg-Maduell index as of the fourth quarter of 2009 do not reflect the publication of the ADIA's annual report in March 2010 (see box 5.2).

32. Galani and Nixon (2008) developed an SWF risk index that focuses on the economic and political risks associated with 20 funds. They score funds on only three dimensions: transparency of investment criteria, extent of control of investments, and the nature of the home country's political system. Not surprisingly, Norway's Government Pension Fund-Global receives the highest score and China's CIC receives the lowest, though the scale is inverted. As of mid-2010, the index had not been updated.

Figure 5.3 Sovereign wealth fund scoreboard and reputation

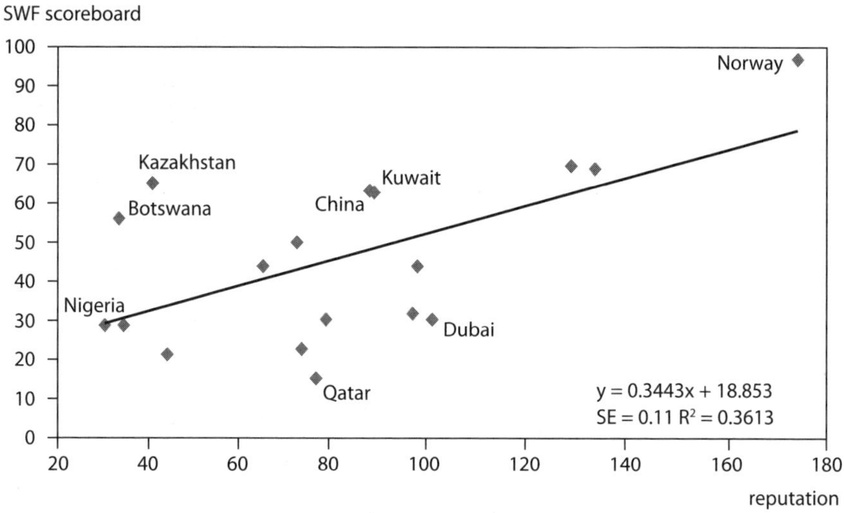

SWF scoreboard

$$S_i = c + bI_i + u_i,$$

Source: Hill & Knowlton and Penn Schoen Berland (2010) for reputation.

of those global norms for the 37 home countries to funds included in the scoreboard and each fund's score. We ran simple regressions of the form:

$$S_i = c + bI_i + u_i,$$

where S is the fund's score on the scoreboard, I is the country's score on some other index, i refers to a particular fund or average of funds in each country, and u is an error term.[33] The results are summarized in table 5.10 using the scores of the 40 nonpension SWFs as the dependent variable. The first set of tests, shown on the left-hand side of the table, was preformed with the total SWF scores as the dependent variable.

The strongest relationship is between the World Bank's governance indicator for voice and accountability and the SWF scoreboard results. This is reassuring given the emphasis in the scoreboard on accountability. As might be expected, and as others have found (Setser 2008b), a high score on the Heritage Foundation's well-known index of economic freedom also is significantly correlated with the relevant country's SWF score. The World Bank's indicator of the ease of doing business is in the same ballpark, and

---

33. Where the SWF scoreboard includes more than one fund from the country, we averaged the scores for the dependent variable. We also adjusted the independent variables to a scale of 100 so that the coefficients could be interpreted as the effect of a change of a single point in that independent variable on the SWF scoreboard.

Table 5.10   Sovereign wealth fund scoreboard index and other indicators

Independent variable indicator	Dependent variable					
	Scoreboard total			Accountability and transparency subset		
	Coefficient	Standard error	R^2	Coefficient	Standard error	R^2
Transparency International corruption perceptions index	0.344*	0.170	0.12	0.499**	0.222	0.14
Heritage index of economic freedom	0.567**	0.239	0.12	0.982***	0.341	0.18
World Economic Forum global competitiveness index	0.341	0.332	0.05	0.425	0.459	0.05
World Bank						
Ease of doing business	0.299**	0.142	0.15	0.429**	0.183	0.17
Worldwide governance indicators						
Voice and accountability	0.764***	0.165	0.40	0.908***	0.239	0.32
Government effectiveness	0.466**	0.176	0.18	0.659**	0.238	0.20
Regulatory quality	0.438**	0.176	0.16	0.689***	0.238	0.23
Rule of law	0.398**	0.190	0.13	0.516**	0.248	0.12
Control of corruption	0.364*	0.183	0.12	0.497*	0.243	0.12
Political stability	0.323	0.203	0.08	0.34	0.273	0.05

* = significant at 10 percent level; ** = significant at 5 percent level; *** = significant at 1 percent level.

most other elements of the set of World Bank governance indicators are in the same range of significance. The exceptions are the indicator of political stability, which has no significance, and control of corruption, whose significance is only at the 10 percent level. Interestingly, the relationship of Transparency International's corruption perceptions index with the scoreboard results is also significant but only at that lower level. The World Economic Forum's global competitiveness index does not appear to be significantly related to the SWF scoreboard results.

The right-hand panel focuses just on the category of accountability and transparency on the SWF scoreboard as the dependent variable. The pattern is not substantially altered. While the R-squares are essentially the same, the significance of the Heritage Foundation's index of economic freedom, the World Bank's indicator of regulatory quality, and Transparency International's corruption perceptions index are each increased a notch. Including the 13 pension SWFs on the scoreboard boosts the correlations across the board because those observations tend to be more heavily concentrated in the funds and countries that score highly on both variables.

These results are consistent with findings by Aizenman and Glick (2009) using, in part, a subsample of 26 countries with SWFs in the 2008 SWF scoreboard (Truman 2008a) and the World Bank governance indicators. Aizenman and Glick find a weak positive correlation between the overall scoreboard result for these countries and the average of the six World Bank governance indicators, but it is not significant. However, they find a strong relationship between the overall governance score and the probability that a country will have an SWF and a strong positive correlation between the 2008 SWF scoreboard result and the World Bank governance component indicator of voice and accountability. Table 5.10 in effect replicates this result for the updated SWF scoreboard. Aizenman and Glick interpret their results through the prism of a few fuel-producing countries with older SWFs that have reasonably good governance scores but weaker voice and accountability scores. They link the latter not only to the strength of governance in the countries but also to relatively low levels of democracy, such as in Russia, Kazakhstan, Azerbaijan, and Timor-Leste. At the same time, some of the countries with newer SWFs may have relatively low democracy scores but higher SWF scoreboard results. The authors speculate that countries with newer funds have a greater incentive to foster more globalization by fostering more transparency and accountability in their funds. A supporting observation is the fact that these four countries were more engaged with the IMF and World Bank, and thus with international norms and standards, when they were setting up their funds.

Arguments against the Scoreboard Approach

A number of arguments have been put forward disparaging an agreed-upon global standard such as the SWF scoreboard presented in this chapter. They fall under four headings: unnecessary, undesirable, inappropriate, and unenforceable.

As was discussed in chapter 3, observers such as El-Erian (2008) think that the scoreboard approach sets up an *unnecessary* arbitrary standard for SWFs, which are entities that knowledgeable market participants are fully capable of assessing on their own. That argument not only flies in the face of the general demand for greater transparency and accountability that has been a feature of, and positive trend in, global finance for more than a decade, but it also rings a bit hollow in 2010 when markets and important players in markets have lost some of their luster, and along with it the willingness of outsiders to trust existing institutions to be entirely self-policing.

It also is argued that the scoreboard approach is *undesirable* because it would hamper funds from discharging their obligation to maximize returns to their beneficiaries, the residents of their home countries.[34] The way one

---

34. Interestingly, the survey by Norton Rose (2008) described in chapter 3 found that more than 60 percent of non-SWF respondents thought that the imposition by a jurisdiction of disclosure and transparency requirements would discourage SWF investments there, while more than 70 percent of SWF respondents said it would not, of course depending on the nature of the requirements.

hears this argument is that forcing SWFs to disclose their investment strategies and intentions will undercut their profit opportunities.[35] For example, Lou Jiwei of the CIC was quoted in late 2007 as saying, "We will increase transparency without harming the commercial interests of CIC. That is to say it will be a gradual process. Transparency is a really tough issue. If we are transparent on everything, the wolves will eat us up."[36] More aggressively against the rising demands for increased transparency, Bader M. Al-Sa'ad of the Kuwait Investment Authority said in January 2008, "We are concerned about what they mean when they call for transparency. Do we have to announce every investment before we make it?"[37]

It is reasonable to ask whether SWFs that have higher figures on the scoreboard have lower returns. This is not an easy question to answer without access to a dataset covering many funds over an extended period of time standardized on their portfolio preferences. Those data are not in the public domain. We looked at a limited amount of data for a small subset of the funds in terms of their 2007 returns—not a very satisfactory set of evidence. What we found was that there was no correlation one way or the other between the 2007 financial performances of SWFs and how they ranked on the 2009 SWF scoreboard. For 11 pension SWFs, the coefficient on the total scoreboard's score as the independent variable was negative but not significantly different from zero. For a dozen nonpension SWFs, the coefficient was positive, but also not significantly different from zero. Using the accountability and transparency score alone produced similar results.

We do have some indirect evidence on the importance of an SWF's performance on the scoreboard. Kotter and Lel (2010), using a dataset of 358 announced investments in 40 countries by 22 SWFs of 15 countries from 1988 to February 2009, find that the announcements are associated with a positive initial impact on stock prices, looking principally at a two-day window. This finding is not surprising; studies involving other types of large investors yield similar results, and those results can be explained by anything from insider information to market respect for the due diligence of the investor. What is more surprising and relevant in the context of the SWF scoreboard is that the stock-price effect is stronger and statistically significant for the funds that have a better record of accountability and

---

35. A related argument is that SWFs will increase the frequency and rapidity of their adjustments to market conditions as a result of having to disclose their short-term results and contribute to greater market volatility. The appropriate response is that opacity has never helped markets and the owners and managers of SWFs should be able to do the right thing for their citizens and the financial system as a whole without having to retreat into darkness.

36. As quoted in Marin Arnold, "China Fund Warns on National Security," *Financial Times*, December 11, 2007, 4.

37. Henny Sender, "KIA Chief Focuses on Long-Term Opportunities," *Financial Times*, January 2, 2008, 20.

transparency as indicated by their scores on that component of the 2008 edition of the SWF scoreboard (Truman 2008a).[38]

Bortolotti et al. (2009) look at similar evidence for a slightly larger sample of SWF investments, which is still a very small portion of total SWF portfolios—$141 billion, or less than 5 percent of the overall total even for a narrow definition of SWFs. They find that SWFs tend to invest in listed companies that have a history of low returns compared with investments in matched targets and with other standards. They find, as do Kotter and Lel (2010), that those investments are significantly associated with immediate positive returns. For Bortolotti et al., this effect is not significantly enhanced or reduced by an SWF's score on the 2008 edition of the scoreboard or any of its components. The reason for the apparent conflict with the Kotter-Lel results may be that Bortolotti et al. introduce as a separate independent variable whether the investment is in a financial institution.[39] Finally, Bortolotti et al. look at longer-term returns of up to 24 months and find that those returns are substantially negative compared with matched targets and with other standards. Although a fund's score on the governance component of the 2008 edition of the scoreboard has a significant positive influence, its score on the accountability and transparency component goes the other way at least at the 6- and 12-month time horizons, providing a bit of evidence that transparency may hurt returns. Bortolotti et al. (2009, 28) conclude that poor stock picking by SWFs "could be a consequence of political pressures which led SWFs to invest in distressed industries in order to minimize target-country regulatory and political opposition." It should be noted that a quarter of their overall sample of 1,216 investments involved domestic investments, but this did not show up as a significant explanatory variable.

Is it *inappropriate* to ask SWFs to practice a high degree of accountability and transparency under something like the SWF scoreboard approach? The results of Bortoloti et al. are insufficient to support that case. My answer is no for three reasons.

First, no one is asking a fund to reveal its investment intentions, and thus to set itself up for front running. The approach involves only ex post reporting. Moreover, a large fund can hardly disguise its investments, and many now announce their significant investments, providing the information for the limited number of statistical studies of the effects of those investments.

Second, these are governmental institutions, and they should be held to the highest standards even if it proves to be embarrassing to their boards

---

38. Separate regressions with each of the 33 elements of the 2008 SWF scoreboard produce statistical significant results for 14 of those elements, and all 14 are included in the updated scoreboard presented in this chapter.

39. Kotter and Lel find that their results are robust to excluding those investments.

and managers when they incur losses. As I have argued (Truman 2007), over the longer run an established track record of accountability and disclosure protects managers from unjustified criticism. Many officials of SWFs with whom I have spoken over the past three years have confirmed this judgment.

Third, as for the rest of the argument that hedge funds and private equity firms do not practice such accountability and transparency, the pendulum is swinging in that direction. I have long argued that hedge funds and private equity firms should provide more public disclosure. John Gieve, speaking in early 2008 as the deliberations of the IWG were about to begin, turned this argument around saying that there should be a level playing field. He reminded his listeners that efforts were then under way in the United Kingdom to promote greater transparency on the part of hedge funds and private equity funds.[40]

Those efforts produced a report on transparency and disclosure by UK portfolio companies and private equity firms (Walker Group 2007) and a report on hedge fund standards (Large Group 2008). The Walker Group report prescribed the types of information that should be in the public annual reports of portfolio companies under the UK Companies Act of 2006 and recommended that private equity firms publish annual reviews on their websites communicating specific types of information, including investment strategies, portfolios, and partners. The Large Group report (2008) on hedge funds went into much greater detail, but limited its call for public disclosure to a call for hedge fund managers "to carry on their websites an appropriate amount of information about themselves" and for the sector as a whole to provide more generic information about the sector and individual firms. The UK groups also put forward the useful concept of "comply or explain" why you are not complying, which should be adopted by the owners of SWFs.

A parallel exercise in the United States instigated by the President's Working Group on Financial Markets produced two reports on hedge funds in April 2008 (Asset Managers' Committee 2008, Investors' Committee 2008). These reports, while going into considerable detail about disclosures to counterparties and information that should be made available to investors, did not directly address the issue of standards of public disclosure. Thus, they did not go as far in this direction as was recommended for the United States or globally in the wake of the Long-Term Capital Management episode (President's Working Group on Financial Markets 1999, Financial Stability Board 2000). However, those recommendations were not fully implemented because of resistance from representatives of financial institutions. In 2004, the SEC moved toward regulating hedge funds more

---

40. John Gieve, "Sovereign Wealth Funds and Global Imbalances," speech to the Sovereign Wealth Management Conference, London, March 14, 2008, available at www.bankofengland.co.uk (accessed on July 12, 2010).

formally by issuing a rule requiring them to register as investment advisors. This rule was struck down by the courts in 2006, responding to the hedge funds. In a similar vein of resistance to regulation, in the middle of the global economic and financial crisis of 2007–09, the Institute of International Finance (2009b) released a report that cautioned against the unintended consequences of substantially increased disclosure under pillar 2 of the Basel II capital framework that applies to regulating the banking sector.

I am confident that when all the dust settles from the global economic and financial crisis, hedge funds and private equity firms, as well as more comprehensively regulated financial institutions, will be subject to a great deal more in the way of public disclosure requirements than was the case in 2007 before the crisis broke. Although the exact modalities have yet to be established, and they may not be consistent with nondiscrimination and a level playing field, both the United States and the European Union will subject hedge funds or alternative investment managers to a higher degree of disclosure as well as oversight than has been the case.

These actions with respect to hedge funds and similar entities are occurring despite the fact that many argue, with considerable merit, that hedge funds and private equity firms had little to do with the crisis. Indeed, Mallaby (2010) argues that in the case of hedge funds, incentives were better aligned than they were in large, publicly traded financial institutions that came under severe stress to the point of collapse during the crisis.

What about the *enforceability* of a scoreboard approach to best practices for SWFs? It is necessary to recognize that SWFs are owned and controlled by sovereign governments. International leverage over sovereign governments is constrained by that reality unless a country wants to impose a unilateral prohibition on such investments. In that context, various international agreements and conventions operate as restraints on the other side.[41] Thus, the principal mechanism of enforcement is peer pressure, possibly reinforced by naming and shaming. In general, countries with low scores on international indicators do not like the negative publicity associated with those scores and often respond by trying to raise them. The evidence on improved scores on the SWF scoreboard adduced earlier in this chapter supports this argument. More importantly in this context, each country with an SWF has an interest in encouraging "compliance," for want of a better word, by other countries with SWFs lest they all become tarred with the same brush. This fact reinforces the positive role that transparency about relative performance on the SWF scoreboard can play.

---

41. US Senator Evan Bayh advocated unilateral enforcement of best practices by the United States; countries seeking to invest in the United States would be prohibited from doing so unless they could demonstrate that they adhered to best practices that would be enshrined in US law. It is not clear how the United States would verify compliance with this type of national standard without the cooperation of other countries. See Evan Bayh, "Time for Sovereign Wealth Rules," *Wall Street Journal*, February 13, 2008.

Finally, host countries are not entirely without some leverage. The United States and other similarly situated countries might reasonably decide to take account of a country's voluntary compliance with the international best practices for SWFs as one of a number of factors considered in making determinations about whether a particular fund's investment should be blocked because of a threat to national security. For example, in a March 13, 2008 letter sent to US Treasury Secretary Henry Paulson, Representatives Barney Frank, Carolyn Maloney, and Luis Gutierrez suggested that a country's compliance with aspects of SWF best practices could be used by the CFIUS as a factor in determining whether it should grant that country a waiver from a full investigation of an investment by a government-owned pension fund under the FINSA. A record and a reputation can matter. It is just not enough in this regard for a fund to have established a reputation with market participants alone.

The Scoreboard and Concerns about Sovereign Wealth Funds

Chapter 3 identified five concerns about SWFs: mismanagement of their investments; pursuit of political or economic power objectives; financial protectionism in anticipation of, or in response to, the pursuit by SWFs of political or economic power objectives; market turmoil and uncertainty; and conflicts of interest. I argued in that chapter that the various approaches to dealing with these concerns were either off the mark, infeasible, or counterproductive. How does an agreed-upon international standard for SWFs such as the SWF scoreboard approach measure up?

With respect to the home country's mismanagement of the investments of its SWFs, the scoreboard approach helps to limit the scope of the problem. The scoreboard is built on the concept of accountability and transparency, exploiting the disinfecting and inoculating effects of sunshine. Although it is not possible to exclude the possibility of mismanagement and corruption in the activities of SWFs, the more that is known about them, the more difficult it is for that mismanagement or corruption to occur.

On the pursuit of political or economic power objectives, I have argued that politics is inherent in any government-owned or -controlled economic or financial institution. However, if that institution is accountable not only to its own government and citizens but also to the governments and citizens of countries hosting its investments—which would be aided by the SWF scoreboard approach—then the temptation and scope to use the SWF to achieve this type of objective is reduced. Countries do not in general set up an SWF with a high degree of transparency and accountability to undertake activities that would not be welcome in the countries in which they are investing. I am not saying that countries' motives are always pure, only that they are disinclined to advertise their impurities.

On financial protectionism in anticipation of, or in response to, the pursuit by an SWF of political or economic power objectives, that risk would be reduced to the extent that the home countries were more accountable and transparent about the operations of their SWFs. As El-Erian (2008, 197) put it while defending the inherent respectability of SWFs, "the risk is that the absence of adequate safeguards at the level of the SWF—as opposed to that of the recipient country—will end up feeding general protectionist pressures into the global economy. The specific risk is a proliferation of capital account protectionism and negative externalities in the form of further delays in completing the next stages of trade liberalization." Host countries would have less to fear and, hence, less to protect against.

Market participants would be similarly aided with respect to concerns about potential turbulence and uncertainty on account of SWF activities. Some of the funds are large and could move markets. If the SWFs can establish an open record of credible accountability, then this potential source of disturbance or at least uncertainty would be reduced if not eliminated. This is the rationale behind the scoreboard element focused on whether an SWF has a stated guideline for adjusting its portfolio. As we saw, very few SWFs currently have such a guideline.

Finally, with respect to conflicts of interest, those conflicts involving the funds and agents acting for them in markets should be reduced by the promotion of standards covering their interactions. This is part of the rationale behind the scoreboard element focused on whether an SWF publishes the list of recipients of its mandates. As we saw, compliance with this element is not perfect, but it has increased substantially over the past several years. On the potentially more serious conflicts between home and host governments over the activities of SWFs, the fact that they can jointly agree upon an international standard should promote better understanding and trust among them, or at least reduce misunderstanding and distrust. This is the case whether the standard is described as a scoreboard, a code of conduct, a set of best practices, or the IWG's Generally Accepted Principles and Practices to which I turn in the next chapter, as long as that standard is robust and compliance with it is high.

Appendix 5A
Scoreboard for Sovereign Wealth Funds

This appendix and its accompanying table 5A.1 present the individual elements of the scoreboard described in chapter 5. The scoreboard has evolved since the first edition in 2007, as summarized below.

For each of the 33 elements, posed as questions, if the answer is an unqualified yes, we score it as 1. If the answer is no, we score it as 0. However, partial scores of 0.25, 0.50, and 0.75 are recorded for many elements, indicated by (p) in the descriptions below.

The four categories in the scoreboard are listed below with subcategories where relevant. The words in bold are keyed to the presentation of results in table 5A.1.

Structure

1. Is the SWF's **objective** clearly **stated**? (p)

2. Is there a clear **legal framework** for the SWF? This element was incorporated into the 2008 scoreboard from Santiago Principle 1.1 (see chapter 6).

3. Is the procedure for **changing the structure** of the SWF clear? (p)

4. Is the overall **investment strategy** clearly **stated**? (p)

Fiscal Treatment

5. Is the **source of** the SWF's **funding** clearly specified? (p)

6. Is the nature of the subsequent **use of** the principal and **earnings** of the **fund** clearly specified? (p)

7. Are the SWF's operations appropriately **integrated with fiscal and monetary policies**? (p)

8. Is the SWF **separate from** the country's **international reserves**?

Governance

9. Is the **role of** the **government** in setting the investment strategy of the SWF clearly established? (p)

10. Is the **role of the governing body** of the SWF clearly established? (p) This element was incorporated into the 2008 scoreboard from Santiago Principle 8 (see chapter 6).

11. Is the **role of** the **managers** in executing the investment strategy clearly established? (p)

12. Are **decisions** on specific investments **made by** the **managers**? (p)

13. Does the SWF have **internal ethical standards** for its management and staff? (p) This element was incorporated into the 2008 scoreboard from Santiago Principle 13 (see chapter 6).

14. Does the SWF have in place, and make publicly available, **guidelines for corporate responsibility** that it follows? (p)

15. Does the SWF have **ethical investment guidelines** that it follows? (p)

Transparency and Accountability

Investment Strategy Implementation

16. Do regular reports on investments by the SWF include information on the **categories** of investments? (p)

17. Does the strategy use **benchmarks**? (p)

18. Does the strategy use **credit ratings**? (p)

19. Are the holders of investment **mandates identified**? (p)

Investment Activities

20. Do regular reports on the investments by the SWF include the **size** of the fund? (p)

21. Do regular reports on the investments by the SWF include information on its **returns**? (p)

22. Do regular reports on the investments by the SWF include information on the geographic **location** of investments? (p)

23. Do regular reports on the investments by the SWF include information on the **specific investments**? (p)

24. Do regular reports on the investments by the SWF include information on the **currency composition** of investments? (p)

Reports

25. Does the SWF provide at least an **annual report** on its activities and results? (p)

26. Does the SWF provide **quarterly reports**? (p)

Audits

27. Is the SWF subject to a **regular** annual **audit**? (p)

28. Does the SWF **publish** promptly the **audits** of its operations and accounts? (p)

29. Are the **audits independent**? (p)

Behavior

30. Does the SWF have an operational **risk management policy**? This element was incorporated into the 2008 scoreboard from Santiago Principle 22.2 (see chapter 6).

31. Does the SWF have a **policy on** the use of **leverage**? (p)

32. Does the SWF have a **policy on** the use of **derivatives**? (p)

33. Does the SWF have a guideline on the nature and **speed of adjustment** in its portfolio? (p)

Four elements in the 2008 scoreboard are not included in this scoreboard. Element (a) was also included in the 2007 version. The others were new with the 2008 version.

(a) Are the guidelines for fiscal treatment generally followed without frequent adjustment?

(b) Does the SWF have limits on the size of its stakes?

(c) Does the SWF not take controlling stakes?

(d) Are derivatives used primarily for hedging?

Five elements in this scoreboard and the 2008 version were not included in the 2007 version.

(a) Are decisions on specific investments made by the managers?

(b) Does the strategy use benchmarks?

(c) Does the strategy use credit ratings?

(d) Does the SWF have a policy on the use of leverage?

(e) Does the SWF have a policy on the use of derivatives?

Table 5A.1 Scoreboard for sovereign wealth funds

| | | Structure | | | | Fiscal treatment | | | | |
| | | 1 | 2 | 3 | 4 | 5 | 6 | 7 | 8 | |
Country	Fund	Objective stated	Legal framework	Changing the structure	Investment strategy	Source of funding	Use of fund earnings	Integrated with policies	Separate from international reserves	Sub-total
Algeria	Revenue Regulation Fund	1	1	1	0	1	0.5	0	1	5.5
Australia	Future Fund (PR)	1	1	1	1	1	1	0.5	0.5	7
Azerbaijan	State Oil Fund	1	1	1	0.5	1	1	1	1	7.5
Bahrain	Mumtalakat Holding Company	1	0	0	1	1	0	0	0	3
Botswana	Pula Fund	1	1	0	1	0.5	1	1	0	5.5
Brunei	Brunei Investment Agency	1	1	1	0	0.5	0	0	0	3.5
Canada	Alberta Heritage Savings Trust Fund	1	1	1	1	1	1	1	0.5	7.5
	Caisse de dépôt et placement du Québec (P)	1	1	1	1	1	1	0.5	0.5	7
	Canada Pension Plan (P)	1	1	1	1	1	1	0.5	0.5	7
	Ontario Teachers' Pension Plan (P)	1	1	1	1	1	1	0.5	0.5	7
Chile	Economic and Social Stabilization Fund	1	1	1	0.5	1	1	1	1	7.5
	Pension Reserve Fund (PR)	1	1	1	0.5	1	1	0.5	0.5	6.5
China	China Investment Corporation	1	0	0	1	1	1	1	1	6
	National Social Security Fund (P)	1	1	0.5	1	1	1	0.5	0.5	6.5
France	Fonds de réserve pour les retraites (P)	1	1	1	1	1	1	0.5	0.5	7
Hong Kong	Exchange Fund	1	1	1	1	1	1	1	0	7
Iran	Oil Stabilization Fund	1	1	0.5	0	1	0.5	0	1	5
Ireland	National Pensions Reserve Fund (PR)	1	1	1	1	1	1	0.5	0.5	7
Japan	Government Pension Investment Fund (P)	1	1	1	1	1	1	0.5	0.5	7

(continued on next page)

Table 5A.1 Scoreboard for sovereign wealth funds (continued)

Country	Fund	Structure				Fiscal treatment				Sub-total
		1 Objective stated	2 Legal framework	3 Changing the structure	4 Investment strategy	5 Source of funding	6 Use of fund earnings	7 Integrated with policies	8 Separate from international reserves	
Kazakhstan	National Fund	1	1	0.5	1	1	1	1	1	7.5
Kiribati	Revenue Equalization Reserve Fund	1	1	1	0.5	1	1	1	0	6.5
Korea	Korea Investment Corporation	1	1	1	1	1	0	1	0	6
Kuwait	Kuwait Investment Authority	1	1	1	1	1	0	1	1	7
Malaysia	Khazanah Nasional	1	1	0	0.5	1	0	0	1	4.5
Mexico	Oil Income Stabilization Fund	1	1	0.5	0.5	1	0.5	1	1	6.5
Netherlands	Stichting Pensioenfonds ABP (P)	1	1	1	1	1	1	0.5	0.5	7
New Zealand	Superannuation Fund (PR)	1	1	1	1	1	1	0.5	0.5	7
Nigeria	Excess Crude Account	1	1	1	0	1	1	0	0	5
Norway	Government Pension Fund – Global	1	1	1	1	1	1	1	1	8
Oman	State General Reserve Fund	0.5	1	0.5	0	1	0.5	0.5	1	5
Qatar	Qatar Investment Authority	1	1	0.5	0.25	0	0	0	1	3.75
Russia	Reserve Fund and National Wealth Fund	1	1	1	1	1	0.5	1	0	6.5
São Tomé & Príncipe	National Oil Account	1	1	1	1	1	1	1	1	8
Singapore	Government of Singapore Investment Corporation	1	1	1	1	0.5	1	1	0	6.5
	Temasek Holdings	1	1	1	1	1	0	1	1	7
Sudan	Oil Revenue Stabilization Account	0.5	0	0	0	1	0.5	1	1	4
Thailand	Government Pension Fund (P)	1	1	1	1	1	1	0.5	0.5	7
Timor-Leste	Petroleum Fund	1	1	1	1	1	1	1	1	8

Trinidad & Tobago	Heritage and Stabilization Fund	1	1	1	1	1	1	1	1	8
UAE	Abu Dhabi Investment Authority	0.5	0	0	1	0	0	0	0.5	2
	Dubai International Capital	1	0	1	1	0.5	1	1	0.5	6
	International Petroleum Investment Company	1	0	1	0	1	0	0	0.5	3.5
	Investment Corporation of Dubai	1	1	0	0	1	0	0	0.5	3.5
	Istithmar World	1	0	0	0.5	0.5	0	0	0.5	2.5
	Mubadala Development Company	1	1	0.5	1	1	0	0	0.5	5
United States	Alabama Trust Fund	1	1	1	1	1	1	1	0.5	7.5
	Alaska Permanent Fund	1	1	1	1	1	1	1	0.5	7.5
	California Public Employees' Retirement System (P)	1	1	1	1	1	1	0.5	0.5	7
	New Mexico Severance Tax Permanent Fund	1	1	1	1	1	1	1	0.5	7.5
	Wyoming Permanent Mineral Trust Fund	1	1	1	1	1	1	1	0.5	7.5
Venezuela	Macroeconomic Stabilization Fund	1	1	1	0.5	1	0	0	1	5.5
	National Development Fund	0.5	1	1	0	0.5	0	0	1	4
Vietnam	State Capital Investment Corporation	1	1	1	1	1	0.5	0	1	6.5
Nonpension total[a]		38	33	29	26.75	35	22.5	24.5	25.5	5.86
Pension total[a]		13	13	12.5	12.5	13	13	6.5	6.5	6.92
SWFs total[a]		51	46	41.5	39.25	48	35.5	31	32	6.12
Memorandum										
United Kingdom	Terra Firma	1	1	1	1	1	1	0.5	0.5	7
United States	Harvard University Endowment	1	1	1	1	1	1	0.5	0.5	7
	TIAA-CREF	1	1	1	1	1	1	0.5	0.5	7
	Blackstone	1	1	1	1	1	1	0.5	0.5	7
Total[a]		4	4	4	4	4	4	2	2	7

(continued on next page)

a. For each element, the total is the sum for the relevant funds. For the subtotals category and the grand total, the figures are for the individual fund.

Note: Pension funds (P) and reserve pension funds (PR) shown in italics.

Table 5A.1 Scoreboard for sovereign wealth funds *(continued)*

Country	Fund	Governance							Sub-total
		9 Role of government	**10** Role of governing body	**11** Role of managers	**12** Decisions made by managers	**13** Internal ethical standards	**14** Guidelines for corporate responsibility	**15** Ethical investment guidelines	
Algeria	Revenue Regulation Fund	1	0	1	0	0	0	0	2
Australia	Future Fund (PR)	1	1	1	1	1	1	0	6
Azerbaijan	State Oil Fund	1	1	1	1	0	0	0	4
Bahrain	Mumtalakat Holding Company	0	1	0	0	0	0	0	1
Botswana	Pula Fund	1	1	1	1	0	0	0	4
Brunei	Brunei Investment Agency	0	0	0	0	0	0	0	0
Canada	Alberta Heritage Savings Trust Fund	1	1	1	1	0	0	0	4
	Caisse de dépôt et placement du Québec (P)	1	1	1	1	1	1	1	7
	Canada Pension Plan (P)	1	1	1	1	1	1	1	7
	Ontario Teachers' Pension Plan (P)	1	1	1	1	0	1	1	6
Chile	Economic and Social Stabilization Fund	1	1	1	1	0	0	0	4
	Pension Reserve Fund (PR)	1	1	1	1	0	0	0	4
China	China Investment Corporation	1	1	1	0	0	0.5	0	3.5
	National Social Security Fund (P)	1	1	1	0	0	0	0	3
France	Fonds de réserve pour les retraites (P)	1	1	1	1	1	1	1	7
Hong Kong	Exchange Fund	1	1	1	0	0	0	0	3
Iran	Oil Stabilization Fund	0.5	1	0.5	0	0	0	0	2
Ireland	National Pensions Reserve Fund (PR)	1	1	1	1	1	1	1	7
Japan	Government Pension Investment Fund (P)	1	1	1	1	1	1	0.5	6.5
Kazakhstan	National Fund	1	1	1	1	0	0	0	4

Kiribati	Revenue Equalization Reserve Fund	1	1	1	1	0	0	**4**
Korea	Korea Investment Corporation	1	1	1	1	1	0	**5**
Kuwait	Kuwait Investment Authority	1	1	1	1	0	1	**6**
Malaysia	Khazanah Nasional	0.5	1	0.5	0	0.5	0	**3.5**
Mexico	Oil Income Stabilization Fund	0.5	0.5	0	0	0	0	**1**
Netherlands	*Stichting Pensioenfonds ABP (P)*	1	1	1	0	1	1	**6**
New Zealand	*Superannuation Fund (PR)*	1	1	1	1	1	1	**7**
Nigeria	Excess Crude Account	0.5	1	0	0	0	0	**2.5**
Norway	Government Pension Fund – Global	1	1	1	1	1	1	**7**
Oman	State General Reserve Fund	0	0	0	0	0	0	**0**
Qatar	Qatar Investment Authority	0	1	0	0	0	0	**1**
Russia	Reserve Fund and National Wealth Fund	1	0	1	0	0	0	**2**
São Tomé & Príncipe	National Oil Account	1	1	1	1	0	0	**4**
Singapore	Government of Singapore Investment Corporation	1	1	1	1	1	0	**5**
	Temasek Holdings	1	1	1	1	0.5	0.5	**5.5**
Sudan	Oil Revenue Stabilization Account	0	0	0	0	0	0	**0**
Thailand	*Government Pension Fund (P)*	1	1	1	0	1	1	**6**
Timor-Leste	Petroleum Fund	1	1	0	0	0	0	**3**
Trinidad & Tobago	Heritage and Stabilization Fund	1	1	1	0.5	0	0	**4.5**
UAE	Abu Dhabi Investment Authority	0	1	0	0	0	0	**1**
	Dubai International Capital	1	1	1	1	1	1	**6**
	International Petroleum Investment Company	0.5	0.5	1	0	0	0	**2**
	Investment Corporation of Dubai	0.5	0	0	0	0	0	**0.5**

(continued on next page)

Table 5A.1 Scoreboard for sovereign wealth funds *(continued)*

| | | | Governance | | | | | | |
Country	Fund	9 Role of government	10 Role of governing body	11 Role of managers	12 Decisions made by managers	13 Internal ethical standards	14 Guidelines for corporate responsibility	15 Ethical investment guidelines	Sub-total
	Istithmar World	0	1	0.5	0	0	0	0	1.5
	Mubadala Development Company	1	1	1	0	1	0	0	4
United States	Alabama Trust Fund	1	1	1	1	0	0	0	4
	Alaska Permanent Fund	1	1	1	1	1	1	0	6
	California Public Employees' Retirement System (P)	1	1	1	1	1	1	1	7
	New Mexico Severance Tax Permanent Fund	1	1	1	0.5	0	0	0	3.5
	Wyoming Permanent Mineral Trust Fund	1	1	1	1	1	0.5	1	6.5
Venezuela	Macroeconomic Stabilization Fund	0	1	0	0	0	0	0	1
	National Development Fund	0	1	0	0	0	0	0	1
Vietnam	State Capital Investment Corporation	1	1	1	1	0	0	0	4
Nonpension total[a]		28	32.5	29.5	18	9.5	5	4	3.16
Pension total[a]		13	13	13	12	8	11	9.5	6.12
SWFs total[a]		41	45.5	42.5	30	17.5	16	13.5	3.89
Memorandum									
United Kingdom	Terra Firma	0.5	1	1	1	0	0.25	1	4.75
United States	Harvard University Endowment	0.5	1	1	1	0	1	0	4.5
	TIAA-CREF	0.5	1	1	1	1	1	0.25	5.75
	Blackstone	0.5	1	1	1	0	0	0	3.5
Total[a]		2	4	4	4	1	2.25	1.25	4.625

a. For each element, the total is the sum for the relevant funds. For the subtotals category and the grand total, the figures are for the individual fund.

Note: Pension funds (P) and reserve pension funds (PR) shown in italics.

| Country | Fund | Investment strategy implementation | | | | 20 | 21 | Investment activities | | | Reports | |
		16 Categories	17 Bench-marks	18 Credit ratings	19 Man-dates	Size	Returns	22 Location	23 Specific investments	24 Currency composition	25 Annual	26 Quarterly
Algeria	Revenue Regulation Fund	0.5	0	0	1	0.5	0	0	0	0	0	0
Australia	Future Fund (PR)	1	1	0.5	1	1	1	0	0	0	1	1
Azerbaijan	State Oil Fund	1	1	1	1	1	1	0.5	0	1	1	1
Bahrain	Mumtalakat Holding Company	1	0	0	0	1	1	1	1	0	1	0
Botswana	Pula Fund	1	1	1	0	1	0	0	0	0.5	1	0.5
Brunei	Brunei Investment Agency	0	0	0	1	0	0	0	0	0	0.5	0
Canada	Alberta Heritage Savings Trust Fund	1	1	0.5	0	1	1	1	0	0.5	1	1
	Caisse de dépôt et placement du Québec (P)	1	1	0.5	1	1	1	1	1	1	1	0
	Canada Pension Plan (P)	1	1	1	1	1	1	0.5	1	1	1	1
	Ontario Teachers' Pension Plan (P)	1	1	1	0.5	1	1	0.5	1	1	1	0.5
Chile	Economic and Social Stabilization Fund	1	1	1	1	1	1	1	1	1	1	1
	Pension Reserve Fund (PR)	1	1	1	1	1	1	1	1	1	1	1
China	China Investment Corporation	1	0.5	0	0	1	1	0	0.75	0	1	0
	National Social Security Fund (P)	1	1	1	1	1	1	0.5	0	0	1	1
France	Fonds de réserve pour les retraites (P)	1	1	1	1	1	1	0.5	0	1	1	1
Hong Kong	Exchange Fund	1	1	1	0	1	1	0.5	0	0.5	1	1
Iran	Oil Stabilization Fund	0	0	0	1	0.5	0.5	0	0	0	0.5	0
Ireland	National Pensions Reserve Fund (PR)	1	1	0	1	1	1	1	1	0	1	1
Japan	Government Pension Investment Fund (P)	1	1	1	1	1	1	0.25	0	0	1	1
Kazakhstan	National Fund	0.5	1	1	0	1	1	0.25	0	0.25	0.5	0.5
Kiribati	Revenue Equalization Reserve Fund	0	0	0	0	0	0	0	0	0	0.5	0.5

Accountability and transparency

(continued on next page)

115

Table 5A.1 Scoreboard for sovereign wealth funds *(continued)*

Country	Fund	Investment strategy implementation				Accountability and transparency							
						Investment activities					Reports	
		16 Cate-gories	17 Bench-marks	18 Credit ratings	19 Man-dates	20 Size	21 Returns	22 Location	23 Specific investments	24 Currency composition	25 Annual	26 Quarterly
Korea	Korea Investment Corporation	0.5	0.5	1	0	1	0.25	0	0	0	0.5	0
Kuwait	Kuwait Investment Authority	1	0.5	1	0	1	0.5	0.25	0	0	0.5	0
Malaysia	Khazanah Nasional	0.5	1	0	0	1	1	1	0.5	0	0.5	0
Mexico	Oil Income Stabilization Fund	0	0	0	0	1	1	0	0	1	0.5	0.5
Netherlands	*Stichting Pensioenfonds ABP (P)*	1	1	1	0	1	1	0.5	1	1	1	0.5
New Zealand	*Superannuation Fund (PR)*	1	1	1	1	1	1	1	1	1	1	1
Nigeria	Excess Crude Account	0	0	0	1	0.5	0	0	0	0.5	0	0
Norway	Government Pension Fund – Global	1	1	1	1	1	1	1	1	1	1	1
Oman	State General Reserve Fund	0	0	0	0	0	0	0	0	0	0.5	0
Qatar	Qatar Investment Authority	0	0	0	0	0	0	0	0	0.25	0	0
Russia	Reserve Fund and National Wealth Fund	1	0	1	1	1	0.5	0.5	0	1	0.5	0.5
São Tomé & Príncipe	National Oil Account	0.5	0	0	1	0.5	0	0	0	0	0	0
Singapore	Government of Singapore Investment Corporation	1	1	0.5	0	0	0.5	1	0	0	1	0.5
	Temasek Holdings	1	0.5	0	0.5	1	1	1	0.5	0	1	0
Sudan	Oil Revenue Stabilization Account	0	0	0	1	1	0	0	0	0	0	0
Thailand	*Government Pension Fund (P)*	1	1	1	1	1	1	0.25	1	0	1	1
Timor-Leste	Petroleum Fund	1	1	1	1	1	1	1	1	1	1	1
Trinidad & Tobago	Heritage and Stabilization Fund	1	1	1	1	1	1	1	0	1	1	1
UAE	Abu Dhabi Investment Authority	0.25	0.25	0	0	0	0	0	0	0	0	0

	Dubai International Capital	1	0	0	0.5	1	0	1	1	0	0.5	0
	International Petroleum Investment Company	1	0	0	0.5	0.5	0	0	1	0	0	0
	Investment Corporation of Dubai	1	0	0	0	0.5	0	1	1	0	0	0
	Istithmar World	0.25	0	0	0	0.5	0	0.25	0	0	0	0
	Mubadala Development Company	1	0.5	0	0.5	1	1	1	0.5	1	1	0
United States	Alabama Trust Fund	1	1	1	0	1	1	0	0	0	1	0
	Alaska Permanent Fund	1	1	1	1	1	1	1	1	1	1	1
	California Public Employees' Retirement System (P)	1	1	1	1	1	1	0.5	1	1	1	1
	New Mexico Severance Tax Permanent Fund	1	1	1	1	1	1	0.5	0	1	1	1
	Wyoming Permanent Mineral Trust Fund	1	1	1	1	1	1	0.5	0	0.5	1	1
Venezuela	Macroeconomic Stabilization Fund	0.5	0	0	1	1	1	0	0	0	0	0
	National Development Fund	0.25	0	0	0	1	1	0	0	0	1	0.5
Vietnam	State Capital Investment Corporation	1	0	0	0	0	0	0	0	0	0	0
Nonpension total[a]		26.75	17.75	16	18	29	20.25	16.25	10.25	12	23.5	13.5
Pension total[a]		13	13	11	11.5	13	13	7.5	9	8	13	11
SWFs total[a]		39.75	30.75	27	29.5	42	33.25	23.75	19.25	20	36.5	24.5
Memorandum												
United Kingdom	*Terra Firma*	1	0	0	0.5	1	1	1	1	1	1	0.5
United States	*Harvard University Endowment*	1	1	1	0	1	1	0.25	0	0	1	0
	TIAA-CREF	1	1	1	0	1	1	1	1	0	1	1
	Blackstone	1	0	0	0.5	1	1	1	0.5	0.5	1	1
Total[a]		4	2	2	1	4	4	3.25	2.5	1.5	4	2.5

a. For each element, the total is the sum for the relevant funds. For the subtotals category and the grand total, the figures are for the individual fund.

Note: Pension funds (P) and reserve pension funds (PR) shown in italics.

(continued on next page)

Table 5A.1 Scoreboard for sovereign wealth funds *(continued)*

Country	Fund	Accountability and transparency *(continued)* Audits 27 Regular	28 Published	29 Independent	Sub-total	Behavior Risk 30 Risk management policy	31 Policy on leverage	32 Policy on derivatives	33 Portfolio adjustment	Sub-total	Grand total
Algeria	Revenue Regulation Fund	0	0	0	2	0	0	0	0	0	9.5
Australia	Future Fund (PR)	1	1	1	10.5	1	1	1	0	3	26.5
Azerbaijan	State Oil Fund	1	1	1	12.5	0	0	1	0	1	25
Bahrain	Mumtalakat Holding Company	0	0	0	6	0	0	0	0	0	10
Botswana	Pula Fund	1	0	1	8	0	0	1	0	1	18.5
Brunei	Brunei Investment Agency	1	0	1	3.5	0	0	0	0	0	7
Canada	Alberta Heritage Savings Trust Fund	1	1	1	11	0	1	1	0	2	24.5
	Caisse de dépôt et placement du Québec (P)	1	1	1	12.5	1	1	1	0	3	29.5
	Canada Pension Plan (P)	1	1	1	13.5	1	1	1	0	3	30.5
	Ontario Teachers' Pension Plan (P)	1	1	1	12.5	1	0	1	0	2	27.5
Chile	Economic and Social Stabilization Fund	0.5	0	0.5	12	0	0	0	0	0	23.5
	Pension Reserve Fund (PR)	0.5	0	0.5	12	0	0	0	0	0	22.5
China	China Investment Corporation	1	1	1	8.25	1	0	0	0	1	18.75
	National Social Security Fund (P)	1	1	1	11.5	1	0	1	0	2	23
France	Fonds de réserve pour les retraites (P)	1	1	1	12.5	1	0	1	1	3	29.5
Hong Kong	Exchange Fund	1	1	1	11	1	0	1	0	2	23
Iran	Oil Stabilization Fund	0	0	0	2.5	0	0	0	0	0	9.5
Ireland	National Pensions Reserve Fund (PR)	1	1	1	12	1	0	1	0.5	2.5	28.5
Japan	Government Pension Investment Fund (P)	1	1	1	11.25	1	0	1	1	3	27.75
Kazakhstan	National Fund	1	1	1	9	0	0	1	0	1	21.5

Kiribati	Revenue Equalization Reserve Fund	0	0	0	1	0	0	0	0	0	0	11.5
Korea	Korea Investment Corporation	1	0.5	1	6.25	1	0	1	1	0	2.5	19.75
Kuwait	Kuwait Investment Authority	1	0	1	6.75	0	1	0	0	0	1	20.75
Malaysia	Khazanah Nasional	1	0	0	6.5	0	0	0	0	0	0	14.5
Mexico	Oil Income Stabilization Fund	0.5	0.5	1	6	0	0	1	1	1	1	14.5
Netherlands	*Stichting Pensioenfonds ABP (P)*	1	1	1	12	1	0	1	0	1	3	28
New Zealand	*Superannuation Fund (PR)*	1	1	1	14	1	1	1	1	0	3	31
Nigeria	Excess Crude Account	0	0	0	2	0	0	0	0	0	0	9.5
Norway	Government Pension Fund – Global	1	1	1	14	1	0	1	1	1	3	32
Oman	State General Reserve Fund	1	0	1	2.5	0	0.5	0	0	0.5	0	7.5
Qatar	Qatar Investment Authority	0	0	0	0.25	0	0	0	0	0	0	5
Russia	Reserve Fund and National Wealth Fund	0	0	0	7	0	0	0	0	1	1	16.5
São Tomé & Principe	National Oil Account	1	0	1	4	0	0	1	0	0	0	16
Singapore	Government of Singapore Investment Corporation	1	1	1	8.5	1	0	0	0.5	0	1.5	21.5
	Temasek Holdings	1	1	1	9.5	1	0	0	1	0	2	24
Sudan	Oil Revenue Stabilization Account	0	0	0	2	0	0	0	0	0	0	6
Thailand	*Government Pension Fund (P)*	1	1	1	12.25	0	0	0	0.5	0	0.5	25.75
Timor-Leste	Petroleum Fund	1	1	1	14	1	0	0	1	1	3	28
Trinidad & Tobago	Heritage and Stabilization Fund	1	1	1	13	1	0	0	0	1	2	27.5
UAE	Abu Dhabi Investment Authority	0	0	0	0.5	0	0	0	0	0	0	3.5
	Dubai International Capital	0	0	0	5	1	0	0	0	0	1	18
	International Petroleum Investment Company	0	0	0	3	0	0	0	0	0	0	8.5
	Investment Corporation of Dubai	0	0	0	3	0	0	0	0	0	0	7
	Istithmar World	0	0	0	1	0	0	0	0	0	0	5

(continued on next page)

Table 5A.1 Scoreboard for sovereign wealth funds *(continued)*

Country	Fund	Accountability and transparency *(continued)*					Behavior				Grand total
		Audits									
		27 Regular	28 Published	29 Independent	Sub-total	30 Risk management policy	31 Policy on leverage	32 Policy on derivatives	33 Portfolio adjustment	Sub-total	
	Mubadala Development Company	1	1	1	9.5	1	0	0	0	1	19.5
United States	Alabama Trust Fund	1	1	1	9	0	1	1	0	2	22.5
	Alaska Permanent Fund	1	1	1	14	1	1	1	0	3	30.5
	California Public Employees' Retirement System (P)	1	1	1	13.5	1	1	1	1	4	31.5
	New Mexico Severance Tax Permanent Fund	1	1	1	12.5	0	1	1	1	3	26.5
	Wyoming Permanent Mineral Trust Fund	1	1	1	12	1	1	1	1	4	30
Venezuela	Macroeconomic Stabilization Fund	0	0	0	2.5	0	0	0	0	0	9
	National Development Fund	1	0	0	3.75	0	0	0	0	0	8.75
Vietnam	State Capital Investment Corporation	0	0	0	1	0	0	0	0	0	11.5
Nonpension total[a]		24	16	22.5	6.64	12	6.5	15	5.5	0.98	16.64
Pension total[a]		12.5	12	12.5	12.31	11	5	11.5	4.5	2.46	27.81
SWFs total[a]		36.5	28	35	8.03	23	11.5	26.5	10	1.34	19.38
Memorandum											
United Kingdom	Terra Firma	1	1	1	11	1	0	0.5	0.5	2	24.75
United States	Harvard University Endowment	1	1	1	9.25	1	0	1	0	2	22.75
	TIAA-CREF	1	1	1	12	1	1	1	0	3	27.75
	Blackstone	1	1	1	10.5	1	0	1	0	2	23
Total[a]		4	4	4	10.69	4	1	3.5	0.5	2.25	24.56

a. For each element, the total is the sum for the relevant funds. For the subtotals category and the grand total, the figures are for the individual fund.

Note: Pension funds (P) and reserve pension funds (PR) shown in italics.

6

The Santiago Principles

In response to widespread support for the development of a code of conduct or a set of best practices for sovereign wealth funds, a group of countries with such funds organized themselves into the International Working Group (IWG) of SWFs under the aegis of the International Monetary Fund. In a remarkably short period of time, the group produced a set of Generally Accepted Principles and Practices (GAPP) of SWFs (IWG 2008b), which were released publicly on October 11, 2008 and described as the "Santiago Principles."

This chapter reviews the events leading up to the formation of the IWG and the nature of that group, evaluates the results of its efforts, including some of the more controversial elements, and reviews next steps as the IWG transforms itself into the International Forum of SWFs (IFSWF). My conclusion is that the Santiago Principles are a very important first step toward creating a robust international standard for SWFs. However, the principles can and should be fully implemented as well as improved upon.

International Working Group

Over the course of 2007, as concerns about SWFs began to bubble to the surface and possibly threaten the relatively free flow of international capital, responsible officials mounted a counteroffensive. At the Group of Eight (G-8) Summit on June 7, 2007 in Heiligendamm, Germany, leaders reiterated a commitment "to minimize any national restrictions on foreign investment. Such investments should apply to very limited cases that primarily concern national security." They declared their intention to have their governments "work with the OECD and other fora to develop further our common understanding of transparency principles for market-driven cross-border investment of both private and state-owned enterprises" (Group of Eight 2007, paragraph 11). In June 2007, US Treasury Assistant Secretary Clay Lowery made a more precise proposal that the IMF and World Bank develop best practices for SWFs, stressing the importance of informal consultations on foreign asset accumulation, the need for national governments to ensure that mechanisms to review foreign direct investment preserve national security without creating unnecessary and counterproductive barriers, and the responsibilities of the US government in this regard.[1]

On October 19, 2007 the Group of Seven (G-7) finance ministers and central bank governors declared that "sovereign wealth funds are increasingly important participants in the international financial system and that our economies can benefit from openness to SWF investment flows. We see merit in identifying best practices for SWFs in such areas as institutional structure, risk management, transparency, and accountability. For recipients of government-controlled investments, we think it is important to build on principles such as nondiscrimination, transparency, and predictability" (Group of Seven 2007). The G-7 ministers and governors asked the IMF, World Bank, and OECD to examine these issues.[2]

The next day, October 20, the International Monetary and Financial Committee (IMFC) of the IMF responded, noting "the growing importance of Sovereign Wealth Funds in international financial markets. While recognizing their positive role in enhancing market liquidity and financial resource allocation, the Committee welcomes the work by the IMF to analyze issues for investors and recipients of such flows, including a dialogue on identifying best practices. It stresses the importance of resisting protectionism and maintaining an open global financial system" (IMF 2007a).

The G-7 identified four areas to be covered by best practices: institutional structure, risk management, transparency, and accountability. US Treasury Deputy Secretary Robert Kimmitt (2008) and Assistant Secretary Lowery (2008) outlined four guiding principles for US policy toward SWF best practices: (1) a statement of policies that investment decisions should be based solely on economic grounds rather than political or foreign policy

---

1. Clay Lowery, "Sovereign Wealth Funds and the International Financial System," remarks at the Federal Reserve Bank of San Francisco's Conference on the Asian Financial Crisis Revisited, Washington, June 2, 2007. On June 12 of that same year I argued that the IMF had a positive potential role with respect to developing best practice standards for all cross-border investments. See Edwin M. Truman, "What Should the Fund's Role Be Now?" Remarks at the Bretton Woods Committee 2007 Annual Meeting, June 12, 2007, available at www.piie.com (accessed on July 12, 2010). In August, the Peterson Institute for International Economics released my policy brief on SWFs (Truman 2007) based on a presentation on May 12 on nonrenewable resource funds to the G-20 Workshop on Commodities and Financial Stability in Washington, sponsored by the US Treasury and the Board of Governors of the Federal Reserve System.

2. The World Bank subsequently chose to play a secondary role in this examination.

considerations; (2) world-class institutional integrity, including transparency about investment policies and strong risk management systems, governance structures, and internal controls; (3) fair competition with the private sector; and (4) respect for host-country rules. On March 20, 2008, the US Treasury and the governments of Singapore and Abu Dhabi issued a joint statement embracing these principles. The three countries also laid down principles for countries receiving SWF investments.[3]

In addition, the Commission of the European Communities (2008) on February 28, 2008 spelled out its preferred standards of governance and transparency for SWFs. The EU Council (leaders) endorsed the commission's recommended position on March 14 (Council of the European Union 2008). On governance, the Commission called for a clear allocation and separation of responsibilities (presumably, between the government and the SWF); an investment policy that defines the SWF's overall objectives; operational autonomy to achieve those objectives; public disclosure of the principles governing the relationship between the SWF and its governmental authorities; disclosure of principles of internal governance providing assurances of integrity; and issuance of risk management policies.

On transparency, the Commission called for annual disclosure of investment positions and asset allocations; exercise of ownership rights; disclosure of the use of leverage, the currency composition of assets, and the size and source of the fund's resources; and disclosure of the home country's regulation and oversight governing the SWF.

On April 12, 2008, the IMFC welcomed an IMF initiative to facilitate and coordinate work with SWFs on a set of best practices (IMF 2008a). The welcoming was not unanimous among the members of the IMFC. Sultan bin Nassir Al-Suwaidi (2008), governor of the United Arab Emirates Central Bank, speaking on behalf of his constituency, was critical of the IMF's involvement in this area:

> [W]e reiterate our misgivings regarding the Fund's involvement in setting best practices for Sovereign Wealth Funds (SWFs). The Fund does not have the requisite expertise in the areas of governance and transparency to take the lead in producing a set of best practices for SWFs. We are also concerned that the treatment of SWFs, to the exclusion of other types of institutional investors with a proven track record of excessive risk taking and destabilizing behavior [presumably a reference to hedge funds and private equity funds], would introduce a severe element of bias and lack evenhandedness in financial surveillance. Finally, the timing of this exercise and its political dimensions could inadvertently disrupt the flow of much-needed long-term capital from SWFs to institutions in the U.S. and elsewhere that face both liquidity and capital shortage issues.

The IWG met for the first time on May 1, 2008 to begin work on voluntary SWF principles that properly reflected their investment practices and

---

3. US Treasury, "Treasury Reaches Agreement on Principles for Sovereign Wealth Funds with Singapore and Abu Dhabi," press release HP-881, March 20, 2008.

objectives, with Hamad Al Hurr Al-Suwaidi, the undersecretary of the Abu Dhabi Department of Finance, and Jaime Caruana, then director of the IMF's Monetary and Capital Markets Department, as co-chairs.[4] Twenty-three countries were members of the IWG and three countries were observers.[5] On September 2, the IWG announced the preliminary completion of its work on the GAPP of SWFs and released the principles on October 11 at a meeting of the IMFC. The GAPP cover three areas: (1) legal framework, objectives, and coordination with macroeconomic policies; (2) institutional framework and governance structure; and (3) investment and risk management framework. However, the individual principles and subprinciples are not identified with the three specific areas.

Assessment of the Santiago Principles

My *Blueprint for SWF Best Practices* (Truman 2008a) was designed to influence the deliberations of the IWG. The blueprint suggested three tests for success of the IWG effort: (1) whether the best practices are embraced by substantially all countries with large SWFs; (2) whether they cover substantially all the elements in the scoreboard that was part of the blueprint; and (3) the quality of compliance by the countries embracing the practices.

On the first test of *participation*, the pension and nonpension SWFs of the 23 members of the IWG hold an estimated $3.6 trillion in assets and $2.6 trillion in foreign assets, which represent 61 and 71 percent, respectively, of the totals for all entities listed in table 2.1, excluding those of Saudi Arabia. Each member of the IWG has embraced the GAPP, and the group includes each of the 18 of the 25 countries with nonpension SWFs with more than $10 billion in total assets and some holdings of foreign assets.[6] The IWG also included a number of countries with smaller funds: Botswana, Mexico, Timor-Leste, and Trinidad and Tobago. The individual SWFs explicitly associated with the governments participating in the IWG account for $2.5

---

4. UAE central bank governor Al-Suwaidi and Hamad al Hurr al-Suwaidi are from the same country, but the willingness of an official of the Abu Dhabi government to participate in a leadership role in the IWG did not reflect a consensus of the UAE as a whole.

5. The member countries were Australia, Azerbaijan, Bahrain, Botswana, Canada, Chile, China, Equatorial Guinea, Iran, Ireland, South Korea, Kuwait, Libya, Mexico, New Zealand, Norway, Qatar, Russia, Singapore, Timor-Leste, Trinidad and Tobago, the United Arab Emirates, and the United States. The observer countries were Oman, Saudi Arabia, and Vietnam, and the OECD and the World Bank were also observers. The IMF provided the secretariat.

6. The seven countries or economies with funds with more than $10 billion in total assets that were not part of the IWG are Algeria, Brunei Darussalam, Hong Kong, Kazakhstan, Malaysia, Nigeria, and Venezuela. (I am excluding Saudi Arabia from both groups, but including Australia, Ireland, and New Zealand as noted in the following footnote.) Those countries account for an estimated $376 billion in assets of nonpension SWFs or about 10 percent of the total listed in table 2.1. Only Hong Kong is among the 10 economies with the largest funds.

trillion of estimated total assets and \$2.1 trillion of foreign assets of non-pension SWFs listed in table 2.1, almost 70 percent of the respective totals.[7]

On the second test of *coverage*, the GAPP include 30 principles or sub-principles that correspond to 25 of the 33 elements in the scoreboard presented in chapter 5.[8] Table 6A.1 at the end of this chapter presents the correspondence between the GAPP and the scoreboard with an associated commentary. Thus, the GAPP would receive a score of 76 on the scoreboard if there were full compliance of the funds with its principles. In other words, the GAPP rank 17th on the scoreboard for the 53 funds that we scored.

On the other hand, public disclosure is explicitly recommended for only 17 of those items. This would reduce the score for the GAPP itself to 52 on the scoreboard, slightly below the mean and median for all the funds.

Moreover, of the 30 principles and subprinciples in the GAPP, 10 are essentially meaningless in terms of public transparency and accountability. They deal with topics that are essentially matters between the SWF and its government. For example, principle 5 states "The relevant statistical data pertaining to the SWF should be reported on a timely basis to the owner, or as otherwise required, for inclusion where appropriate in macroeconomic data sets." New Zealand's Superannuation Fund has posted on its website a principle-by-principle concordance between the Santiago Principles and its own practices. On principle 5, the Superannuation Fund merely states "Performance data is reported monthly, publicly via the Fund's website, and directly to the New Zealand Treasury for incorporation within the Crown accounts (which are published on the Treasury Website)."[9] It is notable that this fund also reports these data publicly, and that the fund does not consider it relevant to report to the domestic and international accounts of New Zealand on the size of its portfolio and the location of its investments. However, my basic point is that to satisfy these ten Santiago Principles, the fund merely has to state that it is following them.

Therefore, although I conclude that the Santiago Principles are a very good first step, they are not as comprehensive and robust as they could be. In addition to reconsidering decisions to exclude some elements of the SWF scoreboard from the Santiago Principles, the members of the IFSWF should agree that all the principles should be verifiable via public disclosure according to the principle of "comply or explain."

---

7. In this calculation, we include the pension reserve funds of Australia, Chile, Ireland, and New Zealand in both the numerator and the denominator because they were incorporated in the IWG's definition of SWFs and participated in the IWG.

8. As is detailed in table 6A.1 at the end of this chapter and table 5A.1 in chapter 5's appendix 5A, the 2009 scoreboard explicitly included four elements from the GAPP.

9. See the website of the Superannuation Fund, www.nzsuperfund.co.nz (accessed on June 19, 2010).

On the test of *compliance* with the GAPP, the SWFs have a substantial way to go. Table 6.1 presents a comparison of how the 53 SWFs score on the 25 elements of the SWF scoreboard where there is an intersection or overlap with the Santiago Principles. As with the full scoreboard, the results for the scaled-down Principles are widely dispersed. The simple correlation with the scores on the full SWF scoreboard is 0.99. On average the SWFs score about 3 percentage points higher on the reduced number of elements in the GAPP. This improvement is consistent across pension and nonpension SWFs and for the subset of countries that are members of the IFSWF (the successor body to the IWG) or whose funds are explicitly listed on the IFSWF website. The statistical improvement is more than accounted for by the fact that compliance with each element is worth more when there are only 25 elements normalized to a 100-point scale. On the other hand, the 23 funds that directly participated in the IWG and now participate in the IFSWF score 5 percentage points higher on these 25 elements, and the larger number of funds of the 21 relevant countries that participate in the IFSWF score another point higher.[10]

The pattern of scores on the SWF scoreboard and on the intersection with the Santiago Principles is not uniform across the SWFs. The scores of 15 funds are boosted by 6 percentage points or more. Singapore's GIC, São Tomé and Príncipe's National Oil Account, and the Australian Future Fund lead that group. Eight of the funds do less well on the GAPP intersection with the scoreboard than on the scoreboard itself, but this is largely due to rounding and the fact that the amount of credit for compliance differs between the 33-element scoreboard and the 25-element GAPP intersection with it.

Table 6.2 displays the results for the smaller intersection of the GAPP with only the 17 elements of the scoreboard for which the Santiago Principles explicitly call for public disclosure. Not surprisingly, the average increase in scores compared with the full scoreboard is larger at 7 to 9 percentage points depending on the comparison. This increase slightly exceeds the increase in value on a scale of 100 of compliance with a particular element associated with a reduction from 25 to 17 elements.[11] For the 23 funds specifically linked with the 21 countries that are members of the IFSWF and

10. This comparison treats each of the 25 elements of intersection equally. As detailed in table 6A.1, several of the SWF scoreboard elements are grouped under a single principle or subprinciple of GAPP; the actual number of GAPP principles or subprinciples in the intersection is only 20. Adjusting for this fact by using averages of the SWF scoreboard elements makes no difference in the comparisons shown in the second column of table 6.1. Similarly, considering only the averages for the 16 relevant principles, and ignoring subprinciples, also does not affect the overall results. However, results for individual SWFs could be different.

11. On a 17-element scale, compliance with any element yields 5.88 percentage points, 1.88 percentage points more than on a 25-element scale similarly transformed. The 3 percentage point "improvement" in table 6.1, thus, would translate into a 5.6 percentage point improvement in table 6.2.

Table 6.1 Comparison of the Santiago Principles and the sovereign wealth fund scoreboard (25 elements)

Country[a]	Fund[a]	Scoreboard	Santiago Principles	Difference
Norway	Government Pension Fund-Global	97	96	−1
United States	California Public Employees' Retirement System (P)	95	96	1
New Zealand	Superannuation Fund (PR)	94	98	4
Canada	Canada Pension Plan (P)	92	96	4
United States	Alaska Permanent Fund	92	96	4
	Wyoming Permanent Mineral Trust Fund	91	96	5
Canada	Caisse de dépôt et placement du Québec (P)	89	98	9
France	Fonds de réserve pour les retraites (P)	89	92	3
Ireland	National Pensions Reserve Fund (PR)	86	94	8
Netherlands	Stichting Pensioenfonds ABP (P)	85	84	−1
Timor-Leste	Petroleum Fund	85	80	−5
Japan	Government Pension Investment Fund (P)	84	89	5
Canada	Ontario Teachers' Pension Plan (P)	83	86	3
Trinidad and Tobago	Heritage and Stabilization Fund	83	82	−1
Australia	Future Fund (PR)	80	90	10
United States	New Mexico Severance Tax Permanent Fund	80	80	0
Thailand	Government Pension Fund (P)	78	81	3
Azerbaijan	State Oil Fund	76	76	0
Canada	Alberta Heritage Savings Trust Fund	74	80	6
Singapore	Temasek Holdings	73	82	9
Chile	Economic and Social Stabilization Fund	71	70	−1
China	National Social Security Fund (P)	70	74	4
Hong Kong	Exchange Fund	70	74	4
Chile	Pension Reserve Fund (PR)	68	68	0
United States	Alabama Trust Fund	68	76	8
Kazakhstan	National Fund	65	67	2
Singapore	Government of Singapore Investment Corporation	65	78	13
Kuwait	Kuwait Investment Authority	63	71	8
Korea	Korea Investment Corporation	60	67	7
United Arab Emirates	Mubadala Development Company	59	66	7
China	China Investment Corporation	57	60	3
Botswana	Pula Fund	56	62	6
United Arab Emirates	Dubai International Capital	55	62	7
Russia	Reserve Fund and National Wealth Fund	50	52	2
São Tomé and Príncipe	National Oil Account	48	58	10
Malaysia	Khazanah Nasional	44	48	4
Mexico	Oil Income Stabilization Fund	44	42	−2
Kiribati	Revenue Equalization Reserve Fund	35	44	9
Vietnam[b]	State Capital Investment Corporation	35	42	7
Bahrain	Mumtalakat Holding Company	30	32	2
Algeria	Revenue Regulation Fund	29	32	3
Iran	Oil Stabilization Fund	29	32	3
Nigeria	Excess Crude Account	29	34	5
Venezuela	Macroeconomic Stabilization Fund	27	28	1
	National Development Fund	27	25	−2

(continued on next page)

Table 6.1   Comparison of the Santiago Principles and the sovereign wealth fund scoreboard (25 elements) *(continued)*

Country[a]	Fund[a]	Scoreboard	Santiago Principles	Difference
United Arab Emirates	International Petroleum Investment Company	26	26	0
Oman[b]	State General Reserve Fund	23	26	3
Brunei Darussalam	Brunei Investment Agency	21	28	7
United Arab Emirates	Investment Corporation of Dubai	21	22	1
Sudan	Oil Revenue Stabilization Account	18	16	−2
Qatar	*Qatar Investment Authority*	15	15	0
United Arab Emirates	Istithmar World	15	16	1
	Abu Dhabi Investment Authority	11	12	1
Nonpension total[c]		50	54	3
Pension total[c]		84	88	4
IFSWF country total[c]		64	67	3
IFSWF fund total[c]		63	67	3
SWFs overall total[c]		59	62	3
Memorandum				
United States	TIAA-CREF	86	89	3
United Kingdom	Terra Firma	77	77	0
United States	Blackstone	73	74	1
United States	Harvard University Endowment	72	77	5
Total[c]		77	79	3

a. Countries and their funds that are members of the International Forum of Sovereign Wealth Funds (IFSWF) are shown in italics.

b. These countries were observers in the IFSWF but are not listed as members.

c. For each category the value under total represents the average for the relevant funds.

that we scored, the increase is 7 percentage points on average.[12] On the other hand, four funds now receive perfect scores of 100: those of Norway, New Zealand, and Ireland, and Canada's Caisse de Dépôt and Placement du Québec.[13] The funds of Vietnam, Kiribati, and Malaysia, along with

---

12. Singapore and Chile each have two such funds that we scored.

13. Norway received only partial scores on its policies on the use of leverage and derivatives and the 17-element comparison does not include those elements. New Zealand received a partial score on the integration of its reserve pension fund with its budget because that element is not applicable to the New Zealand fund, and we scored it at 0.5 so as not to bias the overall results for pension funds. (As noted in the text, the New Zealand Superannuation Fund has posted on its website a document detailing its response to the Santiago Principles. The document states that it is for others to judge compliance, but also notes that principle 3, governing macroeconomic implications, is not applicable to its fund.) Ireland received partial scores where the New Zealand fund does. In addition, it does not use credit ratings, does not publish the currency composition of its holdings, and received only a partial score on portfolio adjustment. These three elements do not have counterparts in the GAPP. However, the Irish National Pensions Reserve Fund also does not publish a policy on the use of leverage, which is part of the 25-element overlap between the SWF scoreboard and the GAPP, but not part of the 17-element overlap.

Table 6.2   Comparison of the Santiago Principles and the sovereign wealth fund scoreboard (17 elements)

Country[a]	Fund[a]	Scoreboard	Santiago Principles	Difference
Norway	Government Pension Fund-Global	97	100	3
United States	California Public Employees' Retirement System (P)	95	97	2
New Zealand	Superannuation Fund (PR)	94	100	6
Canada	Canada Pension Plan (P)	92	97	5
United States	Alaska Permanent Fund	92	94	2
	Wyoming Permanent Mineral Trust Fund	91	94	3
Canada	Caisse de dépôt et placement du Québec (P)	89	100	11
France	Fonds de réserve pour les retraites (P)	89	97	8
Ireland	National Pensions Reserve Fund (PR)	86	100	14
Netherlands	Stichting Pensioenfonds ABP (P)	85	97	12
Timor-Leste	Petroleum Fund	85	82	−2
Japan	Government Pension Investment Fund (P)	84	93	9
Canada	Ontario Teachers' Pension Plan (P)	83	97	14
Trinidad and Tobago	Heritage and Stabilization Fund	83	88	5
Australia	Future Fund (PR)	80	88	8
United States	New Mexico Severance Tax Permanent Fund	80	76	−4
Thailand	Government Pension Fund (P)	78	90	12
Azerbaijan	State Oil Fund	76	76	1
Canada	Alberta Heritage Savings Trust Fund	74	82	8
Singapore	Temasek Holdings	73	82	10
Chile	Economic and Social Stabilization Fund	71	79	8
China	National Social Security Fund (P)	70	76	7
Chile	Pension Reserve Fund (PR)	68	79	11
United States	Alabama Trust Fund	68	76	8
Kazakhstan	National Fund	65	72	7
Singapore	Government of Singapore Investment Corporation	65	82	17
Hong Kong	Exchange Fund	64	68	4
Kuwait	Kuwait Investment Authority	63	72	9
Korea	Korea Investment Corporation	60	66	6
United Arab Emirates	Mubadala Development Company	59	71	11
China	China Investment Corporation	57	65	8
Botswana	Pula Fund	56	62	6
United Arab Emirates	Dubai International Capital	55	74	19
Russia	Reserve Fund and National Wealth Fund	50	56	6
São Tomé and Príncipe	National Oil Account	48	62	13
Malaysia	Khazanah Nasional	44	62	18
Mexico	Oil Income Stabilization Fund	44	38	−6
Kiribati	Revenue Equalization Reserve Fund	35	56	21
Vietnam[b]	State Capital Investment Corporation	35	62	27
Bahrain	Mumtalakat Holding Company	30	41	11
Algeria	Revenue Regulation Fund	29	41	12
Iran	Oil Stabilization Fund	29	38	9
Nigeria	Excess Crude Account	29	44	15
Venezuela	Macroeconomic Stabilization Fund	27	35	8
	National Development Fund	27	25	−2

(continued on next page)

Table 6.2   Comparison of the Santiago Principles and the sovereign wealth fund scoreboard (17 elements) *(continued)*

Country[a]	Fund[a]	Scoreboard	Santiago Principles	Difference
United Arab Emirates	International Petroleum Investment Company	26	35	10
Oman[b]	State General Reserve Fund	23	21	−2
Brunei Darussalam	Brunei Investment Agency	21	21	−1
United Arab Emirates	Investment Corporation of Dubai	21	32	11
Sudan	Oil Revenue Stabilization Account	18	12	−6
Qatar	*Qatar Investment Authority*	15	22	7
United Arab Emirates	Istithmar World	15	24	8
	Abu Dhabi Investment Authority	11	18	7
Nonpension total[c]		50	58	7
Pension total[c]		84	93	9
IFSWF country total[c]		64	71	7
IFSWF fund total[c]		63	70	7
SWFs total[c]		59	66	8
Memorandum				
United States	TIAA-CREF	86	93	7
United Kingdom	Terra Firma	77	87	10
United States	Blackstone	73	79	7
United States	Harvard University Endowment	72	87	15
Total[c]		77	86	10

a. Countries and their funds that are members of the International Forum of Sovereign Wealth Funds (IFSWF) are shown in italics.
b. These countries were observers in the IFSWF but are not listed as members.
c. For each category the value under total represents the average for the relevant funds.

Dubai International Capital and Singapore's GIC, receive boosts of 17 percentage points or more compared with their results on the overall scoreboard. The few reductions are marginal and largely due to rounding.

Table 6.3 provides some information on the individual elements in the scoreboard and how all funds compare on those elements with the funds of the relevant 21 countries that are members of the IFSWF[14] and the 23 funds specifically identified with the those countries. The top panel focuses on the 17 elements where the GAPP and the SWF scoreboard overlap and the Santiago Principles clearly call for public disclosure. The second panel looks at the eight elements of overlap but where the Santiago Principles are less clear about public disclosure. The final panel provides information on the remaining eight elements.

Not surprisingly, overall compliance by all funds that we scored of the relevant 21 IFSWF countries is highest in the top panel and lowest in the bottom panel. However, the differences between the three groups of

---

14. Equatorial Guinea and Libya are members of the IFSWF, but there was not enough information about their funds to allow us to score them. In effect, they would score zero on the SWF scoreboard if they were included.

Table 6.3   Performance on elements of the sovereign wealth fund scoreboard (percent of maximum possible points)

Element	All funds	International Forum of Sovereign Wealth Funds	
		21 countries	23 funds
17 elements			
Structure			
Objective stated	96	99	98
Source of funding	91	89	87
Legal framework	87	84	87
Changes in the structure	78	77	76
Investment strategy	74	83	84
Use of fund earnings	67	69	67
Total	82	83	83
Governance			
Role of governance body	86	91	91
Role of managers	80	85	83
Role of government	77	84	83
Decisions made by managers	57	58	65
Guidelines for corporate responsibility	30	31	26
Ethical investment guidelines	25	27	17
Total	59	63	61
Accountability and transparency			
Categories of investments	75	86	82
Returns of fund	63	74	75
Use of benchmarks	58	67	66
Location of investments	45	57	58
Total	60	71	70
Behavior			
Risk management policy	43	54	48
Total 17 elements	67	71	70
8 elements			
Structure			
Integrated with budget	58	66	74
Governance			
Internal ethical standards	33	42	41
Accountability and transparency			
Annual reports	69	78	80
Regular audits	69	72	72
Independent audits	66	73	74
Mandates published	56	55	54
Total	65	70	70

(continued on next page)

Table 6.3 **Performance on elements of the sovereign wealth fund scoreboard** (percent of maximum possible points) *(continued)*

Element	All funds	International Forum of Sovereign Wealth Funds	
		21 countries	23 funds
Behavior			
Policy on derivatives	50	59	57
Policy on leverage	22	31	24
Total	36	45	40
Total 8 elements	53	60	60
8 elements			
Structure			
Separate from international reserves	60	57	63
Accountability and transparency			
Size of fund	79	85	85
Published audits	53	62	57
Use of credit ratings	51	59	59
Quarterly reports	46	53	57
Currency composition	38	47	49
Specific investments	36	45	40
Total	51	59	58
Behavior			
Portfolio adjustment	19	19	17
Total 8 elements	48	53	53
Total 33 elements	59	64	63

funds in each panel are not large. In addition, within each of the panels there is considerable variation in scores on the specific elements.

In the top panel, the IFSWF countries and their funds have similar overall scores with those of the other funds we scored, but four elements in the accountability and transparency category stand out as areas where their scores are higher in the IFSWF groups than for all funds. On the other hand, the 23 IFSWF funds are less likely to have ethical investment guidelines, though more likely to have decisions made by managers.

In the middle panel, the IFSWF countries and their funds record somewhat higher overall scores on these eight elements, even though the Santiago Principles do not appear to require publicly demonstrated compliance with these elements. This positive result is attributable to the fact that on the basis of the public record, their funds are more clearly integrated with their macroeconomic policies, and they more often have internal ethical standards, issue annual reports, have independent audits, and publish policies on their use of derivatives. Box 6.1 provides information on the record of ADIA updated to 2010.

Box 6.1   The Abu Dhabi Investment Authority and the Santiago Principles

On its website and in its March 2010 annual report, the Abu Dhabi Investment Authority (ADIA) has demonstrated a substantial and impressive effort to align its practices with the Santiago Principles. As noted in box 5.2 in chapter 5, the ADIA goes from 11 on SWF scoreboard in 2009 to 58 in 2010, compared with an average of 63 for all SWFs participating in the International Forum of Sovereign Wealth Funds.

On the 25-element intersection of the SWF scoreboard with the Santiago Principles, the ADIA scores 71, compared with 67 for all the participating SWFs. Collapsing the 25 elements to the 20 principles and subprinciples raises the ADIA's score to 73, and further collapsing the subprinciples into the 16 relevant principles raises the ADIA's score to 84. On the narrower 17-element intersection, the ADIA scores 78, compared with 70 for all the participating SWFs. These comparisons illustrate not only the ADIA's compliance with the Santiago Principles but also the fact that SWFs may "game" how they present their compliance.

The ADIA provides no details in its annual report or on its website on how it manages its risk exposure and possible use of leverage (GAPP 18.1) or on its use of external managers (GAPP 18.2), but it does provide a statement of its investment policy. In our assessment, the statement of the ADIA's policy purpose or objectives is not as comprehensive as for many funds, which is why we continue to give it only partial credit on this element of the scoreboard and, therefore, for GAPP 2. We reach similar conclusions of partial compliance with respect to coordination with domestic macroeconomic policies, the source and uses of the ADIA's funds, the extent of the financial information that it publishes, how it deals with noneconomic investment issues, and how it exercises its ownership rights.

Like New Zealand's Superannuation Fund, the ADIA has a document on its website describing how it complies with the Santiago Principles. However, unlike the New Zealand fund, it does not provide a principle-by-principle correspondence and leaves several principles out entirely, though those are mostly of the type where all an SWF has to do to comply is to state that it does so. In a few other cases, the ADIA complies, but the website does not say so (e.g., the website does not say that the ADIA now issues an annual report).

Thus, on the third test of *compliance* with the Santiago Principles, the SWFs have a ways to go. Compliance is uneven whether one looks at the funds from the standpoint of the GAPP or the standpoint of the SWF scoreboard as a whole. It should be noted that the IWG document describing the Santiago Principles states that members have either implemented or *aspire* to implement the GAPP. In several places, the text notes the need for a transitional period in particular for the newer funds (IWG 2008b). Moreover, as detailed in the discussion in chapter 5, there has been considerable progress, as measured by the three SWF scoreboards, over the past several years.

On the other hand, Behrendt (2010) reaches a more negative judgment about the Santiago Principles and compliance of SWFs with them. He scores 24 of the funds that participate in the IFSWF, including the two Russian funds individually, and creates a Santiago compliance index. Scores range from more than 90 to about 15. The ranking of compliance of the funds on the whole is broadly consistent with the results presented in tables 6.1 and 6.2.

However, there are some important differences. Behrendt scores Australia's Future Fund, the CIC, and the Korea Investment Corporation considerably higher than we do. He also scores Botswana's Pula Fund, the Kuwait Investment Authority, Alaska's Permanent Fund, Singapore's Temasek, and the Petroleum Fund of Timor-Leste considerably lower than we do. Some but not all of these differences may reflect the fact that Behrendt scores the funds based on the principles and subprinciples in the GAPP, while I prefer to use the intersection of the GAPP with the 25 elements in the SWF scoreboard. The differences may also reflect our interpretation of the available information.

I do disagree with the thrust of Behrendt's (2010, 1) basic conclusion that "Some eighteen months after the publication of the Santiago Principles, their implementation is highly uneven." Yes, implementation to date is uneven, but performance on accountability and transparency has been uneven since the SWF scoreboard was first published three years ago. That is old news. What is important is that performance, or compliance, has been steadily improving, including spectacularly for some funds as detailed in chapter 5. Eighteen months after the publication of the Santiago Principles, there has been progress. What is important is that progress continues.

Discussion of the Santiago Principles

Looking at the four categories in the SWF scoreboard and comparing them with the GAPP, the least amount of detailed correspondence is in the category of accountability and transparency. In his presentation to the IMFC on October 11, IWG Co-chair Al-Suwaidi (2008) addressed the issue of accountability and transparency with nuance:

> Accountability and transparency are key elements of the Santiago Principles. The IWG members have affirmed their commitment to openness and disclosure to the owners of the SWFs, and also to provide information to recipient country regulators and make disclosures as applicable under local laws and regulations. The IWG members have also agreed to publish relevant financial information that demonstrates the economic and financial orientation of SWFs' investment operations.

Under this formulation, accountability and transparency are key, but the owners, the regulators in recipient countries, and the general public are each in a separate category.

Thus, it is not surprising that only eight of the 14 elements in this category in the SWF scoreboard can be identified in the GAPP, and for half of them public disclosure is not explicitly recommended (see table 6A.1). Four of the accountability and transparency elements are captured by the single GAPP principle on public disclosure of relevant financial information. Judging by the lack of detail, this area appears to have been the most contentious in the IWG discussions.

The most prominent omission is any recommendation that an SWF should publicly disclose its overall size rather than leave it to the market and to experts to make estimates. As we know from the results presented in chapter 5, 26 of the 40 nonpension SWFs that we scored disclose complete information about their size to the citizens of the home country as well as the general public, and only eight funds provide no information. Four funds in that latter group are located in countries that are members of the IFSWF: Singapore's GIC, Qatar's Investment Authority, the Abu Dhabi Investment Authority, and the Investment Corporation of Dubai. Given the progress over the past several years on this element, as reported in table 5.9 in chapter 5, a reasonable prediction is that within five years all SWFs will publicly disclose the size of their total assets at least once a year.

The issue of political motivation for investments was discussed extensively in chapter 3. The GAPP (IWG 2008b, 4) list as a guiding objective for SWFs "to invest on the basis of economic and financial risk- and return-related considerations." However, GAPP 19.1 states, "If investment decisions are subject to other than economic and financial considerations these should be clearly set out in the investment policy and publicly disclosed." My interpretation of this principle is that it recognizes the reality that SWFs are political entities because of their ownership, and the GAPP put the best face on that reality by adopting a principle along the lines of element 15 in the SWF scoreboard, calling for an SWF to disclose the ethical investment guideline that it may follow, which may involve a political dimension.

This is a complicated issue. On the one hand, most observers want SWFs to be apolitical. On the other hand, SWFs are viewed as a source of funding for worthy causes that often have a political dimension, such as investing in the promotion of climate change or more generally in developing countries.[15]

---

15. A third group argues that both governments through their SWFs (e.g., Norway's Government Pension Fund-Global) and purely private investors seek to influence (regulate) their environments through their actions. Backer (2009) argues that an SWF can no more be a state organization acting as an idealized private investor than can or will a private investor in today's world refrain from trying to influence the public operating environment.

For example, World Bank President Robert Zoellick called for a "one percent solution" for equity investment in Africa in which SWFs invest 1 percent of their assets, then estimated at $3 trillion, in Africa through investment platforms and benchmarks created by the World Bank Group.[16] Zoellick was clearly making a political pitch to the SWFs and their governments, even though the appeal was couched in the language of achieving attractive financial returns, promoting transparency, and achieving best practices by avoiding politicization.[17]

The report by then UK prime minister Gordon Brown (2009) to the September 2009 G-20 summit in Pittsburgh on the international financial institutions advocated the "innovative use of financing by sovereign wealth funds" and proposed that the World Bank support a mechanism "financed and managed by the private sector to attract investments from sovereign wealth funds so that reserves can be invested more efficiently in developing country infrastructure."

On the other hand, Curto (2010), while noting that SWFs could facilitate more South-South cooperation, warned that some of the proposed recipient countries are already burdened with heavy domestic debts and other economic problems and lack the institutional capacity to select high rate-of-return projects, and that if SWFs shift from debt investments in the North to equity investments in the South they may increase the borrowing costs of developing countries. In two of these three arguments, Curto is saying that it is unrealistic to think that SWFs in their search for higher risk-adjusted returns on their assets will find them in the short run in investments in the poorer developing countries.

The line is very fine and cuts both ways because many of the government owners of SWFs are developing countries. It is natural for those governments to think in development terms, whether investing in development banks or developing countries. Santiso (2008) and Griffith-Jones and Ocampo (2008) are prominent examples of advocacy of SWFs investing for development. On the other hand, Avendaño and Santiso (2009), comparing SWFs and mutual funds with respect to the political bias in their investments, find no significant difference but caution SWFs of developing countries to "resist requests calling to make investments without a good financial rationale to do so."

My conclusion with respect to the Santiago Principles is that the US authorities did not get their way in the GAPP on the principle that SWF

---

16. Robert B. Zoellick, "A Challenge for Global Statecraft," remarks delivered at the Center for Global Development, April 2, 2008.

17. Zoellick (2010) expanded on this theme with the announcement that the IFC Sovereign Fund Initiative—established in 2009 by the International Finance Corporation's Asset Management Company to make equity investments in Africa, Latin America, and the Caribbean—attracted $800 billion from state-owned investment funds, including the Korean and Azerbaijani SWFs, the Netherlands state pension fund, and Saudi Arabia.

investment decisions should be based solely on economic grounds rather than political or foreign policy considerations. However, two of the other principles recommended by Kimmitt (2008) and Lowery (2008)—respect for host-country rules and fair competition with the private sector—found their way into the GAPP in principles 15 and 20. As noted in table 6A.1, these are essentially empty statements to promote good intentions that cannot be verified ex ante. Only ex post would it be possible to ascertain if an SWF has observed these principles in practice. Even that would be difficult without at least a forum to which to bring complaints and review compliance with the principles.

On the other hand, the GAPP's treatment of how SWFs should exercise their ownership rights displays substantial, useful nuance, as well as consistency with US views (Lowery 2008), as discussed in chapter 5. It is recommended in principle 21 that SWFs disclose in advance their policies on whether and how they will exercise their voting rights and approach to board membership. It is also suggested that SWFs could make ex post disclosures to illustrate the economic and financial criteria that they follow in their voting, an indirect way of getting at the politicization issue.

Next Steps

The GAPP falls short of the SWF scoreboard, but the Santiago Principles are very good as a starting point toward making the world safer for SWFs.[18] What comes next?

In the Kuwait Declaration on April 6, 2009 (IWG 2009a), the 23 members of the IWG announced the formation of the IFSWF with David Murray of Australia's Future Fund as chair and Jin Liquen of the CIC and Bader M. Al-Sa'ad of the Kuwait Investment Authority as deputy chairs. This voluntary organization will accept other eligible members that endorse the Santiago Principles. The IFSWF intends to promote an exchange of ideas and views among SWFs, share views on the application of the Santiago Principles, and encourage cooperation with recipient countries.

The IFSWF met for the first time in Baku, Azerbaijan, on October 9, 2009. In their statement, the members again encouraged recipient countries to make their investment regimes more transparent and nondiscriminatory, avoiding financial protectionism in the context of the global financial crisis. They also agreed to continue to assess the application of the Santiago Principles and place emphasis on operational controls, risk management, and accountability, and to encourage capacity building among IFSWF members. They noted that some members had moved forward on implementation

---

18. The Norton Rose (2008) survey described in chapter 3 reported that 60 percent of all SWF and non-SWF respondents thought that lack of disclosure and transparency by SWFs would likely induce host countries to further restrict or inhibit SWF investments.

and stressed the importance of improved communication with domestic stakeholders. One blogger, Ashby Monk of the Oxford SWF Project, reported that there was discussion of the issue of quarterly reporting, which is not recommended under the Santiago Principles, but this was resisted as promoting short-termism when SWFs are supposed to be long-term investors.[19] As discussed in chapter 5, the two should not be incompatible. Monk also reported that some participants continue to be worried that excessive transparency will promote front-running of SWF investments by other market participants. This problem is not unique to SWFs. It is a feature of all investment organizations that manage large amounts of financial resources.

The IFSWF met again on May 6–8, 2010, in Sydney, Australia. It is my understanding that Malaysia was welcomed as a new member of the IFSWF and that the Oman State General Reserve Fund, Kiribati Revenue Equalization Reserve Fund, Brunei Investment Agency, and representatives of Papua New Guinea participated. However, the IFSWF's statement issued and posted on the IFSWF website did not include this information, which in itself is important.[20] Expanded participation in the IFSWF is important, and it should not be downplayed.

The Sydney statement did note that some members had issued their first annual reports or reviews of their funds' activities and increased the information available on their websites. The forum also agreed to conduct a survey on experiences with application of the Santiago Principles and to "publish relevant parts of it." The survey is to be completed in time for the next meeting in Beijing in April 2011 and should be welcomed. However, the limited commitment to publication is disturbing. As one close observer put it to me, the Santiago Principles should not be seen as a beauty contest, doing better than your peers, or as a menu, doing what suits the government and management of individual funds; rather, the principles should be seen as an absolute standard to which funds should comply within a reasonable time period, or explain why they are not complying. It will take time to get all funds to where they should be, but progress should be steady and continuous. Moreover, the Santiago Principles should not be static, they should be improved as I have suggested.

It follows from the analysis presented above that enhanced application of the Santiago Principles will be an important test for the IFSWF and its members. In the absence of progress based either on the SWF scoreboard presented in the previous chapter or on the testable elements of the GAPP examined in this chapter, the process of making the world safer for SWFs will be set back. In this context, the IFSWF can be viewed, and I would say it should be viewed, as an organization of peers. Each of those peers has

---

19. Oxford SWF Project, University of Oxford, available at http://oxfordswfproject.com.

20. See IFSWF, Sydney Statement by the International Forum of Sovereign Wealth Funds, May 8, 2010, available at www.ifswf.org/pr/pr4.htm (accessed on July 19, 2010).

an interest in the operations and behavior of each of the other members. In other words, what a particular SWF may or may not do with respect to compliance with the GAPP will reflect on Norway and New Zealand with high GAPP compliance as well as on the home country itself. Thus, we can expect some peer pressure to be applied over time.

On the other hand, it is not clear in all cases who the relevant peers are. The United States is represented in the IFSWF by the US Treasury and Alaska's Permanent Fund, but what does this imply about the other US nonpension SWFs of Wyoming, New Mexico, and Alabama? Similarly, the ADIA participates in the IFSWF, but have the governments of the United Arab Emirates, Abu Dhabi, and Dubai accepted that the Santiago Principles apply to the other, at least five, SWFs in Abu Dhabi and Dubai (see table 2.1)? I have heard reports that some of those funds would like to differentiate themselves from SWFs. In effect, regulatory arbitrage allows them to avoid peer pressure.

Meanwhile, reciprocal responsibility by definition is two-way. Governments with SWFs are justified in remaining concerned about the openness of other countries to SWF investments. In presenting the Santiago Principles to the IMFC in October 2008, Hamad Al Hurr Al-Suwaidi (2008) addressed this point directly:

> [W]e believe that the Santiago Principles should mitigate . . . concerns [of recipient countries] about the motives and potential investments of Sovereign Wealth Funds. Thus, in the Santiago Principles, there are provisions confirming the IWG's expectations that recipient countries will not subject the SWFs to discriminatory measures to which other foreign or domestic investors in similar circumstances are not subjected. We trust the recipient countries will support these provisions.

The reference to similar circumstances leaves these expectations open to a range of interpretations. The next chapter turns more generally to host-country responses to SWFs.

Appendix 6A

Table 6A.1   Correspondence between the Santiago Principles and elements of the sovereign wealth fund (SWF) scoreboard

Santiago Principle	Scoreboard element	Comment
1.1. The legal framework for the SWF should ensure legal soundness of the SWF and its transactions.	2. Is there a clear **legal framework** for the SWF?	This element was added to the scoreboard in light of the GAPP. Though not explicitly stated, we assume that the legal framework should be **publicly disclosed** under the GAPP.
1.2. The key features of the SWF's legal basis and structure, as well as the legal relationship between the SWF and other state bodies, should be **publicly disclosed.**	3. Is the procedure for **changing the structure** of the SWF clear?	This correspondence is not perfect. In the scoreboard, element 2 refers to the *framework* and element 3 to *changing* the framework.
2. The policy purpose of the SWF should be **publicly disclosed.**	1. Is the SWF's **objective** clearly **stated**?	
3. Where the SWF's activities have significant domestic macroeconomic implications, those activities should be closely coordinated with the domestic fiscal and monetary authorities, so as to ensure consistency with the overall macroeconomic policies.	7. Are the SWF's operations appropriately **integrated with fiscal and monetary policies**?	In the 2008 scoreboard, this element referred only to fiscal policy. This change in terminology has been made in the 2009 scoreboard. It is appropriate to include other macroeconomic policies, but more difficult to determine whether this is done.
4.1. The source of SWF funding should be **publicly disclosed**.	5. Is the **source of** the SWF's **funding** clearly specified?	The commentary on this principle touches on scoreboard element 8 calling for a separation from international reserves. The GAPP merely recommend that to the extent that some SWF assets are also classified as international reserves, the relationship should be clarified.
4.2. The general approach to withdrawals from the SWF and spending on behalf of the government should be **publicly disclosed**.	6. Is the nature of the subsequent **use** of the principal and **earnings of** the **fund** clearly stated?	The commentary on this principle also touches on scoreboard element 7.

Table 6A.1 (continued)

Santiago Principle	Scoreboard element	Comment
5. The relevant statistical data pertaining to the SWF should be reported on a timely basis to the owner, or as otherwise required, for inclusion where appropriate in macroeconomic data sets.	None	In principle, it would be desirable to include this element in the scoreboard. However, in no case could we find information to confirm that an SWF does so. The commentary on the principle mentions the issue of confidentiality.
6. The governance framework for the SWF should be sound and establish a clear and effective division of roles and responsibilities in order to facilitate accountability and operational independence in the management of the SWF to pursue its objectives.	11. Is the **role of** the **managers** in executing the investment strategy clearly established?	GAPP principles 6–9 overlap roughly with scoreboard elements 9–12. Here the emphasis is on the operational independence of the management of the SWF to establish the point of correspondence. **Public disclosure** follows from principle 16.
7. The owner should set the objectives of the SWF, appoint the members of its governing body(ies) in accordance with clearly defined procedures, and exercise oversight over the SWF's operation.	9. Is the **role of** the **government** in setting the investment strategy of the SWF clearly established?	GAPP principles 6–9 overlap roughly with scoreboard elements 9–12. Here the emphasis is on setting the investment objectives of the SWF to establish the point of correspondence. **Public disclosure** follows from principle 16.
8. The governing body(ies) should act in the best interests of the SWF, and have a clear mandate and adequate authority and competency to carry out its functions.	10. Is the **role of** the **governing body** of the SWF clearly established?	GAPP principles 6–9 overlap roughly with scoreboard elements 9–12. This element was added to the scoreboard in light of the GAPP. The commentary states that information on the governing body's roles and responsibilities should be **publicly available**, which also follows from principle 16.

(continued on next page)

Table 6A.1   Correspondence between the Santiago Principles and elements of the sovereign wealth fund (SWF) scoreboard *(continued)*

Santiago Principle	Scoreboard element	Comment
9. The operational management of the SWF should implement the SWF's strategies in an independent manner and in accordance with clearly defined responsibilities.	12. Are **decisions** on specific investments **made by** the **managers?**	The correspondence here may be overly generous to the GAPP. "Independent manner" is not the same as full independence, and the commentary refers only to protection from "undue and direct political influence." **Public disclosure** follows from principle 16.
10. The accountability framework for the SWF's operation should be clearly defined in the relevant legislation, charter, other constitutive documents, or management agreement.	None	Because the commentary makes clear that this principle applies primarily to relations between an SWF and its government, and only tangentially to the public, it does not correspond to a specific element in the scoreboard.
11. An annual report and accompanying financial statements on the SWF's operations and performance should be prepared in a timely fashion and in accordance with international or national accounting standards in a consistent manner.	25. Does the SWF provide at least an **annual report** on its activities and results?	The GAPP are silent on whether the annual report should be published, which is required by the scoreboard. The GAPP call for use of a consistent accounting system, but it can be to a national or an international standard, though the financial statements are to be prepared according to international financial reporting standards.
12. The SWF's operations and financial statements should be audited annually in accordance with recognized international or national auditing standards in a consistent manner.	27. Is the SWF subjected to a **regular** annual **audit?** 29. Are the **audits independent?**	The accounting standards can be either international or national. The commentary is clear that the audit should be independent, but unclear about how the public is to confirm this.

Table 6A.1   *(continued)*

Santiago Principle	Scoreboard element	Comment
13. Professional and ethical standards should be clearly defined and made known to the members of the SWF's governing body(ies), management, and staff.	13. Does the SWF have **internal ethical standards** for its management and staff?	This element was added to the scoreboard in light of the GAPP. The scoreboard's presumption is that the standards are publicly disclosed, but that does not appear to be what the GAPP intended.
14. Dealing with third parties for the purpose of the SWF's operational management should be on economic and financial grounds, and follow clear rules and procedures.	None	This principle deals with conflicts of interest. It overlaps with principle 13 and element 15 in the scoreboard. It also bears tangentially on element 19 in the scoreboard. No other direct correspondence.
15. SWF operation and activities should be conducted in compliance with all regulatory and disclosure requirements of the countries in which they operate.	None	There is little content in this principle. All investors are required by laws and regulations to be in compliance with such requirements, and there is no way of confirming whether they are or not. The commentary does add a useful point about national treatment of the SWFs in this regard.
16. The governance framework and objectives, as well as the manner in which the SWF's management is operationally independent from the owner, should be **publicly disclosed**.	None	This principle adds public disclosure to principles 6–9, but it does not add a separate point of correspondence.

(continued on next page)

Table 6A.1 Correspondence between the Santiago Principles and elements of the sovereign wealth fund (SWF) scoreboard *(continued)*

Santiago Principle	Scoreboard element	Comment
17. Relevant financial information regarding the SWF should be **publicly disclosed** to demonstrate its economic and financial orientation, so as to contribute to stability in international financial markets and enhance trust in recipient countries.	16. Do regular reports on investments by the SWF include information on the **categories** of investments? 17. Does the strategy use **benchmarks**? 21. Do regular reports on the investments by the SWF include information on its **returns**? 22. Do regular reports on the investments by the SWF include information on the geographical **location** of investments?	The principle is quite broad. In light of the subsequent commentary on principle 18 and its subprinciples, this principle can be interpreted as including these four separate elements in the scoreboard. That may be a generous interpretation. The commentary introduces the qualification "normally." The body of the IWG report states that this principle involves an element of aspiration and transition for some SWFs.
18.1. The investment policy should guide the SWF's financial risk exposures and the possible use of leverage.	31. Does the SWF have a **policy on** the use of **leverage**? 32. Does the SWF have a **policy on** the use of **derivatives**?	The commentary mentions both leverage and derivatives, which are used to establish this correspondence. The scoreboard presumes public disclosure.
18.2. The investment policy should address the extent to which internal and/or external managers are used, the range of their activities and authority, and the process by which they are selected and their performance monitored.	19. Are the holders of investment **mandates identified**?	This correspondence is not perfect, but the principle mentions external managers and their activities. The scoreboard presumes public disclosure.
18.3. A description of the investment policy should be **publicly disclosed**.	4. Is the overall **investment strategy** clearly **stated**?	See comment on principle 17 above.

Santiago Principle	Scoreboard element	Comment
19.1. If investment decisions are subject to other than economic and financial considerations, these should be clearly set out in the investment policy and **publicly disclosed**.	15. Does the SWF have **ethical investment guidelines** that it follows?	This correspondence is not perfect, but the scoreboard element is intended to identify restrictions on investments for social, ethical, environmental, or religious reasons, which are all mentioned in the commentary on the subprinciple.
19.2. The management of an SWF's assets should be consistent with generally accepted sound asset management principles.	None	This principle involves internal management issues separate from the ethical standards of principle 13. Although the intent is laudable, the language does not point to anything that is verifiable.
20. The SWF should not seek to take advantage of privileged information or inappropriate influence by the broader government in competing with private entities.	None	This principle identifies a serious issue, but it points to no mechanism to verify whether an SWF is following the principle.
21. SWF's view shareholder ownership rights as a fundamental element of their equity investments' value. If an SWF chooses to exercise its ownership rights, it should do so in a manner that is consistent with its investment policy and protects the financial value of its investments. The SWF should **publicly disclose** its general approach to voting securities of listed entities, including the key factors guiding its exercise of ownership rights.	14. Does the SWF have in place, and make publicly available, **guidelines for corporate responsibility** that it follows?	Though the language is somewhat different, this correspondence appears to be appropriate, in particular because the commentary mentions ex ante as well as ex post disclosure.

(continued on next page)

**Table 6A.1 Correspondence between the Santiago Principles
and elements of the sovereign wealth fund (SWF)
scoreboard** *(continued)*

Santiago Principle	Scoreboard element	Comment
22.1. The risk management framework should include reliable information and timely reporting systems, which should enable the adequate monitoring of and management of relevant risks within acceptable parameters and levels, control and incentive mechanisms, codes of conduct, business continuity planning, and an independent audit function.	None	The description and commentary touch on principles included elsewhere in the GAPP, such as an independent audit function. No additional content is provided by this principle.
22.2. The general approach to risk management should be **publicly disclosed**.	30. Does the SWF have an operational **risk management policy**?	This element was added to the scoreboard in light of the GAPP despite the fact that it is difficult in practice to assess risk management policies from the outside.
23. The assets and investment performance (absolute and relative to benchmarks, if any) should be measured and reported to the owner according to clearly defined principles and standards.	None	The reporting under this principle is solely to the owner and covers material captured by other principles.
24. A process of regular review of implementation of the GAPP should be engaged in by or on behalf of the SWF.	None	This is a good principle, but it looks to the future. Therefore, it is not useful for assessing SWFs today.
Scoreboard elements with no correspondence with the Santiago Principles		
	8. Is the SWF **separate from the country's international reserves**?	Touched upon in subprinciple 4.1 but less prescriptively.
	18. Does the strategy use **credit ratings**?	The GAPP might be interpreted as covering this element implicitly, but there is no explicit mention.

Santiago Principle	Scoreboard element	Comment
	20. Do regular reports on the investments by the SWF include the **size** of the fund?	It is understood that the omission of this element was deliberate, though funds are free to disclose this information and many do.
	23. Do regular reports on the investments by the SWF include information on **specific investments**?	The provision of such information would be consistent with principle 17, but it is not mentioned.
	24. Do regular reports on the investments by the SWF include information on the **currency composition** of investments?	The provision of such information would be consistent with principle 17, but it is not mentioned.
	26. Does the SWF provide **quarterly reports**?	The GAPP are silent on reports other than annual reports, though they might be encompassed in 22.1, but without public release.
	28. Does the SWF **publish** the **audits** of its operations and accounts?	This element might logically follow from principle 12, but publication is not mentioned in the principle or the commentary on it.
	33. Does the SWF indicate the nature and **speed of adjustment** in its portfolio?	This element would be consistent with principle 17, which mentions financial market stability, and subprinciples 22.1 and 22.2 on risk management, but the concept addressed in the scoreboard is not mentioned in the document on the Santiago Principles.

7

Host-Country Responses to Sovereign Wealth Funds

The global distribution of income and wealth has shifted away from the traditional industrial countries, and that trend is likely to continue. At the same time, governments are becoming more important players in managing national financial wealth. It is natural that the policy framework governing the investment activities of sovereign wealth funds and other government entities has come under review in SWF host countries at the same time that countries that own SWFs have been pressed to be more accountable and transparent about the activities of their funds. Some authors have advocated a grand bargain between home and host countries (Roeller and Véron 2008). I prefer to use language of reciprocal responsibility (Truman 2008b, 2008c),[1] which is not to be confused with formal reciprocity in the treatment applied to investments in the home countries of the SWFs. Berrigan, Bertoldi, and Bosma (2008) refer to joint ownership by home and host countries.

It is useful to remember that host countries to SWF investments are home countries to SWFs as well. Eleven of the 54 countries with SWFs or the equivalent that are listed in table 2.1 are members of the OECD and a number of the remaining members have pension funds that are not listed in the table but are similar to those listed.[2] Seven of those OECD countries

1. See also Edwin M. Truman, "Sovereign Wealth Funds: New Challenges for a Changing Landscape," testimony before the Subcommittee on Domestic and International Monetary Policy, Trade and Technology, Financial Services Committee, US House of Representatives, September 10, 2008, available at www.piie.com (accessed July 12, 2010).

2. Two of the OECD members that were also members of the IWG have joined the OECD since the mid-1990s (Korea and Mexico), and Chile is on its way to joining.

also were members of the IWG and will continue to participate in the IFSWF. Despite this confluence of interests, it is no accident that the IWG meeting in Kuwait City on April 6, 2009 (IWG 2009b), welcomed the April 2 G-20 Communiqué and its pledge to do whatever is necessary to promote global trade and investment and reject protectionism. One complicating factor when considering the stance of OECD countries toward SWFs is that the principal issues for host countries involve foreign direct investment and the control of the investment targets, or at least significant stakes in them, by government entities other than SWFs when SWF investments may not take that form at all. However, the focus of much of the debate about SWF investments tends to be on foreign direct investment regimes and on the OECD as a forum to discuss those regimes.

OECD Response

The major instruments in the agreed-upon OECD investment framework are the Code of Liberalization of Capital Movements adopted in 1961 (OECD 1961) and the Declaration on International Investment and Multinational Enterprises adopted in 1976 and revised in 2000 (OECD 2000). The key principles are nondiscrimination among OECD members and best endeavors to extend such nondiscrimination to nonmembers, transparency of information, progressive liberalization, a standstill (freeze) on new restrictions, and unilateral liberalization extended to all members (OECD 2008c).

Notwithstanding these fine principles, many of which have been established for decades, an OECD (2006) study suggests that there is a long way to go in applying them. The study looks at self-reported departures from national treatment by member and nonmember countries on limitations on ownership, screening and notification procedures, and management and operational restrictions. It finds that across 15 sectors for 29 of the 30 OECD members (Luxembourg was not included), 18 members had restrictions in at least one sector, and in two cases more than four sectors, at or above the halfway point between zero (no restrictions) and one (completely restricted). The study also reports essentially no changes since 1999–2000, when an earlier report was published.

Meanwhile, Marchick and Slaughter (2008) document that there have been protectionist shifts in policies toward foreign direct investment in 11 major countries that accounted for 40 percent of world foreign direct investment inflows in 2006. They argue that this shift has been accelerated by concerns over SWFs and massive pools of capital controlled by governments.

It was in this deteriorating environment that members of the OECD in June 2006 launched a broad project on freedom of investment, national security, and "strategic" industries. In 2007, the project was blessed by the

Group of Eight (2007, paragraph 11) countries meeting at Heiligendamm, Germany and extended implicitly to embrace SWFs:

> [W]e remain committed to minimize any national restrictions on foreign investment. Such restrictions should apply to very limited cases which primarily concern national security. The general principles to be followed in such cases are nondiscrimination, transparency and predictability. In any case, restrictive measures should not exceed the necessary scope, intensity and duration. Applicable treaties relating to investment remain unaffected. We encourage the OECD to continue its work on these issues, especially by identifying best practices and by further developing general principles. We will work with the OECD and other fora to develop further our common understanding of transparency principles for market-driven cross border investment of both private and state-owned enterprises.

In response, in 2008, members of the OECD engaged in a parallel process looking at investment regimes for SWFs while the IWG was meeting under the aegis of the IMF. The organizations coordinated to some extent, and the overlap in membership was important to the rapid progress made by the IWG. For its part, the OECD sought, with reportedly less-than-complete success, to engage some nonmembers in its discussions.

The basic task that the OECD countries set for themselves was to consider whether SWF investments in member countries should be subject to a special regime. The good news is that OECD members concluded in the negative. The OECD Ministerial Council Meeting in Paris on June 4–5, 2008 adopted a Declaration on Sovereign Wealth Funds (OECD 2008a) that stated:

> SWFs have become a key player in the new financial landscape. Ministers welcomed the benefits that SWFs bring to home and host countries and agreed that protectionist barriers to foreign investment would hamper growth. They recognized the rapidity by which the OECD has responded to the mandate given by the G7 Finance Ministers and other OECD Members. Ministers praised the Report by the Investment Committee on SWFs and the guidance they give to recipient countries on preserving and expanding an open environment for investments by SWFs while protecting legitimate national security interests. They expressed their support for the work at the IMF on voluntary best practices for SWFs as an essential contribution and welcomed the continuing co-ordination between the OECD and the IMF. Ministers looked forward to future work on freedom of investment by the OECD, including surveillance of national policy developments. They adopted the OECD Declaration on SWFs and Recipient Country Policies and were joined by Ministers from Chile, Estonia and Slovenia, who adhered to the Declaration. This Declaration constitutes another example of the OECD's capacity to set international standards.

Thus, existing OECD investment principles, codes, and declarations were judged to be sufficient to provide an appropriate framework for reviewing SWF investments. When the focus of the OECD's Freedom of Investment initiative was shifted in 2007 to include consideration of this type of investment, this nonnegative outcome was far from assured.

As part of its broader program reviewing investment regimes, the OECD in October 2008 issued Guidelines for Recipient Country Investment Policies Relating to National Security that advocated nondiscrimination, transparency and predictability in procedures and outcomes, proportionality where remedies are sought, and accountability internally and externally (OECD 2008b). The guidelines apply to all types of investments, not only to government-controlled or SWF investments. The guidelines were essentially an elaboration and codification of the OECD-recommended regime; they were not part of an effort to encourage OECD members as a group to be more receptive to foreign investment by government or nongovernment investors.[3]

As reported in chapter 6, the joint statement by the US Treasury and the governments of Singapore and Abu Dhabi on SWF investment covered policy principles for countries receiving SWF investment as well as for countries that originate such investments.[4] The principles called for recipient countries not to erect protectionist barriers to portfolio or foreign direct investment, and for predictable investment regimes, nondiscrimination among investors, equal treatment for like-situated investors, unintrusive investment regimes, and proportional restrictions on investments that raise national security concerns. To their credit, the US authorities were trying to convey in these principles a continued openness to foreign investment in general.

Assessment of Collective Actions

On the basis of the available public record, we can conclude that no effort to strengthen the collective openness of national investment regimes to SWFs or any other forms of investment from governmental or nongovernmental investors was considered as part of the OECD process. Notwithstanding the use of the phrase "expanding an open environment for investments by SWFs" in the June 2008 OECD declaration, no actions resulted from these fine words. I disagree with Berrigan, Bertoldi, and Bosma (2008), who opine that the OECD action "provides sovereign wealth funds and their sponsor countries with a clear, predictable and stable investment framework."

A number of initiatives would have been desirable. First, the nondiscrimination provisions of OECD investment codes and standards are binding, in the loosest sense of that word because they are enforced only via

---

3. The adoption of these guidelines in October 2008 was initially at the level of officials of the OECD Investment Committee, but OECD ambassadors in May 2009 endorsed them as an OECD Recommendation, which raises the guidelines' political and policy profile.

4. US Treasury, "Treasury Reaches Agreement on Principles for Sovereign Wealth Funds with Singapore and Abu Dhabi," Press Release HP-881, March 20, 2008.

peer reviews, only on members of the OECD alone. Demarolle (2008) uses the word "mandatory" to describe the OECD regime and contrasts that with the voluntary nature of the then-proposed best practices for SWFs. However, the comparison is not particularly apt because the OECD framework of nondiscrimination is extended to nonmembers, if they are also members of the IMF, only on a best-endeavors basis. It would have been desirable to explore the possibility of broadening this nondiscrimination to the SWFs of nonmember countries, perhaps with an implicit quid pro quo in terms of the best practices for such funds that were then being worked out in the IWG and ultimately became the Santiago Principles. This would have enhanced the stability and predictability of investment regimes in OECD countries.

Second, under the circumstances, including the crisis that was then breaking over the global economy and financial system, it is unfortunate that the OECD countries did not call for a meaningful standstill on new restrictive measures governing investment, instead of merely referencing a commitment to a standstill that had been observed in the breach for some time.

Third, individual OECD countries have invoked multiple exceptions to the investment principles and guidelines even as they apply to OECD members. In other words, what is weakly binding and mandatory has many loopholes. It is unfortunate in this context that no effort apparently was made to limit those exceptions or, at a minimum, shine more light on them. The peer review processes at the OECD take the status quo, which includes exceptions, as the baseline and examine members' policy actions against that baseline of national treatment, which is not a zero baseline. This is not a predictable investment framework.

Fourth, the new guidelines on foreign investment and national security concerns were a step forward in that they at least codified the issues, but this area remains a major obstacle toward the creation of a level playing field. National security is a huge loophole in national investment policies through which financial and other forms of protectionism can expand.

Consider some of the sectors that are exempted on national security grounds. In the United States, restrictions on foreign investment are justified on "essential security" grounds in three sectors: air and maritime transport; radio, broadcasting, and telephone; and (my favorite) maritime dredging and salvaging (OECD 2007b). In the United Kingdom, there is a broad exclusion for controlling investments that are "contrary to the interests of the United Kingdom or a substantial part of it."

In general, the investment policies of many OECD members are inconsistent with the Investment Committee's aforementioned guidelines (OECD 2008b) and its call for regulatory proportionality: "Restrictions on investment, or conditions on transaction, should not be greater than the need to protect national security and they should be avoided when other existing measures are adequate and appropriate to address a national security concern." National security morphs into essential security. Essential security for some countries morphs into public security (France), public order (France, Germany, and Japan), public safety (Germany and Japan), net benefits (Canada), gross benefits (New Zealand), and national interest (Australia).

These are broader issues, but in the context of reciprocal responsibility between home and host countries for SWF investments, several points stand out. Declared national and economic security interests are essentially unchallengeable under international law (OECD 2007a). However, that fact does not prevent the OECD from covering them under its peer-review processes, and those processes could be opened up routinely to nonmember countries with SWFs of significant size. Marchick and Slaughter (2008) paint a gloomy picture of the protectionist drift in national policies on inward foreign direct investment and prescribe a much longer list of desirable reforms, including a code of conduct covering national investment reviews, which they argue should be narrowly tailored and focus on national security and not on economic factors. However, they do not propose that the OECD itself should get into this area in its peer reviews. In their laudable interest in transparency, they lose sight of the fact that it is accountability for a government's policies and actions that should be the goal. Transparency is only a means to that end.

Actions by Individual Countries

Sovereign wealth funds have been caught up in the concern, some would say hysteria, about controlling or substantial investments by governments using vehicles other than SWFs. In Europe, this debate often is a carryover from earlier debates about privatization. The argument asks why it is good for another government to own a country's water company, for example, when it is bad for one's own government to do so (Berrigan, Bertoldi, and Bosma 2008). The answer, of course, turns first on the issue of economic efficiency, which is hampered by political employment- and price-related interventions when the home country owns and manages the company. It also turns on the strength and appropriateness of the regulatory regime accompanying any privatization that would apply to the new owner foreign or domestic.

Most seriously, several countries have acted in recent years to block foreign investments and tighten their foreign investment regimes. In 2008, Canada prevented Alliant Techsystems of the United States from buying the space technology division of MacDonald Dettwiler, which specializes in satellites and space robotics, on national security grounds. One would not have thought that such close neighbors and allies would have national security concerns vis-à-vis each other; and one *would* have thought that if those concerns took the form of continuing access to technology, the issue could be covered by a mitigation arrangement. As another example, Japan rejected the Children's Investment Fund's expanded investment in a Japanese power producer on the grounds that the investment met the test of a potential disruption of "public order." (The Children's Investment Fund is a hedge fund, not an SWF.) Finally, New Zealand prevented the Canada Pension Plan, a pension SWF that registers above 90 on the scoreboard presented in chapter 5, from buying a substantial stake in the Auckland airport because the investment failed to meet the test of being a "benefit" to New Zealand. Each of these examples illustrates the proposition that all politics is local, and international policies and standards can be sideswiped or subverted by domestic political pressures.

Those same pressures have led in recent years to a general tightening of national standards and procedures with respect to foreign direct investment. In the United States in 2007, as has already been reviewed in chapter 4, the Congress passed the FINSA, which revised the framework and procedures of the CFIUS in the wake of the controversy over the proposed Dubai Ports World investment in the management of six US ports in February 2006. This act was passed before the full force of concern about SWFs had surfaced. The result was a tightening of US procedures, but again without special application to SWFs, though the procedures applied to investments by governments were strengthened.

The number of cases submitted to the CFIUS for what in effect is prior approval has ballooned, not since September 11, 2001, but since the Dubai Ports episode in 2006. The CFIUS process has become not a disapproval process with respect to government investments but a de facto approval process, creating a qualified safe harbor for those investments where the CFIUS has completed action or the president has not exercised his authority to block the action even though it may have been recommended by the CFIUS.[5] At a minimum, the transaction costs of investing in the United States have been raised, in particular for government investors, and some are unwilling to pay those financial and political costs. The perception alone of an increase in protectionism is enough to trigger responses, and Chinese officials have been particularly outspoken about the new US CFIUS regime. The head of the CIC commented in late 2007, "If an economy will use national security as a criteria [sic] for entry [of] sovereign wealth funds, we will be reluctant to tap the market because you are not sure what will happen."[6]

The US Treasury released the first report on CFIUS transactions covering the period 2005–07 in December 2008, and the second report in December 2009 (US Treasury 2008a, 2009). These releases appear to have been nonevents with limited press coverage. The 2008 report documents the doubling, from 64 to 138, between 2005 and 2007 of notices to the

---

5. The safe haven is qualified because even when an investment has not been disapproved, the US government reserves the right to reopen the CFIUS review.

6. Leonora Walet, "China Investment Corporation Warns Western Governments Against Protectionism," *Forbes*, December 10, 2007.

CFIUS under section 721 of the Defense Production Act of 1950 as amended by the FINSA legislation. Notices increased a further 12 percent in 2008, the first full year after passage of the FINSA. The share of all notices that were subject to investigations rose to 15 percent in 2008 from 4 percent in 2007. Partial data available for 2009 indicate that, while the overall number of notices declined to 65 in the context of the global economic and financial crisis, the share of those notices that triggered investigations rose to 38 percent. None of the reports on the activities of the CFIUS, of course, are informative about how many investments were discouraged by the process because of the added costs of those investments in time (which can be as long as 150 days) and financial resources (legal fees and other expenses).[7] Between 2007 and 2008, the share of notices that were withdrawn, presumably because they would otherwise have been disapproved or subject to substantial mitigation restrictions, rose from 7 to 12 percent, only to drop to 8 percent in 2009.[8]

By law, the CFIUS must pay particular attention to acquisitions of control by an entity controlled by a foreign government, such as an SWF, but the unclassified CFIUS reports do not provide information on the nature of the investors. Seventeen percent of the 404 CFIUS notices during 2006–08 were from the 15 countries with SWFs, or the equivalent, of significant size—more than $50 billion, as reported in table 2.1. In 2008, a total of 165 acquisitions involved critical technologies. Sixteen came from the countries with the largest SWFs.

A fuller treatment of recent developments with the CFIUS can be found in Moran (2009), who identifies three potential threats with which the CFIUS has to struggle: (1) acquisitions that increase US dependence on a foreign-controlled supplier of critical goods or services; (2) those that would allow transfer of technology or other expertise that could be used against the United States; and (3) those that have the potential for infiltration, surveillance, or sabotage. He analyzes cases with respect to the criticality of the goods or services involved and the availability of alternatives. He suggests two useful tools in this process: concentration ratios, as represented by the Herfindahl-Hirschman index, and strategic trade theory. He concludes that the former may be more useful than the latter. He also concludes that in cases involving the first and third threats it may

---

7. The initial review process can take up to 30 days. If there is a subsequent investigation, it can take up to 45 days unless a resubmission involves an extension of 30 days. In the rare cases when the review goes to the president for a decision, that can take 15 days.

8. Plotkin and Fagan (2010), lawyers experienced in handling these cases, hypothesize that the increase in the number of second-stage investigations in 2009 may have been due to a combination of the changeover in administrations, the more formal establishment of a presumption of investigation under FINSA (and the continued flow of sovereign investments in 2009), and tighter bureaucratic controls. Nevertheless, they argue "CFIUS in many ways remains a model for preserving open investment while balancing national security considerations."

be impossible and undesirable to separate a national security threat from potential damage to the US economy. But he does not advocate rewriting the CFIUS legislation unless this broadening were itself narrowly circumscribed to limit the scope for simple protectionism.

With respect to other major countries, inward foreign investment policies have been under scrutiny and/or revision. As discussed in chapter 5, the European Union has been grappling with the question of who should do what with respect to these policies in the face of concerns about foreign investment by SWFs and other vehicles of governments that are not considered entirely friendly. Roeller and Véron (2008) lay out three alternatives for an EU-wide policy framework on SWFs: continuing the practice of legislation and implementation at the level of the member state; common legislation at the EU level with implementation and review of applications at the member level; and EU-level legislation and implementation. This sensible suggestion has not been adopted.[9] Aside from some general principles governing the financial sector and competition embodied in the various EU treaties, policy decisions are made and executed at the national level.

The European framework constrains national governments to a greater degree than other governments. Moreover, under the Lisbon Treaty, which went into force on December 1, 2009, the European Union in the form of the European Commission has exclusive competence on foreign direct investment into the European Union. The exercise of this authority applies to negotiations with third parties. This new power is expected to be implemented in an evolutionary manner, but the potential exists for future conflicts between EU agreements with third parties and existing agreements of the member states. Prior to the entry into force of the Lisbon Treaty, the Treaty of the European Union stated "all restrictions on the movement of capital between Member States and between Member States and third countries shall be prohibited." However, the treaty also stated "The provisions ... shall be without prejudice to the right of Member States ... to take measures which are justified on grounds of public policy or public security." Mezzacapo (2009, 55) reports that the European Court of Justice has found that measures justified on grounds of public policy or public security must be strictly applied. On the other hand, European legislation also offers national authorities a framework for the application of what are in effect suitability requirements with respect to investments in the financial sector (Mezzacapo 2009, 58). Mezzacapo recommends that at present the European Union rely on the soft-law approach of the Santiago Principles on the one hand, and the OECD approach to investment on the other.

---

9. Writing in the *Financial Times* on August 12, 2009, "Europe Needs to Screen Chinese Investments," two Dutch researchers, Maaike Okano-Heijmans and Frans-Paul van der Patten, again advocated a common European approach that more closely resembles the US CFIUS, particularly to defuse anxieties about China's foreign investment activities.

In Germany, legislation was adopted that gives the government the power to block all acquisitions from outside the European Union and the European Free Trade Association of stakes of more than 25 percent using a test of national interest defined in terms of public order and safety. One issue was whether job preservation explicitly would be part of the test. In the end, it was not, but the breadth of the definition of national interest suggests that employment considerations could be involved in practice.

At the end of 2005, France published a decree requiring the minister of economy to approve, including with restrictions, non-EU foreign investments in 11 sectors or activities. Seven involved public security (ranging from gambling to information systems) and four involved national defense directly. As reported by Demarolle (2008), over 2006–07 the minister acted on 69 transactions (31 in 2006 and 38 in 2007). Only one did not involve national defense. Although none was disapproved, somewhat more than half involved undertakings to mitigate the risks involved. As discussed in chapter 4, Demarolle also advocated a reciprocity dialogue by France and the European Union with countries with SWFs that want to invest in the European Union in order to increase access by EU investors to those countries. France also established in late 2008 its own Strategic Investment Fund. At the time it was seen as a device to take controlling shares in strategic enterprises to prevent them from falling into foreign hands. In practice, it has been used to provide financial support to mid-sized companies.

In July 2008, the Italian government established an Interministerial Strategic Committee for Development and Protection Abroad of Economic National Interests that included policies with respect to SWF investments. The general thrust was to welcome only investments that were limited to less than 5 percent in any given entity. However, in reviewing other investments by SWFs, compliance with Santiago Principles was to be taken into account (Mezzacapo 2009).

The new German, French, and Italian policies were scrutinized by European Commission officials and reportedly adjusted in some cases. In the case of Greece, which has sought to impose restrictions on investments in strategic companies via ex ante authorization of voting rights of more than 20 percent and ex post approval of certain corporate decisions, the Commission has objected and reserved the possibility of taking the Greek government to the European Court of Justice.

Elsewhere, Australia announced a new investment-screening regime on February 17, 2008. The announcement left Australian policy substantially unchanged, but the adjective applied to that policy in the announcement was "enhanced." This illustrates how sensitive these issues are, leading to words being carefully scrutinized. The Australian approach potentially allows substantial case-by-case discretion on the part of the authorities and, in principle, can be used to block any controlling or noncontrolling foreign investment deemed by the treasurer, after receiving the advice of the Foreign Investment Review Board, not to be consistent with Australia's national interest, including but not limited to its national security. It is of some relevance in the context of SWFs, often financed by earnings on natural resources, that much of the debate in Australia revolves around the issue of control over the wealth below ground embodied in the country's vast natural resources.

Finally, in March 2009, Canada passed a substantial amendment to its Investment in Canada Act (ICA), which in principle applies a "net benefits" test to foreign direct investment in Canada, including with respect to preserving jobs. The first direct use of the ICA in 20 years, other than probably discouraging some investments, was in connection with the proposed acquisition by Alliant Techsystems in 2008, noted above. The new act raises some thresholds and establishes clearer procedures for the direct application of a national security test along the lines of the CFIUS. The Canadian authorities retain broad discretion to block investments, including investments in cultural businesses initially screened by the Minister of Canadian Heritage (Battacharjee 2009). As reported in the *Financial Times* on August 7, 2009, the Canadian government recently has stepped up its enforcement of conditions or undertakings associated with foreign investments in Canada, particularly with respect to employment matters.[10]

Reciprocal Responsibility

The process of reciprocal responsibility between home and host countries as it applies to SWFs has a long way to go before success is assured. Roeller and Véron (2008) caution that cultural differences, incentive differences, and a lack of leverage on host countries tend to limit the scope for rapid progress in opening up further to foreign investment or maintaining existing openness. Moreover, the SWF-specific issues get caught up with broader issues of politics and economic and financial interaction in a changing world.

The authorities of newly more-wealthy countries detect a double standard being applied to their investors, as documented by Mattoo and Subramanian (2008). When they were recipients of investments, these countries were encouraged to be more open. When the other foot acquires some shoes, the investor is told to be careful about where he treads. Mattoo and Subramanian argue for a comprehensive multilateral approach to reciprocal responsibilities that would be established under the World Trade Organization (WTO) to blunt protectionist tendencies, avoid the proliferation of heterogeneous national standards, and strengthen the monitoring of compliance.[11] They note the precedent of the General Agreement on Trade in

---

10. "Fear of Corporate 'Predators' Jangles Canadian Nerves," *Financial Times*, August 7, 2009.

11. They also propose a grand bargain in which countries such as China would agree to give the WTO jurisdiction over exchange rate policies in return for WTO protection against discriminatory actions with respect to SWF investments.

Services (GATS) as part of the WTO because many of the SWF-related issues involve investments in service industries. They also note two other precedents: under the General Agreement on Tariffs and Trade (GATT) there are rules that can be applied to state trading enterprises, and more recently the Government Procurement Agreement was established under the WTO. The WTO subsidies code might also be relevant to the activities of SWFs that are viewed as distorting competition via their financial assistance to national champions.

Given the progress associated with the Santiago Principles, on the one hand, and the restraint associated with the decisions taken by OECD countries, on the other, one can hope that home and host countries will continue to work together in the new International Forum of SWFs, the OECD, and possibly the WTO to make further progress.

8

The Future for Sovereign Wealth Funds

Sovereign wealth funds are a permanent, prominent feature of the international financial landscape. As countries become wealthier, and governments expand their responsibilities for the long-term welfare of their citizens, it is highly likely that those citizens will look to their governments to help manage their countries' financial wealth, including wealth associated with natural resources, for themselves and for future generations.

These trends are not set in stone. Responsibility could devolve back onto the citizens themselves, but that is less likely. Moreover, as societies become wealthier, the scale of government involvement in managing their wealth will increase, even if, contrary to recent trends, it does so less than proportionately.

Despite the potential setback to international financial integration as a consequence of the global economic and financial crisis of 2007–09, the financial case for globalizing the allocation of all forms of financial investment via diversification remains overwhelming. Thus, three trends interact to suggest that SWFs are here to stay: the expanding wealth of all societies, growing involvement of governments in managing that wealth, and increasing recognition of the benefits of international portfolio diversification. At the same time, SWFs are instruments of "big money," and big money is distrusted whether in the hands of governments, banks, hedge funds, or other private investment vehicles.

SWFs are not the only mechanisms through which governments actively manage the wealth of their countries on behalf of their citizens. Government pension funds are essentially the same as SWFs except where they are invested solely in government paper or the beneficiaries make the investment choices. However, governments have other mechanisms at their disposal. They generally manage their international reserves more conservatively, and manage other government-owned or -controlled financial or nonfinancial institutions with greater attention to return and less attention to risk, than in the case of SWFs. However, such generalizations can be deceiving because distinctions between these three broad types of governmental financial activity are blurred. Specifics depend on the country and its culture, history, political structure, and economic and financial circumstances. The potential for institutional or regulatory arbitrage is a significant concern in the future. For some countries, a standard such as the Santiago Principles increases the incentive to establish government-controlled investment pools that fall outside the definition of SWFs used by the IFSWF.

Setting aside those complications, and concentrating for the moment on SWFs themselves, distrust of these funds has been substantially defused since they burst into the global consciousness five years ago. The general public and its political representatives know more about what SWFs are and what they are not.

The growth of SWFs slowed with the diminished external surpluses that feed some of the funds, the reduced rate of accumulation of reserves by most countries, and the financial losses that many SWFs suffered during the global economic and financial crisis. This has helped to temper, but again not to eliminate, some of the exaggerated fears promulgated under the heading of state capitalism operating through the channel of SWFs. On the other hand, the philosophical, political, and economic contest between the traditional model of mature industrial economies, with their reliance on markets, and state capitalism, with its appeal to power and nationalism, is far from settled in many emerging-market economies in particular.

The economic and financial threats to both SWF home and host countries that some observers saw in their activities also have not generally materialized. Chapter 3 summarized those concerns under five headings: (1) mismanagement of SWF investments; (2) pursuit of political or economic power objectives; (3) exacerbation of financial protectionism; (4) contribution to financial market turmoil and uncertainty; and (5) conflicts of interest, in particular between home and host countries. Nevertheless, as with much about the complex world today, it is impossible to remove these potential concerns from the economic, financial, and political landscape.

One important contribution to clarifying the role and responsibilities of SWFs and institutionalizing their participation in the international financial system has been the promulgation of the Santiago Principles for such funds. As shown in chapter 6, the Santiago Principles conform broadly to the structure of the SWF scoreboard presented in chapter 5. Moreover, over the past several years the ratings on that scoreboard have significantly improved for a number of SWFs. Nevertheless, the Santiago Principles should be made more comprehensive and robust, and the record of compliance with them by the major SWFs must continue to improve.

The SWF scoreboard and the Santiago Principles are built on the concept of accountability and transparency both to citizens of the home country as well as to citizens and governments of host countries. This approach reduces the risk of mismanagement of SWF investments. The structure of most SWFs, along with their transparency, if practiced, also reduces the possibility that a country will use the funds as a mechanism to pursue economic power objectives. On the other side, with less of a perceived threat, host countries should be less inclined to resort to financial protectionism to guard against such risks. Similarly, financial market participants should be reassured if SWFs adhere to a high degree of accountability and transparency regarding their activities and business practices. All of this should build trust and reduce the scope for conflicts of interest for each SWF and between the home and host country of those funds' investments.

On the side of the host countries, their collective and individual actions over the past several years have been less than impressive. Collectively, the members of the OECD have agreed that a separate regime for SWF investments in their economies is not required. Instead, existing codes and standards governing government investments should be sufficient. Unfortunately, the OECD members did not take advantage of their review of policies in this area to strengthen their openness to government investments. Perhaps, this was inevitable given the increased involvement of the governments of many countries that are not members of the OECD in international investment activities. It is a point of tension that these nonmember countries have not participated in writing the rules of the OECD, which until its recent expansion was an exclusive group of mature industrial countries. This change in the landscape also helps to explain, if not to excuse, the tendency of many individual OECD countries to establish, clarify, or otherwise tighten their policies on foreign direct investment, particularly when that investment involves governmental entities, including but not even primarily SWFs.

On the one hand, SWFs are more trusted than five years ago; on the other, concerns about investment by SWFs and other governmental entities, while somewhat reduced, have not been eliminated. These concerns have been reinforced by the tendency of SWFs to partner with other investors, thus perhaps disguising their intentions. Such partnering by SWFs is of greater concern when it takes the form of co-investment with another state-owned enterprise and involves sensitive sectors such as natural resources or strategic sectors such as electronics.

Thus, policymakers in countries that are home to SWFs should not declare victory. What is required to build on the progress that has been made? I recommend action in four areas: an upgrade of the Santiago Principles and compliance with them; greater reciprocal responsibility by host countries to SWF investments; improvements in related data collection and disclosure; and pursuit of a comprehensive framework governing all forms of government investment as the ultimate goal.

Upgrading the Santiago Principles

Using the framework of the IFSWF, countries with SWFs must be diligent in promoting adherence to the Santiago Principles, upgrading the ratings of their funds on those principles, and enhancing the principles so that they conform more closely to the SWF scoreboard. Unless sustained progress in this area is achieved, observers in countries receiving SWF investments will be justified in their cynicism about the process that led to the promulgation of the Santiago Principles. I expect continued progress, but I am prepared to be disappointed.

The IFSWF should be diligent in encouraging all countries with large SWFs to join the IFSWF and adhere to the Santiago Principles. Economies with estimated total assets of more than $25 billion in their SWF that are not members of the IFSWF are Hong Kong, Algeria, Brunei Darussalam, Kazakhstan, and Malaysia—in order of the size of their funds listed in table 2.1. In addition, Saudi Arabia has a large investment portfolio that is often viewed as similar to an SWF. Saudi Arabia, which was an observer in the IWG that produced the Santiago Principles, should clarify the management of its portfolio of foreign assets and conform their management to international norms of disclosure. Finally, major SWF countries with multiple funds, including the United States and the United Arab Emirates, should ensure that each of their funds complies with the Santiago Principles.

Going forward, as part of the IFSWF's peer review processes that body must actively consider improvements in the Santiago Principles, which are only a good first start toward meeting the standards outlined in the SWF scoreboard presented in chapter 5. As noted in chapter 6, for only 17 of the 25 principles where there is an overlap with the elements in the SWF scoreboard do the Santiago Principles explicitly require public disclosure of compliance with the principle. Given that many of the funds of member countries of the IFSWF already publicly disclose how they implement the eight other principles, there is no reason why the Santiago Principles should not recommend public disclosure of how an SWF complies with a principle that has already been established.

The most important of the principles where public disclosure should be recommended is the release of the SWF's annual report. This is the easiest path to increased accountability and transparency. The vast majority of funds do so already.

The next most important elements for which public disclosure should be made explicit are those covering independent audits of the funds. The

Santiago Principles endorse the principle of independent audits, but they are silent about public disclosure, one of the eight elements of the SWF scoreboard not included in the principles.

The Santiago Principles should also embrace the public disclosure of mandates given to outside managers rather than just calling for a description of the extent and nature of such mandates. This is important to limit opportunities for corruption and conflicts of interest.

The Santiago Principles should incorporate the public disclosure of how the operation of the funds is integrated with the fiscal and monetary policies of the government. This is crucial to the goal of not undermining macroeconomic stability of the home country.

In addition to calling for funds to have policies on leverage and the use of leverage, those policies should be made public. This is an important part of good risk management practices.

Finally, it is not enough that a fund declares that it has internal ethical standards as recommended by the Santiago Principles. The fund should also make those standards public.

With respect to the elements in the SWF scoreboard that were omitted from the Santiago Principles, the two most important of these, after the publication of independent audits, are disclosure of the size of the fund at least annually and establishment of a public policy on the speed of adjustment of the fund's portfolio. The first is widely practiced now and enhances the credibility of each fund's overall disclosure policy. The second would help provide greater confidence that the fund as a good public citizen is dedicated to minimizing market turmoil.

Augmented Reciprocal Responsibility

My second recommendation is that countries receiving SWF investments should develop a mechanism, for example within the OECD Investment Committee, for deeper peer reviews of the adherence by OECD members to its codes and practices. These peer reviews should routinely involve nonmembers of the OECD, including representatives of the largest SWFs or their governments. They should also cover cases where investments have been disallowed because of exceptions to the principle of national treatment based on national security or broader economic or social criteria.

While sovereign governments must make their own decisions, consistent with their own laws and regulations, they should be held responsible to the broader community of governments as well as to official and private investors for justifying and defending their actions. Reciprocal responsibility on the part of host and home countries to SWF investments requires greater accountability and transparency by both groups of countries. The Santiago Principles are a step in this direction by the home countries, and the host countries should more fully reciprocate.

Improving Data Collection and Related Disclosures

My third area of recommendations focuses on the principal reason why SWFs attract so much political attention: they are instruments of cross-border governmental investment activity. Government investors by their nature are faced with a different set of incentives than private investors. In addition, their actions are interpreted as being politically motivated even when they are not. Moreover, to the extent that one vehicle of cross-border investment, such as SWFs, comes under closer examination, governments have an incentive to shift to the use of other vehicles.

It is well known that the managers of the international reserves in a growing number of countries follow investment strategies similar to those of many SWFs. For example, the investments of China's State Administration of Foreign Exchange (SAFE) include those via the SAFE Investment Company said to have about $350 billion in assets under management. The SAFE Investment Company is sometimes classified as an SWF. The Data Template on International Reserves and Foreign Currency Liquidity (IMF 2000), the international disclosure standard that covers some countries' international reserves, is less detailed and comprehensive than the Santiago Principles, and China in particular is not a participant. The Reserves Template, as the international standard is known, was designed to encourage countries to be more transparent and disciplined about their release of information about international reserves and to provide more confidence that those reserves were readily available to meet the country's international obligations. It was not designed to inform the public about investment strategies. For example, the Reserves Template does not distinguish between reserves held in securities in the form of bonds or equities, to say nothing of equity stakes that are significant and might be controlling.

A decade after the Reserves Template was agreed upon, its content should be updated to include more information on the nature of countries' reserve holdings, in particular when those holdings may be indistinguishable from the holdings of any country's or the same country's SWF. At the same time, countries that have large SWFs should be encouraged to adhere to the revised Reserves Template, starting with the United Arab Emirates, China, Kuwait, Libya, Qatar, and Algeria.[1] In addition, as recommended above, Saudi Arabia should become a full participant in the IFSWF as well as adhere to the Reserves Template. Adherence to the IMF's Special Data Dissemination Standard, which is voluntary, requires adherence to the Reserves Template, but not vice versa. One objective of this recommendation is to limit the scope for institutional or regulatory arbitrage as is already readily apparent in China.

---

1. Each of these countries, with the exception of Algeria, is already a member of the IFSWF.

In the same spirit, countries should agree to a broader effort to record and track all forms of international investment by governments and government-owned or -controlled financial or nonfinancial institutions. The *Sixth Balance of Payments and International Investment Position Manual* (BPM6) (IMF 2009a) recognizes that some governments may create "special purpose government funds, usually called sovereign wealth funds." The BPM6 focuses on whether the assets in such funds can be classified as reserve assets and suggests the application of the test of whether they are readily available to the monetary authorities and whether there is a liquid claim of a resident entity on a nonresident that is denominated in foreign currency. The BPM6 goes on to state with respect to such funds: "Some of these assets may be included in reserve assets or possibly in other functional categories. Where the funds are significant, the special purpose government fund's foreign assets not included in reserve assets *can* be shown separately as a supplementary item" (IMF 2009a, 130; emphasis added). One would hope that the international assets of SWFs would be included somewhere in a country's international investment position. The quoted passage is less prescriptive than is desirable. In any case, the guidance does not indicate that SWF assets should be separately identified.

The approach of the BPM6 to the suggested treatment or nontreatment of SWF assets also is recommended for all international assets of governments with the exception of reserves. Those other assets are to be included in the category for the particular type of asset (securities, direct investment, etc.) rather than being shown separately, or in a supplemental item, as government assets. Where the amounts are significant, foreign-government-owned assets and liabilities to foreign governments should be separately recorded and reported.

US statistical treatment of government assets and liabilities to foreign governments is somewhat more informative than is recommended by the BPM6. All US government assets are reported either as reserve assets or other US government assets. However, this treatment applies only to federal government assets and not to the general government category, which includes state and local governments. As reported in chapter 2, US state and local pension funds and SWFs hold substantial international assets—more than $400 billion. On the liability side, the United States reports foreign official holdings by category of asset, such as US treasury securities, under the heading "foreign official assets in the United States." The subcategory of "other foreign official assets" has grown quite rapidly recently and includes SWF holdings of assets other than US government securities or other liabilities reported by banks, as reported in chapter 2. Again, this category generally does not include subnational government entities such as pension funds or nonpension SWFs. Thus, Australia's Future Fund is included, but the holdings of assets in the United States by the Canada Pension Plan or Alberta Heritage Savings Trust Fund are not. One exception involves the United Arab Emirates, where eight of the nine

UAE entities listed in table 2.1 are included in the US Treasury's instructions for what is an official entity.[2]

In light of the increased attention and concern about the international economic and financial role of governments, whether benign or as a manifestation of state capitalism with potential malign overtones, it would be appropriate for the home and host countries to have more comprehensive data on the international assets of governments on both the asset and liability side. This would help to further build trust in SWFs as well as in government investments in other forms, such as direct investment, in particular via mechanisms of institutional or regulatory arbitrage that seek to avoid the inconvenience of SWF reporting standards under the Santiago Principles.

A Comprehensive Investment Framework as the Ultimate Goal

The recommendation on improved data and disclosure leads to my final recommendation: the development of a comprehensive framework governing all forms of government investment in other countries.

Perceptions of SWFs have been adversely affected by the international investment activities of other governmental entities, ranging from institutions managing international reserves to government-owned banks and nonfinancial institutions. If SWFs are to have a safe future, home and host governments should comprehensively approach the broader issues associated with capital flows and international investments by governments.

Preferably this activity would lead to an international investment treaty or at least a more comprehensive approach to governmental investment flows than today is the case. That broader approach should encompass the revision of the IMF's Articles of Agreement to square them with the positive and negative realities of international capital flows—in other words, revival of the capital account amendment proposal that was abandoned in 1997. The broader approach should also encompass standards governing both the behavior and treatment of government investments. The standards could be developed under the aegis of the OECD as long as nonmembers were included in the process. If these standards were to be enforced, the WTO would be a logical place to lodge them because that organization has a proven track record on enforcing international agreements.

---

2. The exception is the Emirates Investment Authority.

References

ADIA (Abu Dhabi Investment Authority). 2010. *ADIA Annual Review 2009*. Available at www.adia.ae (accessed on July 12, 2010).

Aizenman, Joshua. 2007. *Large Hoarding of International Reserves and the Emerging Global Economic Architecture*. NBER Working Paper 13277. Cambridge, MA: National Bureau of Economic Research.

Aizenman, Joshua, and Reuven Glick. 2007. *Sovereign Wealth Funds: Stumbling Blocks or Stepping Stones to Financial Globalization?* FRBSF Economic Letter 2007–38. San Francisco: Federal Reserve Bank of San Francisco.

Aizenman, Joshua, and Reuven Glick. 2008. *Sovereign Wealth Funds: Stylized Facts about Their Determinants and Governance*. Working Paper 14562 (December). Cambridge, MA: National Bureau of Economic Research.

Aizenman, Joshua, and Reuven Glick. 2009. Sovereign Wealth Funds: Stylized Facts about Their Determinants and Governance. *International Finance* 12, no. 3: 351–86.

Aizenman, Joshua, and Jaewoo Lee. 2005. *International Reserves: Precautionary vs. Mercantilist Views: Theory and Evidence*. IMF Working Paper 05/198. Washington: International Monetary Fund.

Aizenman, Joshua, Yeonho Lee, and Yeongseop Rhee. 2004. *International Reserves Management and Capital Mobility in a Volatile World: Policy Considerations and a Case Study of Korea*. NBER Working Paper 10534. Cambridge, MA: National Bureau of Economic Research.

Aizenman, Joshua, and Nancy Marion. 2003. The High Demand for International Reserves in the Far East: What Is Going On? *Journal of the Japanese and International Economies* 17, no. 3: 370–400.

Al-Suwaidi, Hamad Al Hurr. 2008. Statement before the IMF International Monetary and Financial Committee on behalf of the International Working Group of Sovereign Wealth Funds (October 11). Washington. Available at www.iwg-swf.org (accessed on July 12, 2010).

Al-Suwaidi, Sultan bin Nassir. 2008. Statement before the IMF International Monetary and Financial Committee on behalf of Bahrain, Egypt, Iraq, Jordan, Kuwait, Lebanon, Libya, Maldives, Oman, Qatar, Syria, United Arab Emirates, and Yemen, April 12, Washington. Available at www.imf.org (accessed on July 12, 2010).

Arezki, Rabah, and Markus Brückner. 2009. *Oil Rents, Corruption, and State Stability: Evidence from Panel Data Regressions*. IMF Working Paper 09/267. Washington: International Monetary Fund.

Asset Managers' Committee. 2008. Best Practices for the Hedge Fund Industry (April 15). Available at www.amaicmte.org (accessed on July 12, 2010).

Avendaño, Rolando, and Javier Santiso. 2009. *Are Sovereign Wealth Funds' Investments Politically Biased? A Comparison with Mutual Funds.* OECD Development Center Working Paper 283 (December). Paris: Organization for Economic Cooperation and Development. Available at www.oecd.org (accessed on July 12, 2010).

Backer, Larry Catá. 2009. Sovereign Wealth Funds as Regulatory Chameleons: The Norwegian Sovereign Wealth Funds and Public Global Governance Through Private Global Investment. ExpressO. Available at http://works.bepress.com/larry_backer/9 (accessed on July 12, 2010).

Bakker, Age. 2007. Reserve Management in the Eurosystem: From Liquidity to Return. In *Sovereign Wealth Management*, eds. Jennifer Johnson-Calari and Malan Rietveld. London: Central Banking Publications.

Bakker, Age, and Ingmar van Herpt. 2007. Central Bank Reserve Management: Trends and Issues. In *Central Bank Reserve Management: New Trends, from Liquidity to Return*, eds. Age F. P. Bakker and Ingmar R.Y. van Herpt. Cheltenham, UK: Edward Elgar.

Beck, Roland, and Michael Fidora. 2008. *The Impact of Sovereign Wealth Funds on Global Financial Markets.* ECB Occasional Paper Series 91 (July). Frankfurt: European Central Bank.

Behrendt, Sven. 2010. *Sovereign Wealth Funds and the Santiago Principles: Where Do They Stand?* Carnegie Papers 22 (May). Washington: Carnegie Endowment for International Peace. Available at www.carnegieendowment.org (accessed on July 12, 2010).

Bernstein, Shai, Josh Lerner, and Antoinette Schoar. 2009. *The Investment Strategies of Sovereign Wealth Funds.* NBER Working Paper 14861. Cambridge, MA: National Bureau of Economic Research.

Berrigan, John, Moreno Bertoldi, and Chris Bosma. 2008. A Common European Union Approach to Sovereign Wealth Funds. In *New Perspectives on Sovereign Asset Management*, ed. Malan Rietveld. London: Central Banking Publications.

Bhattacharjee, Subrata. 2009. *National Security with a Canadian Twist: The Investment Canada Act and the New National Security Review Test.* Columbia FDI Perspectives (July). Available at www.vcc.columbia.edu (accessed on July 12, 2010).

Birdsall, Nancy, and Arvind Subramanian. 2004. Saving Iraq from Its Oil. *Foreign Affairs* 83, no. 4: 77–89.

Blundell-Wignall, Adrian, Yu-Wei Hu, and Juan Yermo. 2008. *Sovereign Wealth and Pension Fund Issues.* Paris: Organization for Economic Cooperation and Development. Available at www.oecd.org (accessed on July 12, 2010).

Board of Governors of the Federal Reserve System. 2010. *Flow of Funds Accounts of the United States.* Washington. Available at www.federalreserve.gov (accessed on July 12, 2010).

Bortolotti, Bernardo, Veljko Fotak, William Megginson, and William Miracky. 2009. *Sovereign Wealth Fund Investment Patterns and Performance.* Fondazione Eni Enrico Mattei Working Paper 22. Available at www.feem.it (accessed on July 12, 2010).

Brahmbhatt, Milan, Otaviano Canuto, and Ekaterina Vostroknutova. 2010. *Dealing with Dutch Disease.* World Bank Poverty and Economic Management Network Economic Premise 16 (June). Washington: World Bank. Available at www.worldbank.org/economic premise (accessed on July 10, 2010).

Braunstein, Jürgen. 2009. Sovereign Wealth Funds: The Emergence of State-Owned Financial Power Brokers. PhD dissertation. University of Vienna and the Australian National University.

Bremmer, Ian. 2010. *The End of the Free Market: Who Wins the War between States and Corporations?* New York: Penguin Publishing.

Brown, Gordon. 2009. *Supporting Global Growth: A Preliminary Report on the Responsiveness and Adaptability of the International Financial Institutions by the Chair of the London Summit.* London: HM Publishing. Available at www.g20.org (accessed on July 12, 2010).

Buiter, Willem. 2007. Taming Sovereign Wealth Funds in Two Easy Steps. Posting on Maverecon, July 22. Available at http://maverecon.blogspot.com/2007/07/taming-sovereign-wealth-funds-in-two.html (accessed on July 22, 2010).

Caballero, Ricardo J., Emmanuel Farhi, and Pierre-Olivier Gourinchas. 2007. An Equilibrium Model of Global Imbalances and Low Interest Rates. Paper presented at the Bank of Korea International Conference, Seoul (June).

Citi Global Banking. 2007. *Sovereign Wealth Funds: A Growing Global Force* (October 18).

Cohen, Benjamin J. 2008. Sovereign Wealth Funds and National Security: The Great Trade-off. University of California, San Diego. Available at www.polsci.ucsb.edu/faculty/cohen (accessed on July 12, 2010).

Collier, Paul. 2007. *The Bottom Billion: Why the Poorest Countries Are Failing and What Can Be Done About It.* Oxford, UK: Oxford University Press.

Commission of the European Communities. 2008. A Common European Approach to Sovereign Wealth Funds. Communication from the Commission to the European Parliament, the Council, the European Economic and Social Committee and the Committee of the Regions. Document COM (2008) 115 (February 27), Brussels.

Committee on Infrastructure Financing. 2007. Report of the Committee on Infrastructure Financing. New Delhi, India (May).

Corden, W. Max, and J. Peter Neary. 1982. Booming Sector and Deindustrialization in a Small Open Economy. *Economic Journal* 92 (December): 825–48.

Council of the European Union. 2008. Presidency Conclusions. Document 7652/08, March 13–14. Available at http://europa.eu (accessed on July 12, 2010).

Cowper, Steve. 2007. A Word to the Wise: Managing Alaska's Oil Wealth. In *Sovereign Wealth Management*, eds. Jennifer Johnson-Calari and Malan Rietveld. London: Central Bank Publications.

Cox, Christopher. 2007a. The Rise of Sovereign Business. Speech at the American Enterprise Institute (December 5). Available at www.sec.gov (accessed on July 12, 2010).

Cox, Christopher. 2007b. The Role of Governments in Markets. Speech at the John F. Kennedy School of Government (October 24). Available at www.sec.gov (accessed on July 12, 2010).

Curto, Stefano. 2010. *Sovereign Wealth Funds in the Next Decade.* The World Bank Poverty Reduction and Economic Management Network. Economic Premise 8 (April). Available at www.worldbank.org/economicpremise (accessed on July 12, 2010).

Das, Udaibir S., Yinqui Lu, Christian Mulder, and Amadou Sy. 2009. *Setting up a Sovereign Wealth Fund: Some Policy and Operational Considerations.* IMF Working Paper 09/179. Washington: International Monetary Fund.

Davis, Jeffrey, Rolando Ossowski, James Daniel, and Steven Barnett. 2001. *Stabilization and Savings Funds for Nonrenewable Resources: Experience and Fiscal Policy Implications.* IMF Occasional Paper 205. Washington: International Monetary Fund.

Davis, Jeffrey, Rolando Ossowski, and Annalisa Fedlino. 2003. *Fiscal Policy Formulation and Implementation in Oil-Producing Countries.* Washington: International Monetary Fund.

Demarolle, Alain. 2008. Report to the Government of France on Sovereign Wealth Funds (May). Photocopy.

Dewenter, Kathryn, and Paul H. Malatesta. 2000. State-owned and Privately-owned Firms: An Empirical Analysis of Profitability, Leverage, and Labor Intensity. *American Economic Review* 91, no. 1: 320–34.

Dooley, Michael, David Folkerts-Landau, and Peter Garber. 2003. *An Essay on the Revived Bretton Woods System.* NBER Working Paper 9971. Cambridge, MA: National Bureau of Economic Research.

Dooley, Michael, David Folkerts-Landau, and Peter Garber. 2007. *The Two Crises of International Economics* (June 8). Frankfurt: Deutsche Bank.

Drezner, Daniel W. 2008. Sovereign Wealth Funds and the (in)Security of Global Finance. *Journal of International Affairs* 62, no. 1: 115–31.

Ebrahim-zadeh, Christine. 2003. Back to Basics: Dutch Disease. Too Much Wealth Managed Unwisely. *Finance and Development*, 40, no. 1: 50–51.

El-Erian, Mohamed. 2008. Toward a Better Understanding of Sovereign Wealth Funds. In *Debating China's Exchange Policy*, eds. Morris Goldstein and Nicholas Lardy. Washington: Peterson Institute for International Economics.

Farrell, Diana, Susan Lund, Eva Gerlemann, and Peter Seeburger. 2007. *The New Power Brokers: How Oil, Asia, Hedge Funds, and Private Equity Are Shaping Global Capital Markets*. San Francisco: McKinsey Global Institute.

Financial Stability Board. 2000. *Report of Working Group on Highly Leveraged Institutions* (April). Basel.

Fleischer, Victor A. 2008. How Should We Tax Sovereign Wealth? *Yale Law Journal* 118, Pocket Part: 93–97.

Fleischer, Victor A. 2009. A Theory of Taxing Sovereign Wealth. *New York University Law Review* 84, no. 2 (May): 440–513.

Flood, Robert, and Nancy Marion. 2002. Holding International Reserves in an Era of High Capital Mobility. In *Brookings Trade Forum 2001*, ed. Susan M. Collins and Dani Rodrik. Washington: Brookings Institution.

Frenkel, Jacob A., and Boyan Jovanovic. 1981. Optimal International Reserves: A Stochastic Framework. *Economic Journal* 91, no. 362: 507–14.

Galani, Una, and Simon Nixon. 2008. Sovereign Wealth Fund Risk Index (January). Available at www.breakingviews.com (accessed on July 12, 2010).

García, Pablo, and Claudio Soto. 2006. Large Hoardings of International Reserves: Are They Worth It? In *External Vulnerability and Preventive Policies*, eds. Ricardo Caballero, César Calderón, and Luis Felipe Céspedes. Santiago: Central Bank of Chile.

Gelb, Alan, and Associates. 1988. *Oil Windfall: Blessing or Curse?* Washington: World Bank.

Gelpern, Anna. Forthcoming. Sovereignty, Accountability, and the Wealth Fund Governance Conundrum. *Asian Journal of International Law* 1, no. 1.

Genberg, Hans, Robert McCauley, Yung Chul Park, and Avinash Persaud. 2005. Official Reserves and Currency Management in Asia: Myth, Reality and the Future. *Geneva Reports on the World Economy* 7. Geneva: International Center for Monetary and Banking Studies.

Gilson, Ronald J., and Curtis J. Milhaupt. 2008. Sovereign Wealth Funds and Corporate Governance: A Minimalist Response to the New Mercantilism. *Stanford Law Review* 60, no. 5 (March): 1345–369.

Graham, Edward M., and Paul R. Krugman. 1995. *Foreign Direct Investment in the United States*, 3rd edition. Washington: Institute for International Economics.

Graham, Edward M., and David M. Marchick. 2006. *US National Security and Foreign Direct Investment*. Washington: Peterson Institute for International Economics.

Greene, Edward F., and Brian A. Yeager. 2008. Sovereign Wealth Funds: A Measured Assessment. *Capital Markets Law Journal* 3, no. 3: 247–74.

Griffith-Jones, Stephany, and José Antonio Ocampo. 2008. *Sovereign Wealth Funds: A Developing Country Perspective*. Working Paper (April), Financial Markets Reform Program. Columbia University Initiative for Policy Dialogue. Available at www.gsb.columbia.edu/ipd.

Group of Eight (G-8). 2007. Growth and Responsibility in the World Economy. G-8 Summit Declaration (June 7), Heiligendamm, Germany. Available at www.g8.utoronto.ca (accessed on July 12, 2010).

Group of Seven (G-7). 2007. Statement of G-7 Finance Ministers and Central Bank Governors (October 19). Washington. Available at www.g8.utoronto.ca.

Group of 22 (G-22). 1998. *Report of the Working Group on Transparency and Accountability*. Basel: Bank for International Settlements. Available at www.bis.org.

Hamada, Koichi, and Kazuo Ueda. 1977. Random Walks and the Theory of Optimal International Reserves. *Economic Journal* 87, no. 848: 722–42.

Hammer, Cornelia, Peter Kunzel, and Iva Petrova. 2008. *Sovereign Wealth Funds: Current Institutional and Operational Practices*. IMF Working Paper 08/254. Washington: International Monetary Fund.

Heller, H. Robert. 1966. Optimal International Reserves. *Economic Journal* 76, no. 302: 296–311.

Heller, H. Robert, and Malcolm Knight. 1978. *Reserve-Currency Preferences of Central Banks.* Essays in International Finance 131. Princeton, NJ: Princeton University International Finance Section.

Heuty, Antoine, and Juan Aristi. 2009. *Fool's Gold: Assessing the Performance of Alternative Fiscal Instruments during the Commodities Boom and Global Crisis.* New York. Available at www.revenuewatch.org (accessed on July 12, 2010).

Hildebrand, Philipp M. 2007. The Challenge of Sovereign Wealth Funds. Remarks at the International Center for Monetary and Banking Studies, Geneva (December 18). Available at www.snb.ch (accessed on July 12, 2010).

Hill & Knowlton and Penn Schoen Berland. 2010. *Sovereign Brands Survey 2010: Key Findings* (May). London. Available at www.hillandknowlton.com/sovereignbrands (accessed on July 12, 2010).

Humphreys, Macartan, Jeffrey D. Sachs, and Joseph E. Stiglitz, eds. 2007. *Escaping the Resource Curse.* New York: Columbia University Press.

Humphreys, Macartan, and Martin E. Sandbu. 2007. The Political Economy of Natural Resource Funds. In *Escaping the Resource Curse,* eds. Macartan Humphreys, Jeffrey D. Sachs, and Joseph E. Stiglitz. New York: Columbia University Press.

IMF (International Monetary Fund). 2000. Data Template on International Reserves and Foreign Currency Liquidity. Washington. Available at www.imf.org (accessed on July 12, 2010).

IMF (International Monetary Fund). 2003. Issues in Reserve Adequacy and Management. Chapter 2 in *World Economic Outlook,* World Economic and Financial Surveys (September). Washington: International Monetary Fund.

IMF (International Monetary Fund). 2004. *Guidelines for Foreign Exchange Reserve Management.* Washington: International Monetary Fund.

IMF (International Monetary Fund). 2007a. Communiqué of the International Monetary and Financial Committee of the Board of Governors of the International Monetary Fund (October 20). Washington. Available at www.imf.org.

IMF (International Monetary Fund). 2007b. *Guide on Resource Revenue Transparency.* Washington: International Monetary Fund. Available at www.imf.org.

IMF (International Monetary Fund). 2007c. *The Role of Fiscal Institutions in Managing the Oil Revenue Boom* (March 5). Washington: IMF Fiscal Affairs Department. Available at www.imf.org.

IMF (International Monetary Fund). 2007d. Sovereign Wealth Funds. Annex 1.2 in *Global Financial Stability Report,* World Economic and Financial Surveys (September). Washington: International Monetary Fund.

IMF (International Monetary Fund). 2008a. Communiqué of the International Monetary and Financial Committee of the Board of Governors of the International Monetary Fund, April 12. Washington. Available at www.imf.org.

IMF (International Monetary Fund). 2008b. *Sovereign Wealth Funds—A Work Agenda* (February 29). Washington: IMF Monetary and Capital Markets and Policy Development and Review Departments. Available at www.imf.org.

IMF (International Monetary Fund). 2009a. *Sixth Balance of Payments and International Investment Position Manual.* Washington: International Monetary Fund. Available at www.imf.org.

IMF (International Monetary Fund). 2009b. *Currency Composition of Official Foreign Exchange Reserves.* Washington: International Monetary Fund. Available at www.imf.org.

IMF (International Monetary Fund). 2010. *Norway: Staff Report for the 2009 Consultation* (January 5). Washington. Available at www.imf.org.

Institute of International Finance. 2009a. *GCC Regional Overview.* Washington. Available at www.iif.com.

Institute of International Finance. 2009b. Comment Letter on Proposed Enhancement to the Basel II Framework (April). Available at www.iif.com (accessed on July 19, 2010).

Investors' Committee. 2008. *Principles and Best Practices for Hedge Fund Investors* (April 15). Washington. Available at www.amaicmte.org/Investor.aspx (accessed on July 12, 2010).

IWG (International Working Group of Sovereign Wealth Funds). 2008a. *Sovereign Wealth Funds: Current Institutional and Operational Practices* (September). Washington. Available at www.iwg-swf.org (accessed on July 12, 2010).

IWG (International Working Group of Sovereign Wealth Funds). 2008b. *Sovereign Wealth Funds Generally Accepted Principle and Practices "Santiago Principles"* (October). Washington. Available at www.iwg-swf.org.

IWG (International Working Group of Sovereign Wealth Funds). 2009a. Kuwait Declaration. Kuwait City. Available at www.iwg-swf.org.

IWG (International Working Group of Sovereign Wealth Funds). 2009b. Working Group Announces Creation of International Forum of Sovereign Wealth Funds. Press Release 09/01. Kuwait City. Available at www.iwg-swf.org.

Jadresic, Esteban. 2007. The Cost-Benefit Approach to Reserve Adequacy: The Case of Chile. In *Central Bank Reserve Management: New Trends, from Liquidity to Return*, eds. Age F. P. Bakker and Ingmar R.Y. van Herpt. Cheltenham, UK: Edward Elgar.

Jeanne, Olivier. 2007. International Reserves in Emerging Market Countries: Too Much of a Good Thing? *Brookings Papers on Economic Activity* 1: 1–79. Washington: Brookings Institution.

Jeanne, Olivier, and Romain Rancière. 2006. *The Optimal Level of International Reserves for Emerging Market Countries: Formulas and Applications.* IMF Working Paper 06/229. Washington: International Monetary Fund.

Joint Committee on Taxation of the US Congress. 2008. *Economic and US Income Tax Issues Raised by Sovereign Wealth Fund Investment in the United States.* Staff Report JCX-49-08 (June 17). Washington.

Keller, Amy D. 2009. Sovereign Wealth Funds: Trustworthy Investors or Vehicles of Strategic Ambition? *Georgetown Journal of Law and Public Policy* 7, no. 1: 333–72.

Kern, Steffen. 2008. SWFs and Foreign Investment Policies: An Update. Deutsche Bank Research (October 22). Frankfurt: Deutsche Bank Research.

Kern, Steffen. 2010. *The Role of Sovereign Wealth Funds.* Frankfurt: Deutsche Bank Research.

Kester, Anne. 2001. *International Reserves and Foreign Currency Liquidity Guidelines for a Data Template.* Washington: International Monetary Fund.

Kimmitt, Robert M. 2008. Public Footprints in Private Markets: Sovereign Wealth Funds and the World Economy. *Foreign Affairs* 87, no. 1 (January-February): 119–30.

Kotter, Jason, and Ugur Lel. 2010 (forthcoming). Friends or Foes? Target Selection Decisions of Sovereign Wealth Funds and Their Consequences. *Journal of Financial Economics.*

Kozack, Julie, Douglas Laxton, and Krishna Srinivasan. 2009. *The Macroeconomic Impact of Sovereign Wealth Funds.* Washington: International Monetary Fund.

Lane, Philip R., and Gian Maria Milesi-Ferretti. 2006. *The External Wealth of Nations Mark II: Revised and Extended Estimates of Foreign Assets and Liabilities, 1970–2004.* CEPR Discussion Paper 5644. London: Centre for Economic Policy Research.

Large Group. 2008. *Hedge Fund Standards: Final Report.* London: Hedge Funds Standards Board (January). Available at www.hfsb.org (accessed on July 12, 2010).

Linaburg, Carl, and Michael Maduell. 2010. Linaburg-Maduell Transparency Index. 2010. Las Vegas: Sovereign Wealth Fund Institute. Available at www.swfinstitute.org/research/transparencyindex.php (accessed on April 26, 2010).

Le Borgne, Eric, and Paulo Medas. 2007. *Sovereign Wealth Funds in the Pacific Island Countries: Macro-Fiscal Linkages.* IMF Working Paper 07/297. Washington: International Monetary Fund.

Lowery, Clay. 2008. The Role of Sovereign Wealth Funds in the Global Economy. Remarks at Barclays Capital's 12th Annual Global Inflation-Linked Conference, February 25.

Lummis, Cynthia. 2007. Combating the Mineral Curse: The Case of Wyoming. In *Sovereign Wealth Management*, eds. Jennifer Johnson-Calari and Malan Rietveld. London: Central Bank Publications.

Lyons, Gerard. 2007. *State Capitalism: The Rise of Sovereign Wealth Funds.* Standard Chartered Global Research (October 15).

Mallaby, Sebastian. 2010. *More Money Than God: Hedge Funds and the Making of a New Elite.* New York: Penguin Press.

Marchick, David M., and Matthew J. Slaughter. 2008. *Global FDI Policy Correcting a Protectionist Drift.* Council on Foreign Relations Special Report 34 (June). Available at www.cfr.org.

Mattoo, Aaditya, and Arvind Subramanian. 2008. *Currency Undervaluation and Sovereign Wealth Funds: A New Role for the World Trade Organization.* Peterson Institute for International Economics Working Paper 08-02 (January). Washington: Peterson Institute for International Economics. Available at www.piie.com.

Mauck, Nathan, April Knill, and Bong-Soo Lee. 2009. "Sleeping with the Enemy" or "An Ounce of Prevention": Sovereign Wealth Funds Investments and Market Destabilization. Photocopy.

McConnell, J. Michael. 2008. *Annual Threat Assessment of the Intelligence Community for the Senate Armed Services Committee* (February 27). Washington. Available at www.dini.gov/testimonies.

Mendoza, Enrique G., Vincenzo Quadrini, and José-Víctor Ríos-Rull. 2007. *Financial Integration, Financial Deepness and Global Imbalances.* Paper presented at the Bank of Korea International Conference, Seoul (June).

Merrill Lynch. 2007. The Overflowing Bathtub, the Running Tap and SWFs. *Global Economics* (October 5).

Mezzacapo, Simone. 2009. *The So-Called "Sovereign Wealth Funds": Regulatory Issues, Financial Stability, and Prudential Supervision.* Economic Papers 378 (April). Brussels: European Commission.

Miracky, William, and Bernardo Bortolotti. 2010. *Back on Course: Sovereign Wealth Fund Activity in 2009.* Boston: Monitor Group. Available at www.monitor.com (accessed on July 12, 2010).

Miracky, William, Davis Dyer, Drosten Fisher, Tony Goldner, Loic Lagarde, and Vincent Piedrahita. 2008. *Assessing the Risks: The Behaviors of Sovereign Wealth Funds in the Global Economy.* Boston: Monitor Group.

Mohanty, Madhu S., and Philip Turner. 2006. Foreign Exchange Reserve Accumulation in Emerging Markets: What Are the Domestic Implications? *BIS Quarterly Review* (September). Basel: Bank for International Settlements.

Mohi-uddin, Mansoor. 2010. *The Return of Sovereign Wealth Funds.* UBS Investment Research, Foreign Exchange Notes (January 12).

Moran, Theodore H. 2009. *Three Threats: An Analytical Framework for the CFIUS Process.* Washington: Peterson Institute for International Economics.

Morgan Stanley. 2007a. *EM Currencies: Excess Official Reserves.* Morgan Stanley Research Global (July 12).

Morgan Stanley. 2007b. *How Big Could Sovereign Wealth Funds Be by 2015?* Morgan Stanley Research Global (May 3).

Morgan Stanley. 2007c. *Sovereign Wealth Funds and Bond and Equity Prices.* Morgan Stanley Research Europe (May 31).

Moss, Todd, and Lauren Young. 2009. *Saving Ghana from Its Oil: The Case for Direct Cash Distribution.* Center for Global Development Working Paper 186 (October). Washington: Center for Global Development

NACUBO (National Association of College and University Business Officers) and Commonfund. 2010. *2009 Study of Endowments.* Washington: National Association of College and University Business Officers.

NBIM (Norges Bank Investment Management). 2009. Norges Bank's Active Management of the Government Pension Fund Global: Letter to the Ministry of Finance (December 23). Oslo. Available at www.nbim.no (accessed on July 12, 2010).

NBIM (Norges Bank Investment Management). 2010. Government Pension Fund Global: First Quarter 2010. Oslo. Available at www.nbim.no.

Norton Rose. 2008. Sovereign Wealth Funds and the Global Private Equity Landscape. Survey Conducted March-April 2008. Available at www.nortonrose.com (accessed on July 12, 2010).

OECD (Organization for Economic Cooperation and Development). 1961. *Code of Liberalization of Capital Movements.* Paris.

OECD (Organization for Economic Cooperation and Development). 2000. *OECD Declaration on International Investment and Multinational Enterprises and OECD Guidelines for Multinational Enterprises.* Paris.

OECD (Organization for Economic Cooperation and Development). 2006. *OECD's FDI Regulatory Restrictiveness Index: Revision and Extension to More Economies.* OECD Working Paper on International Investment 2006/04. Paris.

OECD (Organization for Economic Cooperation and Development). 2007a. Essential Security Interests under International Investment Law. Part 1, chapter 5 of *International Investment Perspectives: Freedom of Investment in a Changing World.* Paris.

OECD (Organization for Economic Cooperation and Development). 2007b. Freedom of Investment, National Security, and "Strategic" Industries: An Interim Report. Part 1, chapter 3 of *International Investment Perspectives: Freedom of Investment in a Changing World.* Paris.

OECD (Organization for Economic Cooperation and Development). 2008a. Chair's Summary of the OECD Council at Ministerial Level (June 4–5). Paris.

OECD (Organization for Economic Cooperation and Development). 2008b. *OECD Guidelines for Recipient Country Investment Policies Relating to National Security.* OECD Investment Committee Report (October 8). Paris.

OECD (Organization for Economic Cooperation and Development). 2008c. *Sovereign Wealth Funds and Recipient Country Policies.* OECD Investment Committee Report (April 4). Paris.

O'Neill, Jim, Erik F. Nielsen, and Saleem Bahaj. 2008. *In Defense of Sovereign Wealth Funds.* Global Economics Paper No. 167 (May). London: Goldman Sachs.

Ortiz, Guillermo. 2007. A Coordinated Strategy for Assets and Liabilities: The Mexican Perspective. In *Sovereign Wealth Management*, eds. Jennifer Johnson-Calari and Malan Rietveld. London: Central Banking Publications.

Park, Donghyun. 2008. *Capital Outflows, Sovereign Wealth Funds, and Domestic Financial Instability in Developing Asia.* ADB Economics Working Paper 129 (October). Manila: Asian Development Bank.

Pew Research Center for the People & the Press. 2009. Support for Stimulus Plan Slips, But Obama Rides High (April 9). Washington. Available at http://people-press.org/report/490/obama-stimulus (accessed on July 12, 2010).

Pistor, Katharina. 2008. *Global Network Finance: Organizational Hedging in Times of Uncertainty.* Columbia Law and Economics Working Paper 339 (October). New York: Columbia University

Plotkin, Mark E., and David N. Fagan. 2010. Foreign Direct Investment and US National Security: CFIUS under the Obama Administration. *Columbia FDI Perspectives* No. 24 (June 7). Available at www.vcc.columbia.edu/content/fdi-perspectives (accessed on July 12, 2010).

Preqin Equity. 2010. *Sovereign Wealth Funds: SWFs Total Assets Continue to Grow.* Prequin Special Report (May). New York. Available at www.prequin.com.

President's Working Group on Financial Markets. 1999. *Hedge Funds, Leverage, and the Lessons of Long-Term Capital Management* (April). Washington.

Public Strategies. 2008. US National Omnibus Survey Conducted on February 12–13. Available at www.pstrategies.com (accessed on July 12, 2010).

Reuter, Peter, and Edwin M. Truman. 2004. *Chasing Dirty Money: The Fight Against Money Laundering.* Washington: Institute for International Economics.

Rodrik, Dani. 2006. The Social Cost of Foreign Exchange Reserves. *International Economic Journal* 20 (Summer): 253–66.

Roeller, Lars-Hendrik, and Nicolas Véron. 2008. *Safe and Sound: An EU Approach to Sovereign Investment*. Bruegel Policy Brief 2008/08 (November). Brussels: Bruegel.

Rose, Paul. 2008. Sovereigns as Shareholders. *North Carolina Law Review* 87, no. 1: 83–150.

Rozanov, Andrew. 2005. Who Holds the Wealth of Nations? *Central Banking Journal* 15, no. 4 (May): 52–57.

Santiso, Javier. 2008. Sovereign Development Fund: Financial Actors in the Shifting Wealth of Nations. In *New Perspectives on Sovereign Asset Management*, ed. Malan Rietveld. London: Central Banking Publications.

Setser, Brad W. 2008a. Impact of China Investment Corporation on the Management of China's Foreign Assets. In *Debating China's Exchange Policy*, eds. Morris Goldstein and Nicholas Lardy. Washington: Peterson Institute for International Economics.

Setser, Brad W. 2008b. *Sovereign Wealth and Sovereign Power*. Council Special Report 37 (September). New York: Council on Foreign Relations.

Setser, Brad W., and Rachel Ziemba. 2009. *GCC Sovereign Funds: Reversal of Fortune*. Council on Foreign Relations Center for Geoeconomic Studies Working Paper (January). New York: Council on Foreign Relations.

Steil, Benn, and Robert Litan. 2006. *Financial Statecraft*. New Haven: Yale University Press.

Summers, Lawrence H., 2006. Reflections on Global Current Account Imbalances and Emerging Markets Reserve Accumulation. L. K. Jha Memorial Lecture, Reserve Bank of India, Mumbai, March 24.

Summers, Lawrence H. 2007a. Sovereign Funds Shake the Logic of Capitalism. *Financial Times*, July 30.

Summers, Lawrence H. 2007b. Opportunities in an Era of Large and Growing Official Wealth. In *Sovereign Wealth Management*, eds. Jennifer Johnson-Calari and Malan Rietveld. London: Central Banking Publications.

Sun, Tao, and Heiko Hesse. 2009. *Sovereign Wealth and Financial Stability: An Event Study Analysis*. IMF Working Paper 09/239. Washington: International Monetary Fund.

Truman, Edwin M. 2007. *Sovereign Wealth Funds: The Need for Greater Transparency and Accountability*. Policy Brief in International Economics 07-6 (August). Washington: Peterson Institute for International Economics.

Truman, Edwin M. 2008a. *A Blueprint for SWF Best Practices*. Policy Briefs in International Economics 08-3 (April). Washington: Peterson Institute for International Economics.

Truman, Edwin M. 2008b. *Four Myths about Sovereign Wealth Funds* (August 14). Washington. Available at www.piie.com (accessed on July 12, 2010).

Truman, Edwin M. 2008c. The Management of China's International Reserves: China and a Sovereign Wealth Fund Scoreboard. In *Debating China's Exchange Policy*, eds. Morris Goldstein and Nicholas Lardy. Washington: Peterson Institute for International Economics.

Truman, Edwin M. 2008d. The Management of China's International Reserves and Its Sovereign Wealth Funds. Paper prepared for the Chinese Academy of Social Sciences Conference Marking the 30th Anniversary of the Reform and Opening-up (December 16–17). Available at www.piie.com (accessed on July 12, 2010).

Truman, Edwin M. 2010. The International Monetary Fund and Regulatory Challenges. *The International Spectator*, no. 1 (March): 37–58.

Truman, Edwin M., and Anna Wong. 2006. *The Case for an International Reserve Diversification Standard*. Working Paper 06-02. Washington: Peterson Institute for International Economics.

UK Treasury. 2007. Inward Investment and Sovereign Wealth Funds: The UK's Narrative (November). Photocopy.

US Department of the Treasury. 2008a. Committee on Foreign Investment in the United States, Annual Report to Congress, Public Version (December). Washington. Available at www.ustreas.gov (accessed on July 12, 2010).

US Department of the Treasury. 2008b. Regulations Pertaining to Mergers, Acquisitions, and Takeovers by Foreign Persons. Committee on Foreign Investment in the United States (CFIUS) (November 14). Washington. Available at www.ustreas.gov (accessed on July 12, 2010).

US Department of the Treasury. 2009. Committee on Foreign Investment in the United States, Annual Report to Congress, Public Version (November). Washington. Available at www.ustreas.gov.

US House of Representatives Committee on Foreign Relations. 2008. *The Rise of Sovereign Wealth Funds: Impacts on U.S. Foreign Policy and Economic Interests* (May 21). Washington: US Government Printing Office.

Walker Group. 2007. *Guidelines for Disclosure and Transparency in Private Equity* (November). Available at www.walkerworkinggroup.com (accessed on July 12, 2010).

Warrack, Allan A. 2007. Whither a Heritage Fund Public Dividend Policy? In *Alberta's Energy Legacy: Ideas for the Future*, ed. Robert Roach. Calgary: Canada West Foundation. Available at www.cwf.ca (accessed on July 12, 2010).

Wong, Anna. 2007. *Measurement and Inference in International Reserve Diversification*. Working Paper 07–06. Washington: Peterson Institute for International Economics. Available at www.piie.com (accessed on July 12, 2010).

Zoellick, Robert B. 2010. *The End of the Third World? Modernizing Multilateralism for a Multipolar World* (April 14). Washington: World Bank. Available at www.worldbank.org (accessed on July 12, 2010).

Index

Abu Dhabi
    joint statement with US and Singapore, 123, 152
    Mubadala Development Company, 77, 92, 95
    on scoreboard, 75, 77, 96
Abu Dhabi Investment Authority (ADIA)
    asset value, 16, 16*n*, 19
    Citigroup investment, 42, 55
    equity benchmark, 18
    IFSWF participation, 139
    Santiago Principles compliance, 133*b*, 135
    on scoreboard, 75, 76*b*, 96
Abu Dhabi Investment Company (Invest AD), 52
Abu Dhabi Investment Council (ADIC), 52, 75*n*
accountability
    consequences of, 101–103
    international standard for, 5–6, 68
    policy recommendations, 164–68
    Santiago Principles, 125, 131*t*–132*t*, 132, 134–35, 140*t*–147*t*, 164–65
    scoreboard category, 74, 77, 84–88, 85*t*, 92*t*, 93, 107–108, 115*t*–120*t*
    types of, 35*n*
Africa, equity investment in, 136
Alabama, 139
Alaska Permanent Fund, 4, 36, 83, 86, 93, 134, 139
Algeria, 76, 164, 166
Alliant Techsystems, 154, 159
Al-Sa'ad, Bader, 38, 51, 100, 137
Al-Suwaidi, Hamad Al Hurr, 124, 124*n*, 134, 139

Al-Suwaidi, Sultan bin Nassir, 123, 124*n*
annual reports, 87, 107, 142*t*, 164
Asian Development Bank, 36
Asian financial crises, transparency standards and, 69, 70*b*, 86
asset allocations, 18
asset size, 16–19
    disclosure of (*See* transparency)
    on SWF scoreboard, 78, 79*f*
asset value, 1, 2, 11, 12*t*–15*t*, 16–17
audits, 87–88, 108, 142*t*, 147*t*, 164–65
Australia
    foreign investment policies, 158–59
    Future Fund, 18, 75, 93, 126, 134, 137, 167
    IFSWF meeting in, 138
    Queensland Investment Corporation, 16, 71*n*, 75*n*
    on scoreboard, 71*n*, 75, 75*n*, 83
    Victorian Funds Management Corporation, 16
Azerbaijan, 99, 137
    State Oil Fund, 71*n*, 77*n*

Bahrain, Mumtalakat Holding Company, 77*n*, 95
Banamex, 55
behavior. *See also* investment strategies
    code of conduct, 5–6, 68
    Santiago Principles, 131*t*–132*t*, 132, 144*t*–145*t*
    scoreboard category, 88–89, 89*t*, 92*t*, 108
Blackstone Corporation, 11*n*, 76
Blair, Tony, 38
board membership, 63–64, 137

Other Publications from the Peterson Institute for International Economics

WORKING PAPERS

Economic Sanctions Reconsidered (2 volumes) Economic Sanctions Reconsidered: Supplemental Case Histories
Gary Clyde Hufbauer, Jeffrey J. Schott, and Kimberly Ann Elliott
1985, 2d ed. Dec. 1990 ISBN cloth 0-88132-115-X
ISBN paper 0-88132-105-2
Economic Sanctions Reconsidered: History and Current Policy Gary Clyde Hufbauer, Jeffrey J. Schott, and Kimberly Ann Elliott
December 1990 ISBN cloth 0-88132-140-0
ISBN paper 0-88132-136-2
Pacific Basin Developing Countries: Prospects for the Future* Marcus Noland
January 1991 ISBN cloth 0-88132-141-9
ISBN paper 0-88132-081-1
Currency Convertibility in Eastern Europe*
John Williamson, editor
October 1991 ISBN 0-88132-128-1
International Adjustment and Financing: The Lessons of 1985-1991* C. Fred Bergsten, editor
January 1992 ISBN 0-88132-112-5
North American Free Trade: Issues and Recommendations* Gary Clyde Hufbauer and Jeffrey J. Schott
April 1992 ISBN 0-88132-120-6
Narrowing the U.S. Current Account Deficit*
Alan J. Lenz
June 1992 ISBN 0-88132-103-6
The Economics of Global Warming
William R. Cline
June 1992 ISBN 0-88132-132-X
US Taxation of International Income: Blueprint for Reform Gary Clyde Hufbauer, assisted by Joanna M. van Rooij
October 1992 ISBN 0-88132-134-6
Who's Bashing Whom? Trade Conflict in High-Technology Industries Laura D'Andrea Tyson
November 1992 ISBN 0-88132-106-0
Korea in the World Economy* Il SaKong
January 1993 ISBN 0-88132-183-4
Pacific Dynamism and the International Economic System* C. Fred Bergsten and Marcus Noland, editors
May 1993 ISBN 0-88132-196-6
Economic Consequences of Soviet Disintegration* John Williamson, editor
May 1993 ISBN 0-88132-190-7
Reconcilable Differences? United States-Japan Economic Conflict* C. Fred Bergsten and Marcus Noland
June 1993 ISBN 0-88132-129-X
Does Foreign Exchange Intervention Work?
Kathryn M. Dominguez and Jeffrey A. Frankel
September 1993 ISBN 0-88132-104-4
Sizing Up U.S. Export Disincentives*
J. David Richardson
September 1993 ISBN 0-88132-107-9
NAFTA: An Assessment Gary C. Hufbauer and Jeffrey J. Schott, rev. ed.
October 1993 ISBN 0-88132-199-0

Adjusting to Volatile Energy Prices
Philip K. Verleger, Jr.
November 1993 ISBN 0-88132-069-2
The Political Economy of Policy Reform
John Williamson, editor
January 1994 ISBN 0-88132-195-8
Measuring the Costs of Protection in the United States Gary Clyde Hufbauer and Kimberly Ann Elliott
January 1994 ISBN 0-88132-108-7
The Dynamics of Korean Economic Development* Cho Soon
March 1994 ISBN 0-88132-162-1
Reviving the European Union*
C. Randall Henning, Eduard Hochreiter, and Gary Clyde Hufbauer, editors
April 1994 ISBN 0-88132-208-3
China in the World Economy Nicholas R. Lardy
April 1994 ISBN 0-88132-200-8
Greening the GATT: Trade, Environment, and the Future Daniel C. Esty
July 1994 ISBN 0-88132-205-9
Western Hemisphere Economic Integration*
Gary Clyde Hufbauer and Jeffrey J. Schott
July 1994 ISBN 0-88132-159-1
Currencies and Politics in the United States, Germany, and Japan C. Randall Henning
September 1994 ISBN 0-88132-127-3
Estimating Equilibrium Exchange Rates
John Williamson, editor
September 1994 ISBN 0-88132-076-5
Managing the World Economy: Fifty Years after Bretton Woods Peter B. Kenen, editor
September 1994 ISBN 0-88132-212-1
Reciprocity and Retaliation in U.S. Trade Policy Thomas O. Bayard and Kimberly Ann Elliott
September 1994 ISBN 0-88132-084-6
The Uruguay Round: An Assessment*
Jeffrey J. Schott, assisted by Johanna Buurman
November 1994 ISBN 0-88132-206-7
Measuring the Costs of Protection in Japan*
Yoko Sazanami, Shujiro Urata, and Hiroki Kawai
January 1995 ISBN 0-88132-211-3
Foreign Direct Investment in the United States, 3d ed., Edward M. Graham and Paul R. Krugman
January 1995 ISBN 0-88132-204-0
The Political Economy of Korea-United States Cooperation* C. Fred Bergsten and Il SaKong, editors
February 1995 ISBN 0-88132-213-X
International Debt Reexamined*
William R. Cline
February 1995 ISBN 0-88132-083-8
American Trade Politics, 3d ed. I. M. Destler
April 1995 ISBN 0-88132-215-6
Managing Official Export Credits: The Quest for a Global Regime* John E. Ray
July 1995 ISBN 0-88132-207-5
Asia Pacific Fusion: Japan's Role in APEC*
Yoichi Funabashi
October 1995 ISBN 0-88132-224-5

Korea-United States Cooperation in the New World Order*   C. Fred Bergsten and Il SaKong, eds.
February 1996   ISBN 0-88132-226-1
Why Exports Really Matter!*   ISBN 0-88132-221-0
Why Exports Matter More!*   ISBN 0-88132-229-6
J. David Richardson and Karin Rindal
July 1995; February 1996
Global Corporations and National Governments   Edward M. Graham
May 1996   ISBN 0-88132-111-7
Global Economic Leadership and the Group of Seven   C. Fred Bergsten and C. Randall Henning
May 1996   ISBN 0-88132-218-0
The Trading System after the Uruguay Round*   John Whalley and Colleen Hamilton
July 1996   ISBN 0-88132-131-1
Private Capital Flows to Emerging Markets after the Mexican Crisis*   Guillermo A. Calvo, Morris Goldstein, and Eduard Hochreiter
September 1996   ISBN 0-88132-232-6
The Crawling Band as an Exchange Rate Regime: Lessons from Chile, Colombia, and Israel   John Williamson
September 1996   ISBN 0-88132-231-8
Flying High: Liberalizing Civil Aviation in the Asia Pacific*   Gary Clyde Hufbauer and Christopher Findlay
November 1996   ISBN 0-88132-227-X
Measuring the Costs of Visible Protection in Korea*   Namdoo Kim
November 1996   ISBN 0-88132-236-9
The World Trading System: Challenges Ahead   Jeffrey J. Schott
December 1996   ISBN 0-88132-235-0
Has Globalization Gone Too Far?   Dani Rodrik
March 1997   ISBN paper 0-88132-241-5
Korea-United States Economic Relationship*   C. Fred Bergsten and Il SaKong, editors
March 1997   ISBN 0-88132-240-7
Summitry in the Americas: A Progress Report   Richard E. Feinberg
April 1997   ISBN 0-88132-242-3
Corruption and the Global Economy   Kimberly Ann Elliott
June 1997   ISBN 0-88132-233-4
Regional Trading Blocs in the World Economic System   Jeffrey A. Frankel
October 1997   ISBN 0-88132-202-4
Sustaining the Asia Pacific Miracle: Environmental Protection and Economic Integration   Andre Dua and Daniel C. Esty
October 1997   ISBN 0-88132-250-4
Trade and Income Distribution   William R. Cline
November 1997   ISBN 0-88132-216-4
Global Competition Policy   Edward M. Graham and J. David Richardson
December 1997   ISBN 0-88132-166-4

Unfinished Business: Telecommunications after the Uruguay Round   Gary Clyde Hufbauer and Erika Wada
December 1997   ISBN 0-88132-257-1
Financial Services Liberalization in the WTO   Wendy Dobson and Pierre Jacquet
June 1998   ISBN 0-88132-254-7
Restoring Japan's Economic Growth   Adam S. Posen
September 1998   ISBN 0-88132-262-8
Measuring the Costs of Protection in China   Zhang Shuguang, Zhang Yansheng, and Wan Zhongxin
November 1998   ISBN 0-88132-247-4
Foreign Direct Investment and Development: The New Policy Agenda for Developing Countries and Economies in Transition   Theodore H. Moran
December 1998   ISBN 0-88132-258-X
Behind the Open Door: Foreign Enterprises in the Chinese Marketplace   Daniel H. Rosen
January 1999   ISBN 0-88132-263-6
Toward A New International Financial Architecture: A Practical Post-Asia Agenda   Barry Eichengreen
February 1999   ISBN 0-88132-270-9
Is the U.S. Trade Deficit Sustainable?   Catherine L. Mann
September 1999   ISBN 0-88132-265-2
Safeguarding Prosperity in a Global Financial System: The Future International Financial Architecture, Independent Task Force Report Sponsored by the Council on Foreign Relations   Morris Goldstein, Project Director
October 1999   ISBN 0-88132-287-3
Avoiding the Apocalypse: The Future of the Two Koreas   Marcus Noland
June 2000   ISBN 0-88132-278-4
Assessing Financial Vulnerability: An Early Warning System for Emerging Markets   Morris Goldstein, Graciela Kaminsky, and Carmen Reinhart
June 2000   ISBN 0-88132-237-7
Global Electronic Commerce: A Policy Primer   Catherine L. Mann, Sue E. Eckert, and Sarah Cleeland Knight
July 2000   ISBN 0-88132-274-1
The WTO after Seattle   Jeffrey J. Schott, ed.
July 2000   ISBN 0-88132-290-3
Intellectual Property Rights in the Global Economy   Keith E. Maskus
August 2000   ISBN 0-88132-282-2
The Political Economy of the Asian Financial Crisis   Stephan Haggard
August 2000   ISBN 0-88132-283-0
Transforming Foreign Aid: United States Assistance in the 21st Century   Carol Lancaster
August 2000   ISBN 0-88132-291-1
Fighting the Wrong Enemy: Antiglobal Activists and Multinational Enterprises   Edward M. Graham
September 2000   ISBN 0-88132-272-5

NAFTA Revisited: Achievements and
Challenges   Gary Clyde Hufbauer and
Jeffrey J. Schott, assisted by Paul L. E. Grieco and
Yee Wong
October 2005   ISBN 0-88132-334-9
US National Security and Foreign Direct
Investment   Edward M. Graham and
David M. Marchick
May 2006   ISBN 978-0-88132-391-7
Accelerating the Globalization of America: The
Role for Information Technology
Catherine L. Mann, assisted by Jacob Kirkegaard
June 2006   ISBN 978-0-88132-390-0
Delivering on Doha: Farm Trade and the Poor
Kimberly Ann Elliott
July 2006   ISBN 978-0-88132-392-4
Case Studies in US Trade Negotiation, Vol. 1:
Making the Rules   Charan Devereaux,
Robert Z. Lawrence, and Michael Watkins
September 2006   ISBN 978-0-88132-362-7
Case Studies in US Trade Negotiation, Vol. 2:
Resolving Disputes   Charan Devereaux,
Robert Z. Lawrence, and Michael Watkins
September 2006   ISBN 978-0-88132-363-2
C. Fred Bergsten and the World Economy
Michael Mussa, editor
December 2006   ISBN 978-0-88132-397-9
Working Papers, Volume I   Peterson Institute
December 2006   ISBN 978-0-88132-388-7
The Arab Economies in a Changing World
Marcus Noland and Howard Pack
April 2007   ISBN 978-0-88132-393-1
Working Papers, Volume II   Peterson Institute
April 2007   ISBN 978-0-88132-404-4
Global Warming and Agriculture: Impact
Estimates by Country   William R. Cline
July 2007   ISBN 978-0-88132-403-7
US Taxation of Foreign Income
Gary Clyde Hufbauer and Ariel Assa
October 2007   ISBN 978-0-88132-405-1
Russia's Capitalist Revolution: Why Market
Reform Succeeded and Democracy Failed
Anders Åslund
October 2007   ISBN 978-0-88132-409-9
Economic Sanctions Reconsidered, 3d. ed.
Gary C. Hufbauer, Jeffrey J. Schott, Kimberly
Ann Elliott, and Barbara Oegg
November 2007
          ISBN hardcover 978-0-88132-407-5
          ISBN hardcover/CD-ROM 978-0-88132-408-2
Debating China's Exchange Rate Policy
Morris Goldstein and Nicholas R. Lardy, eds.
April 2008   ISBN 978-0-88132-415-0
Leveling the Carbon Playing Field:
International Competition and US Climate
Policy Design   Trevor Houser, Rob Bradley,
Britt Childs, Jacob Werksman, and Robert
Heilmayr
May 2008   ISBN 978-0-88132-420-4
Accountability and Oversight of US Exchange
Rate Policy   C. Randall Henning
June 2008   ISBN 978-0-88132-419-8

Challenges of Globalization: Imbalances and
Growth   Anders Åslund and
Marek Dabrowski, eds.
July 2008   ISBN 978-0-88132-418-1
China's Rise: Challenges and Opportunities
C. Fred Bergsten, Charles Freeman, Nicholas R.
Lardy, and Derek J. Mitchell
September 2008   ISBN 978-0-88132-417-4
Banking on Basel: The Future of International
Financial Regulation   Daniel K. Tarullo
September 2008   ISBN 978-0-88132-423-5
US Pension Reform: Lessons from Other
Countries   Martin N. Baily and
Jacob Kirkegaard
February 2009   ISBN 978-0-88132-425-9
How Ukraine Became a Market Economy and
Democracy   Anders Åslund
March 2009   ISBN 978-0-88132-427-3
Global Warming and the World Trading
System   Gary Clyde Hufbauer,
Steve Charnovitz, and Jisun Kim
March 2009   ISBN 978-0-88132-428-0
The Russia Balance Sheet   Anders Åslund and
Andrew Kuchins
March 2009   ISBN 978-0-88132-424-2
The Euro at Ten: The Next Global Currency?
Jean Pisani-Ferry and Adam S. Posen, eds.
July 2009   ISBN 978-0-88132-430-3
Financial Globalization, Economic Growth, and
the Crisis of 2007–09   William R. Cline
May 2010   ISBN 978-0-88132-4990-0
Russia after the Global Economic Crisis
Anders Åslund, Sergei Guriev, and Andrew
Kuchins, eds.
June 2010   ISBN 978-0-88132-497-6
Sovereign Wealth Funds: Threat or Salvation?
Edwin M. Truman
September 2010   ISBN 978-0-88132-498-3

SPECIAL REPORTS

1   Promoting World Recovery: A Statement
     on Global Economic Strategy*
     by 26 Economists from Fourteen Countries
     December 1982   ISBN 0-88132-013-7
2   Prospects for Adjustment in Argentina,
     Brazil, and Mexico: Responding to the
     Debt Crisis*   John Williamson, editor
     June 1983   ISBN 0-88132-016-1
3   Inflation and Indexation: Argentina, Brazil,
     and Israel*   John Williamson, editor
     March 1985   ISBN 0-88132-037-4
4   Global Economic Imbalances*
     C. Fred Bergsten, editor
     March 1986   ISBN 0-88132-042-0
5   African Debt and Financing*
     Carol Lancaster and John Williamson, eds.
     May 1986   ISBN 0-88132-044-7
6   Resolving the Global Economic Crisis:
     After Wall Street*   by Thirty-three
     Economists from Thirteen Countries
     December 1987   ISBN 0-88132-070-6

7 **World Economic Problems***
Kimberly Ann Elliott and John Williamson, eds.
April 1988   ISBN 0-88132-055-2
Reforming World Agricultural Trade*
by Twenty-nine Professionals from
Seventeen Countries
1988   ISBN 0-88132-088-9
8 **Economic Relations Between the United States and Korea: Conflict or Cooperation?***
Thomas O. Bayard and Soogil Young, eds.
January 1989   ISBN 0-88132-068-4
9 **Whither APEC? The Progress to Date and Agenda for the Future***
C. Fred Bergsten, editor
October 1997   ISBN 0-88132-248-2
10 **Economic Integration of the Korean Peninsula**   Marcus Noland, editor
January 1998   ISBN 0-88132-255-5
11 **Restarting Fast Track***   Jeffrey J. Schott, ed.
April 1998   ISBN 0-88132-259-8
12 **Launching New Global Trade Talks: An Action Agenda**   Jeffrey J. Schott, ed.
September 1998   ISBN 0-88132-266-0
13 **Japan's Financial Crisis and Its Parallels to US Experience**   Ryoichi Mikitani and Adam S. Posen, eds.
September 2000   ISBN 0-88132-289-X
14 **The Ex-Im Bank in the 21st Century: A New Approach**   Gary Clyde Hufbauer and Rita M. Rodriguez, editors
January 2001   ISBN 0-88132-300-4
15 **The Korean Diaspora in the World Economy**   C. Fred Bergsten and Inbom Choi, eds.
January 2003   ISBN 0-88132-358-6
16 **Dollar Overvaluation and the World Economy**   C. Fred Bergsten and John Williamson, eds.
February 2003   ISBN 0-88132-351-9
17 **Dollar Adjustment: How Far? Against What?**   C. Fred Bergsten and John Williamson, eds.
November 2004   ISBN 0-88132-378-0
18 **The Euro at Five: Ready for a Global Role?**
Adam S. Posen, editor
April 2005   ISBN 0-88132-380-2
19 **Reforming the IMF for the 21st Century**
Edwin M. Truman, editor
April 2006   ISBN 978-0-88132-387-0
20 **The Long-Term International Economic Position of the United States**
C. Fred Bergsten, ed.
May 2009   ISBN 978-0-88132-432-7

WORKS IN PROGRESS

China's Energy Evolution: The Consequences of Powering Growth at Home and Abroad
Daniel H. Rosen and Trevor Houser
Global Identity Theft: Economic and Policy Implications   Catherine L. Mann
Growth and Diversification of International Reserves   Edwin M. Truman
Globalized Venture Capital: Implications for US Entrepreneurship and Innovation
Catherine L. Mann
Forging a Grand Bargain: Expanding Trade and Raising Worker Prosperity   Lori Kletzer, J. David Richardson, and Howard Rosen
East Asian Regionalism and the World Economy   C. Fred Bergsten
The Limits of Export-Led Growth: Germany and the Future of Capitalism   Adam S. Posen
Global Forces, American Faces: US Economic Globalization at the Grass Roots
J. David Richardson
Global Services Outsourcing: The Impact on American Firms and Workers
J. Bradford Jensen
Policy Reform in Rich Countries
John Williamson, editor
Banking System Fragility in Emerging Economies   Morris Goldstein and Philip Turner
Witness to Transformation: Refugee Insights into North Korea   Stephan Haggard and Marcus Noland
The Last Shall Be the First   Anders Åslund
The World after the Financial Crisis
Simon Johnson and Arvind Subramanian
Aligning NAFTA with Climate Change Objectives   Jeffrey J. Schott and Meera Fickling
Intellectual Property Rights in the Global Economy   Keith Maskus
The Positive Agenda for Climate and Trade
Trevor Houser
The Implications of China-Taiwan Economic Liberalization   Daniel H. Rosen and Zhi Wang
Stable Prices, Unstable Currencies: The Weak Link between Exchange Rates and Inflation and What It Means for Economic Policy
Joseph Gagnon

DISTRIBUTORS OUTSIDE THE UNITED STATES

Australia, New Zealand,
and Papua New Guinea
D. A. Information Services
648 Whitehorse Road
Mitcham, Victoria 3132, Australia
Tel: 61-3-9210-7777
Fax: 61-3-9210-7788
Email: service@dadirect.com.au
www.dadirect.com.au

Canada
Renouf Bookstore
5369 Canotek Road, Unit 1
Ottawa, Ontario K1J 9J3, Canada
Tel: 613-745-2665
Fax: 613-745-7660
www.renoufbooks.com

India, Bangladesh, Nepal, and Sri Lanka
Viva Books Private Limited
Mr. Vinod Vasishtha
4737/23 Ansari Road
Daryaganj, New Delhi 110002
India
Tel: 91-11-4224-2200
Fax: 91-11-4224-2240
Email: viva@vivagroupindia.net
www.vivagroupindia.com

Japan
United Publishers Services Ltd.
1-32-5, Higashi-shinagawa
Shinagawa-ku, Tokyo 140-0002
Japan
Tel: 81-3-5479-7251
Fax: 81-3-5479-7307
Email: purchasing@ups.co.jp
For trade accounts only. Individuals will find
Institute books in leading Tokyo bookstores.

Mexico, Central America, South America,
and Puerto Rico
US PubRep, Inc.
311 Dean Drive
Rockville, MD 20851
Tel: 301-838-9276
Fax: 301-838-9278
Email: c.falk@ieee.org

Middle East
MERIC
2 Bahgat Ali Street, El Masry Towers
Tower D, Apt. 24
Zamalek, Cairo
Egypt
Tel. 20-2-7633824
Fax: 20-2-7369355
Email: mahmoud_fouda@mericonline.com
www.mericonline.com

Asia (*Brunei, Burma, Cambodia, China,*
Hong Kong, Indonesia, Korea, Laos, Malaysia,
Philippines, Singapore, Taiwan, Thailand,
and Vietnam)
East-West Export Books (EWEB)
University of Hawaii Press
2840 Kolowalu Street
Honolulu, Hawaii 96822-1888
Tel: 808-956-8830
Fax: 808-988-6052
Email: eweb@hawaii.edu

United Kingdom, Europe
(*including Russia and Turkey*), **Africa,**
and Israel
The Eurospan Group
c/o Turpin Distribution
Pegasus Drive
Stratton Business Park
Biggleswade, Bedfordshire
SG18 8TQ
United Kingdom
Tel: 44 (0) 1767-604972
Fax: 44 (0) 1767-601640
Email: eurospan@turpin-distribution.com
www.eurospangroup.com/bookstore

Visit our website at:
www.piie.com
E-mail orders to:
petersonmail@presswarehouse.com

8220